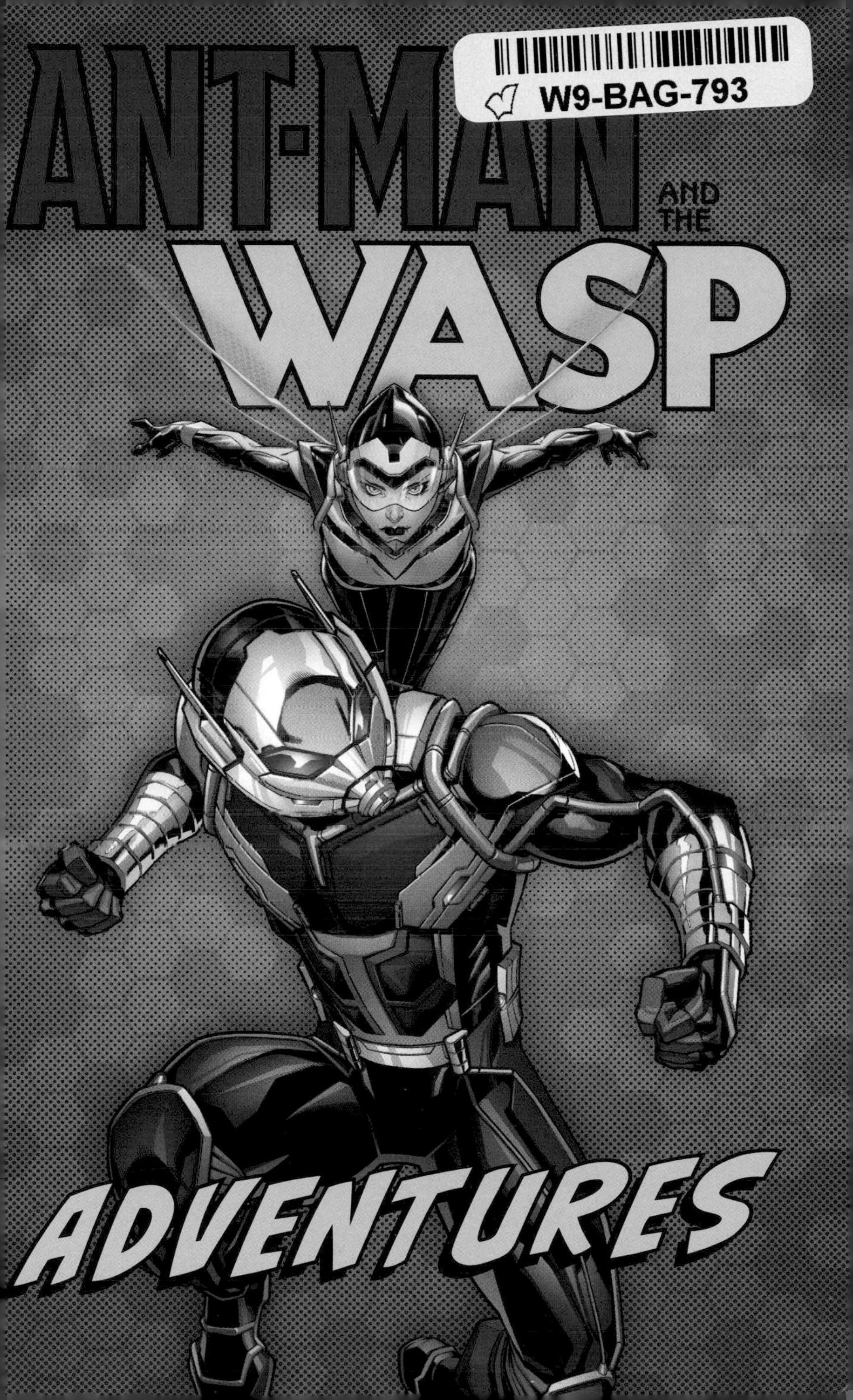
ANT-MAN
AND THE
WASP
ADVENTURES

ANT-MAN AND THE WASP ADVENTURES

Marvel Universe Avengers Assemble Season Two #9
Based on "The New Guy"

Written by **Charlotte Fullerton** & **Kevin Rubio**
Directed by **Tim Eldred**
Art by **Marvel Animation**
Adapted by **Joe Caramagna**
Special thanks to **Henry Ong** & **Product Factory**
Editor **Sebastian Girner**
Consulting Editor **Mark Basso**
Senior Editor **Mark Paniccia**

Avengers: Earth's Mightiest Heroes #2-3

Writer **Christopher Yost**
Penciler **Patrick Scherberger**
Inker **Sandu Florea**
Colorist **Jean-Francois Beaulieu**
Letterers **Dave Sharpe** (#2) &
VC's Joe Sabino (#3)
Editors **Nathan Cosby** & **Michael Horwitz**

Marvel Universe Avengers: Earth's Mightiest Heroes #7

Writer **Christopher Yost**
Penciler **Christopher Jones**
Inker **Victor Olazaba**
Colorist **Sotocolor**
Letterer **VC's Clayton Cowles**
Assistant Editor **Ellie Pyle**
Editor **Tom Brennan**
Senior Editor **Stephen Wacker**

Tales to Astonish #27 & #35

Writer **Stan Lee**
Penciler **Jack Kirby**
Inker **Dick Ayers**
Letterer **Jon D'Agostino**

Tales to Astonish #44

Plot **Stan Lee**
Writer **H.E. Huntley**
Penciler **Jack Kirby**
Inker **Don Heck**
Letterer **Art Simek**

Avengers #223

Writer **David Michelinie**
Penciler **Greg LaRocque**
Inkers **Brett Breeding** & **Crew**
Colorist **Christie Scheele**
Letterer **Rick Parker**
Editor **Mark Gruenwald**

Ant-Man created by **Stan Lee**, **Larry Lieber** & **Jack Kirby**

Wasp created by **Stan Lee**, **Ernie Hart** & **Jack Kirby**

Collection Editor **Jennifer Grünwald**
Assistant Editor **Caitlin O'Connell**
Associate Managing Editor **Kateri Woody**
Editor, Special Projects **Mark D. Beazley**
VP Production & Special Projects **Jeff Youngquist**
SVP Print, Sales & Marketing **David Gabriel**
Book Designer **Adam Del Re**

Editor in Chief **C.B. Cebulski**
Chief Creative Officer **Joe Quesada**
President **Dan Buckley**
Executive Producer **Alan Fine**

ANT-MAN AND THE WASP ADVENTURES. Contains material originally published in magazine form as MARVEL UNIVERSE AVENGERS ASSEMBLE SEASON TWO #9; AVENGERS #223; AVENGERS EARTH'S MIGHTIEST HEROES #2-3; and MARVEL UNIVERSE AVENGERS EARTH'S MIGHTIEST HEROES #7; TALES TO ASTONISH #27, #35 and #44. First printing 2018. ISBN 978-1-302-91204-8. Published by MARVEL WORLDWIDE, INC., a subsidiary of MARVEL ENTERTAINMENT, LLC. OFFICE OF PUBLICATION: 135 West 50th Street, New York, NY 10020. Copyright © 2018 MARVEL. No similarity between any of the names, characters, persons, and/or institutions in this magazine with those of any living or dead person or institution is intended, and any such similarity which may exist is purely coincidental. **Printed in the U.S.A.** DAN BUCKLEY, President, Marvel Entertainment; JOHN NEE, Publisher; JOE QUESADA, Chief Creative Officer; TOM BREVOORT, SVP of Publishing; DAVID BOGART, SVP of Business Affairs & Operations, Publishing & Partnership; DAVID GABRIEL, SVP of Sales & Marketing, Publishing; JEFF YOUNGQUIST, VP of Production & Special Projects; DAN CARR, Executive Director of Publishing Technology; ALEX MORALES, Director of Publishing Operations; DAN EDINGTON, Managing Editor; SUSAN CRESPI, Production Manager; STAN LEE, Chairman Emeritus. For information regarding advertising in Marvel Comics or on Marvel.com, please contact Vit DeBellis, Custom Solutions & Integrated Advertising Manager, at vdebellis@marvel.com. For Marvel subscription inquiries, please call 888-511-5480. Manufactured between 4/13/2018 and 5/15/2018 by SHERIDAN, CHELSEA, MI, USA.

10 9 8 7 6 5 4 3 2 1

MARVEL AVENGERS ASSEMBLE SEASON 2

HERE COMES ANT-MAN!

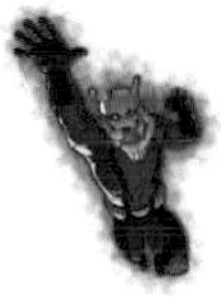

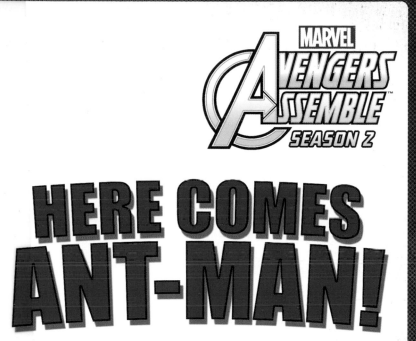

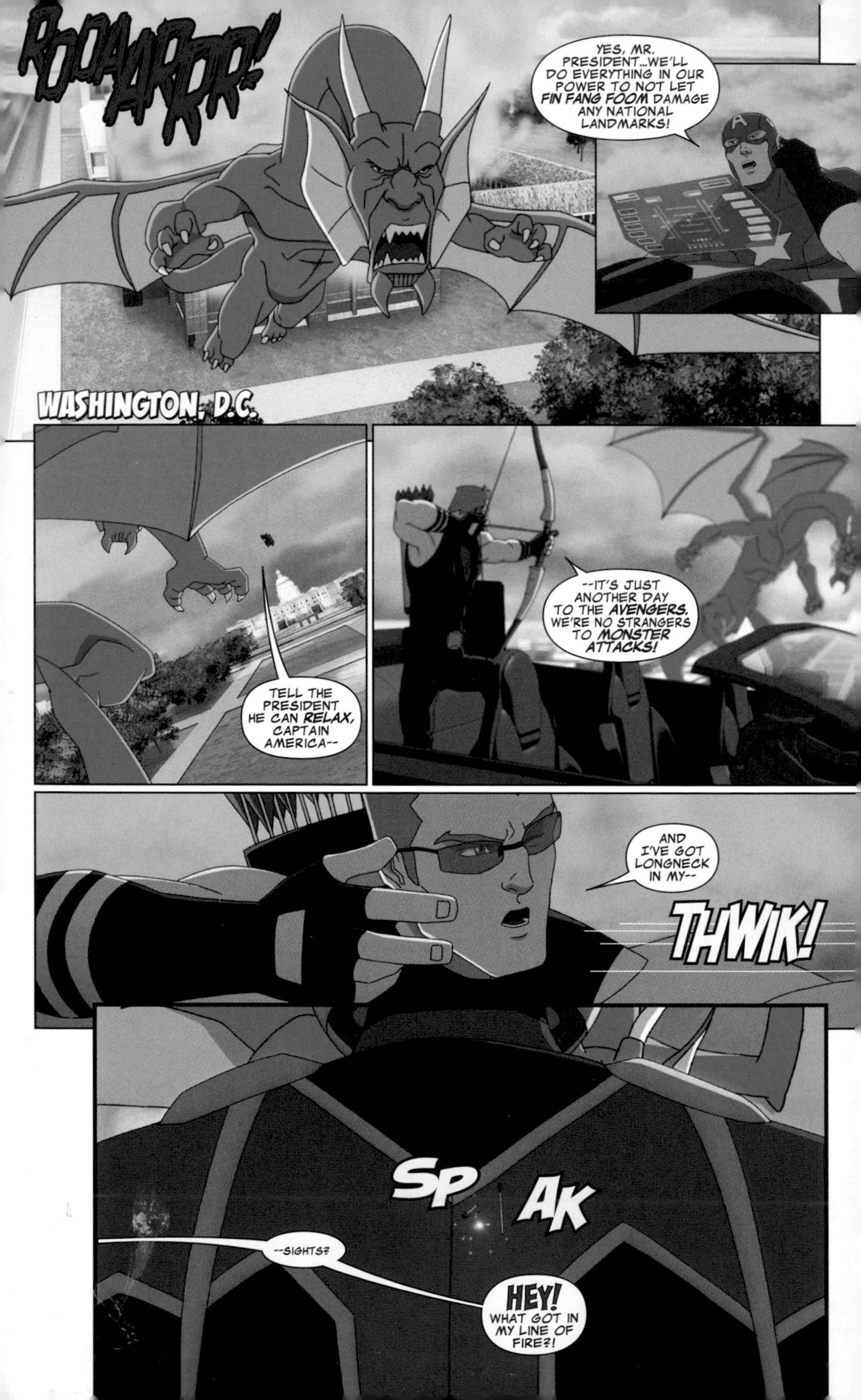
ROOAARRR!
YES, MR. PRESIDENT...WE'LL DO EVERYTHING IN OUR POWER TO NOT LET FIN FANG FOOM DAMAGE ANY NATIONAL LANDMARKS!
WASHINGTON, D.C.
TELL THE PRESIDENT HE CAN RELAX, CAPTAIN AMERICA--
--IT'S JUST ANOTHER DAY TO THE AVENGERS. WE'RE NO STRANGERS TO MONSTER ATTACKS!
AND I'VE GOT LONGNECK IN MY--
THWIK!
SPAK
--SIGHTS?
HEY! WHAT GOT IN MY LINE OF FIRE?!

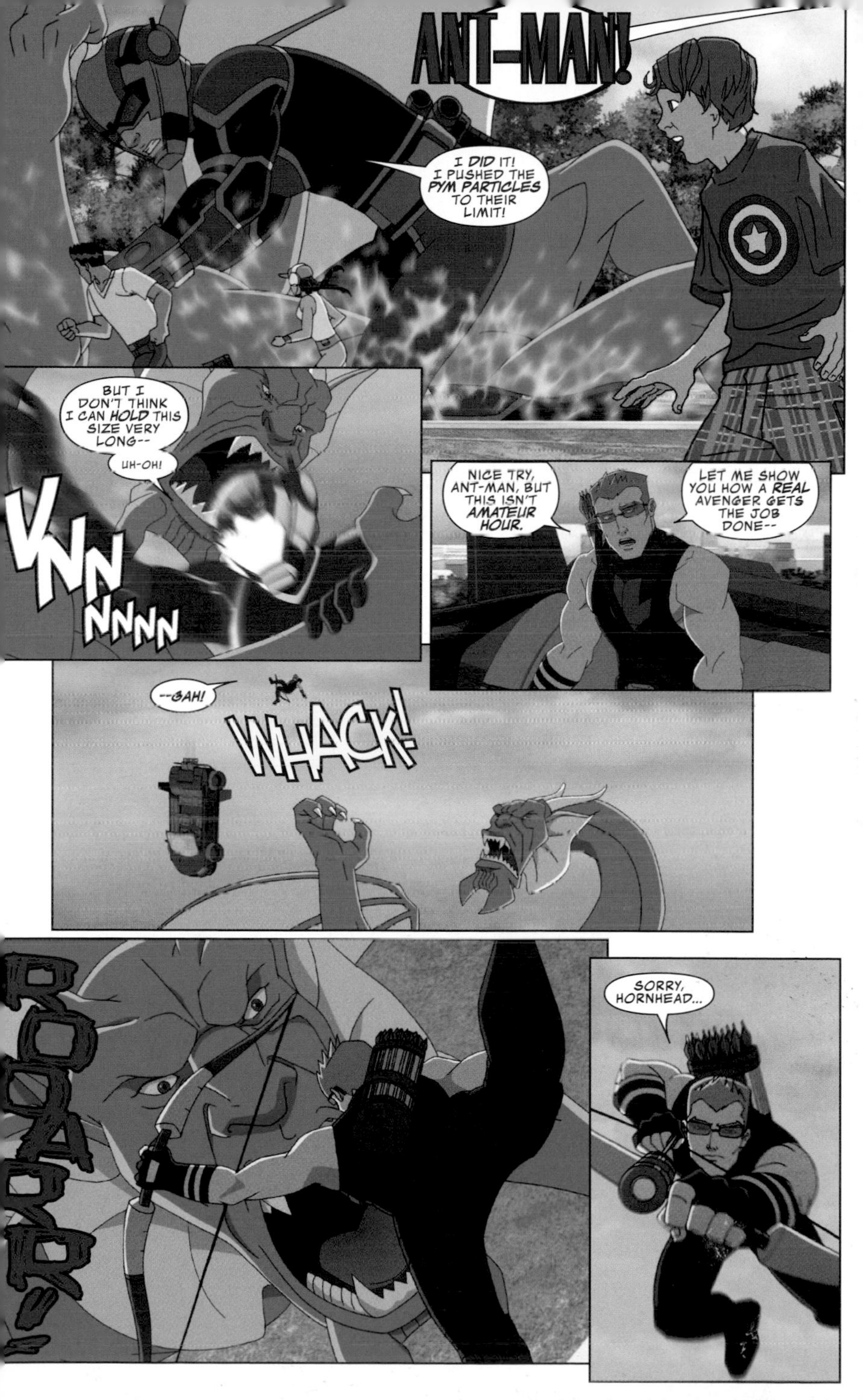
ANT-MAN!
I DID IT! I PUSHED THE PYM PARTICLES TO THEIR LIMIT!
BUT I DON'T THINK I CAN HOLD THIS SIZE VERY LONG--
UH-OH!
VNN NNNN
NICE TRY, ANT-MAN, BUT THIS ISN'T AMATEUR HOUR.
LET ME SHOW YOU HOW A REAL AVENGER GETS THE JOB DONE--
--GAH!
WHACK!
ROOAARR!
SORRY, HORNHEAD...

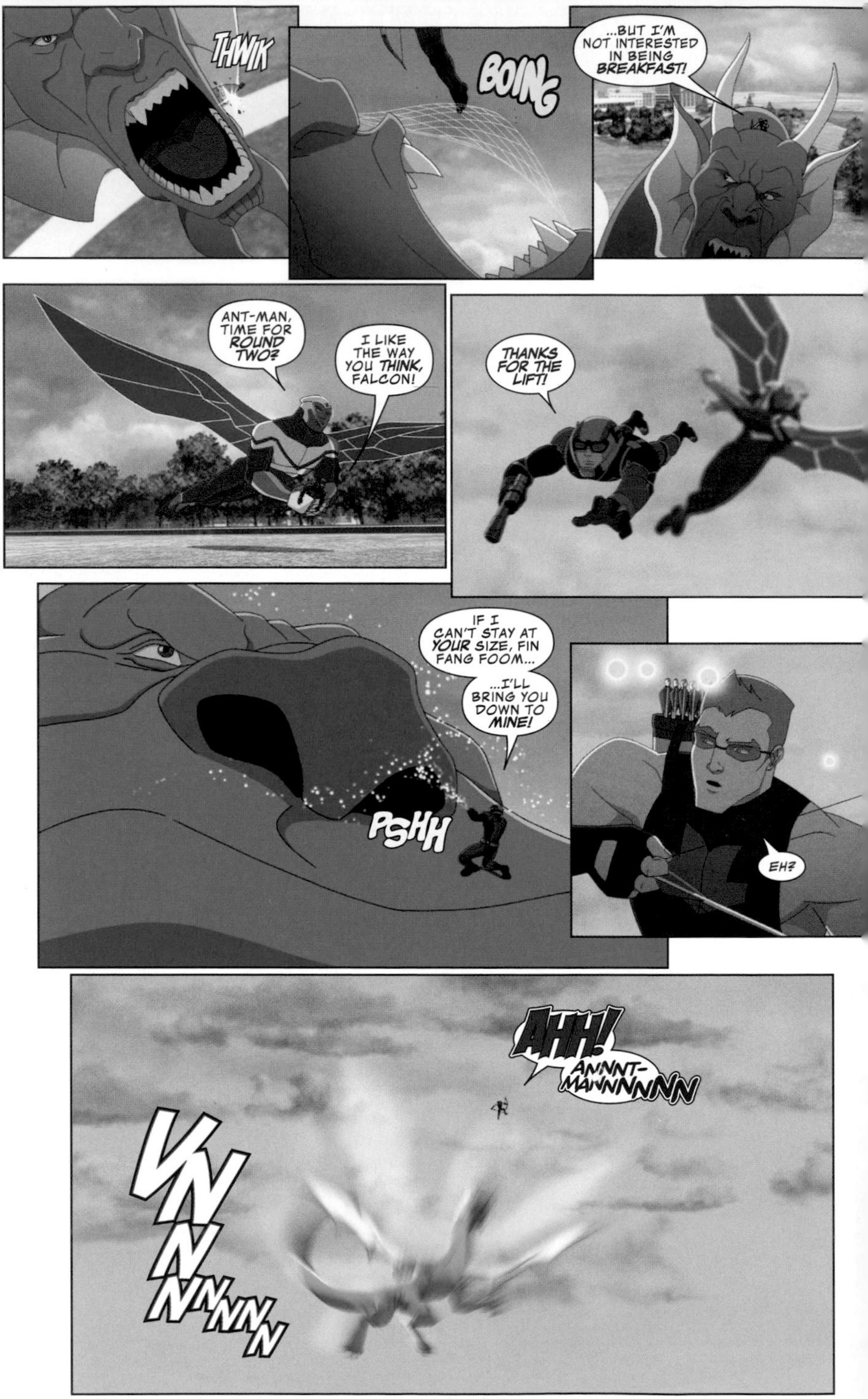
THWIK
BOING
...BUT I'M NOT INTERESTED IN BEING BREAKFAST!
ANT-MAN, TIME FOR ROUND TWO?
I LIKE THE WAY YOU THINK, FALCON!
THANKS FOR THE LIFT!
IF I CAN'T STAY AT YOUR SIZE, FIN FANG FOOM...
...I'LL BRING YOU DOWN TO MINE!
PSHH
EH?
AHH! ANNNT-MANNNNNNN
VNNNNNNN

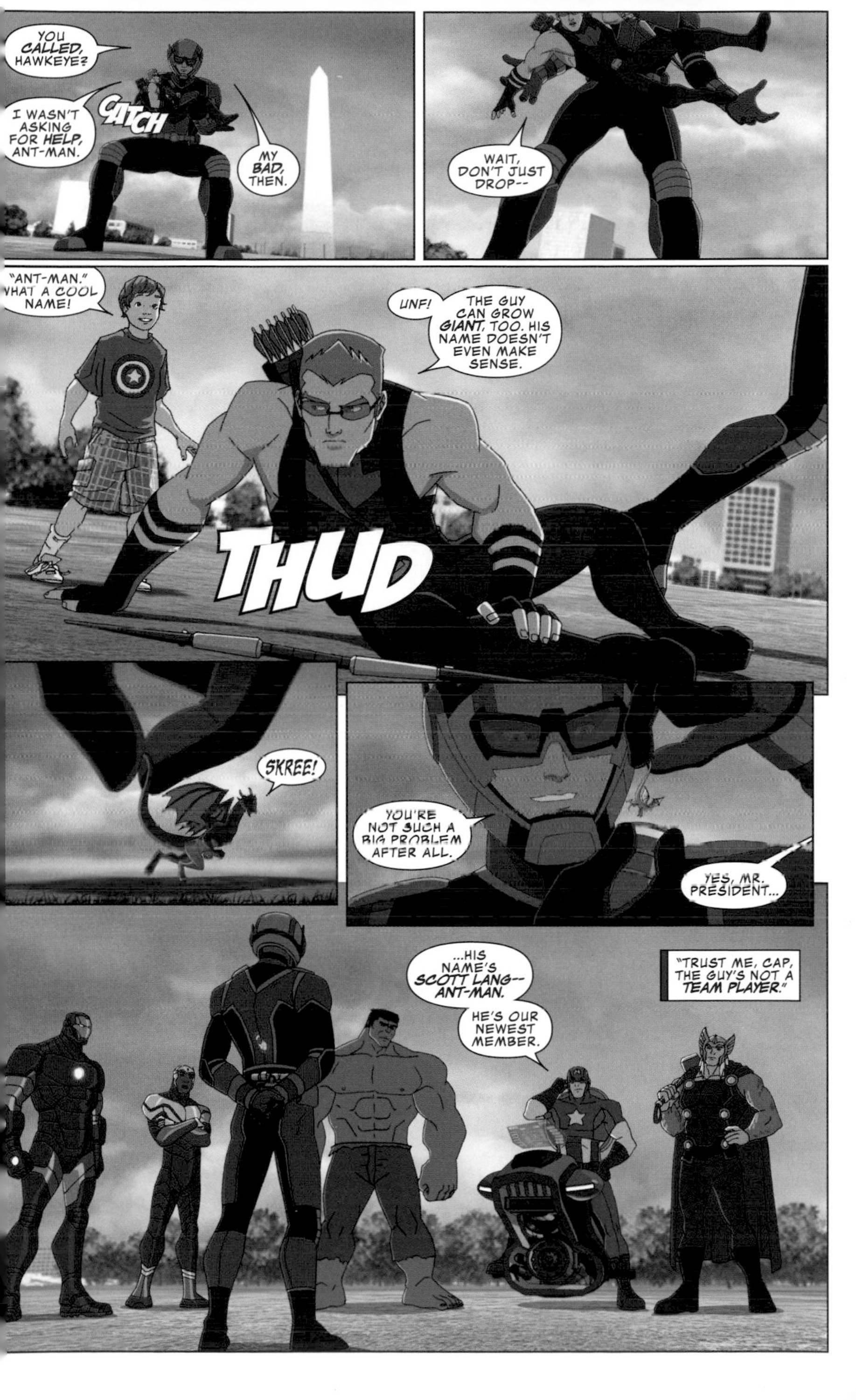
YOU CALLED, HAWKEYE?
I WASN'T ASKING FOR HELP, ANT-MAN.
CATCH
MY BAD, THEN.
WAIT, DON'T JUST DROP--
"ANT-MAN." WHAT A COOL NAME!
UNF!
THE GUY CAN GROW GIANT, TOO. HIS NAME DOESN'T EVEN MAKE SENSE.
THUD
SKREE!
YOU'RE NOT SUCH A BIG PROBLEM AFTER ALL.
YES, MR. PRESIDENT...
"TRUST ME, CAP, THE GUY'S NOT A TEAM PLAYER."
...HIS NAME'S SCOTT LANG-- ANT-MAN.
HE'S OUR NEWEST MEMBER.

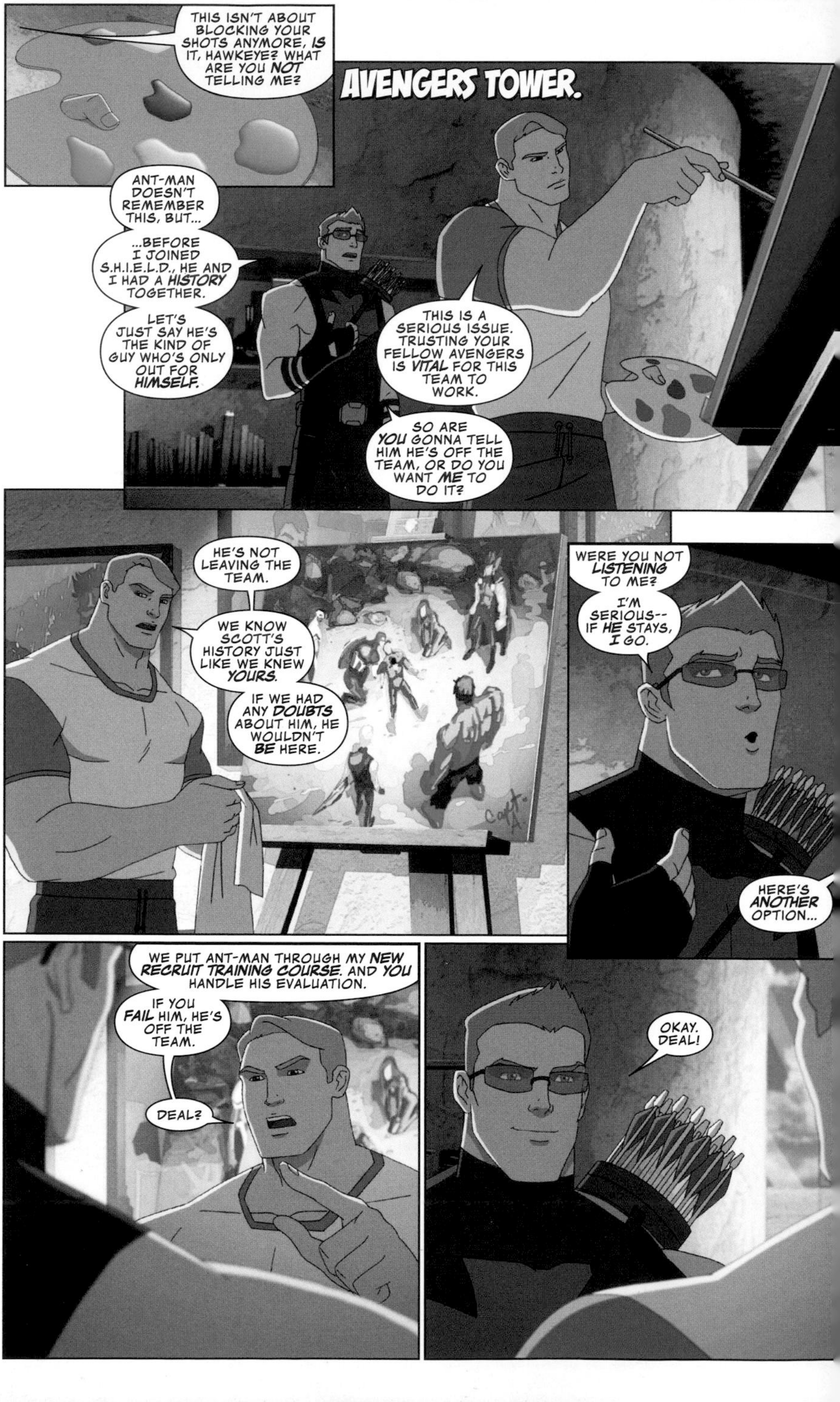
THIS ISN'T ABOUT BLOCKING YOUR SHOTS ANYMORE, IS IT, HAWKEYE? WHAT ARE YOU NOT TELLING ME?
AVENGERS TOWER.
ANT-MAN DOESN'T REMEMBER THIS, BUT...
...BEFORE I JOINED S.H.I.E.L.D., HE AND I HAD A HISTORY TOGETHER.
LET'S JUST SAY HE'S THE KIND OF GUY WHO'S ONLY OUT FOR HIMSELF.
THIS IS A SERIOUS ISSUE. TRUSTING YOUR FELLOW AVENGERS IS VITAL FOR THIS TEAM TO WORK.
SO ARE YOU GONNA TELL HIM HE'S OFF THE TEAM, OR DO YOU WANT ME TO DO IT?
HE'S NOT LEAVING THE TEAM.
WE KNOW SCOTT'S HISTORY JUST LIKE WE KNEW YOURS.
IF WE HAD ANY DOUBTS ABOUT HIM, HE WOULDN'T BE HERE.
WERE YOU NOT LISTENING TO ME?
I'M SERIOUS-- IF HE STAYS, I GO.
HERE'S ANOTHER OPTION...
WE PUT ANT-MAN THROUGH MY NEW RECRUIT TRAINING COURSE. AND YOU HANDLE HIS EVALUATION.
IF YOU FAIL HIM, HE'S OFF THE TEAM.
DEAL?
OKAY. DEAL!

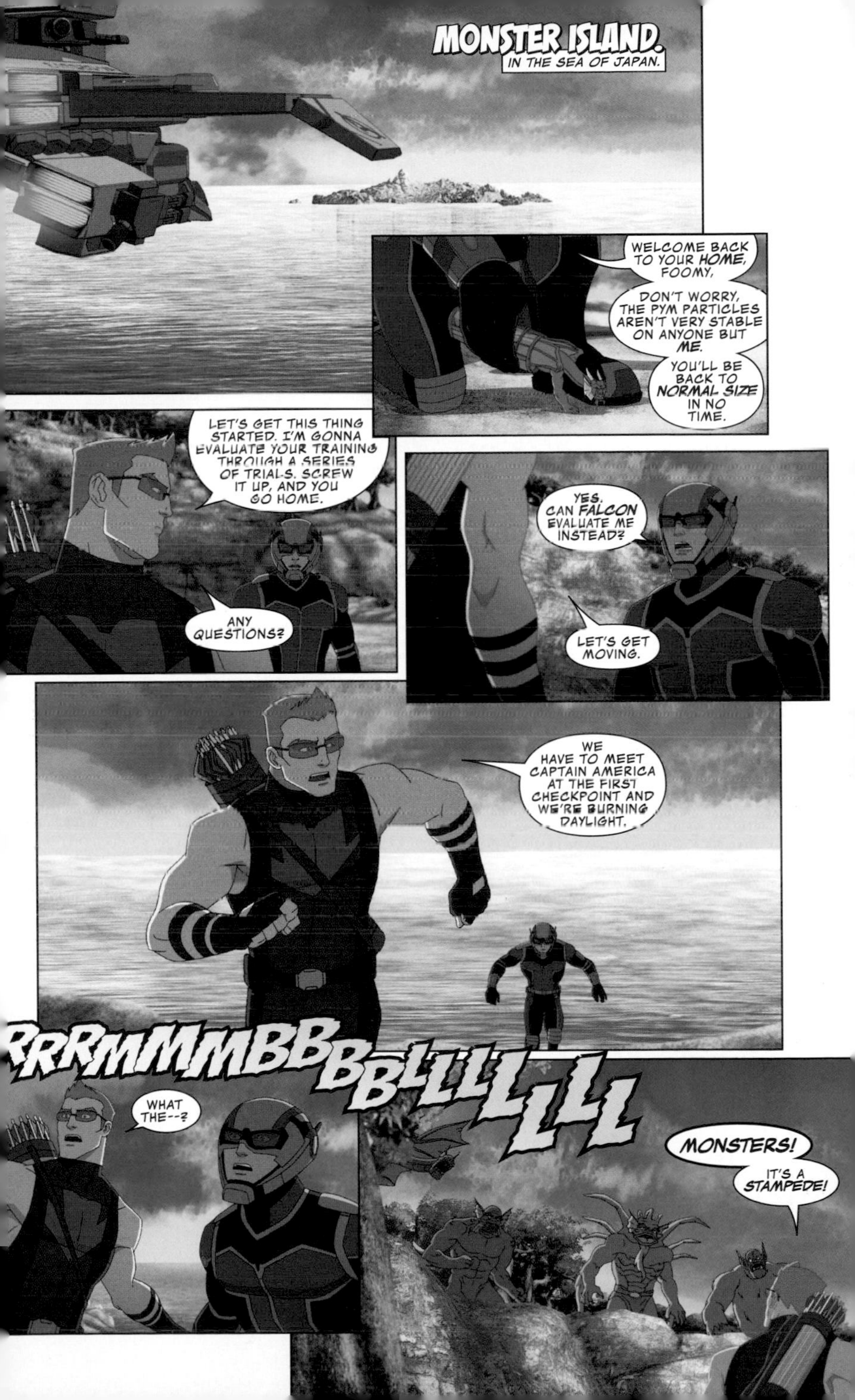
MONSTER ISLAND.
IN THE SEA OF JAPAN.
WELCOME BACK TO YOUR HOME, FOOMY.
DON'T WORRY, THE PYM PARTICLES AREN'T VERY STABLE ON ANYONE BUT ME.
YOU'LL BE BACK TO NORMAL SIZE IN NO TIME.
LET'S GET THIS THING STARTED. I'M GONNA EVALUATE YOUR TRAINING THROUGH A SERIES OF TRIALS. SCREW IT UP, AND YOU GO HOME.
ANY QUESTIONS?
YES. CAN FALCON EVALUATE ME INSTEAD?
LET'S GET MOVING.
WE HAVE TO MEET CAPTAIN AMERICA AT THE FIRST CHECKPOINT AND WE'RE BURNING DAYLIGHT.
RRRMMMMBBBBLLLLLLL
WHAT THE--?
MONSTERS!
IT'S A STAMPEDE!

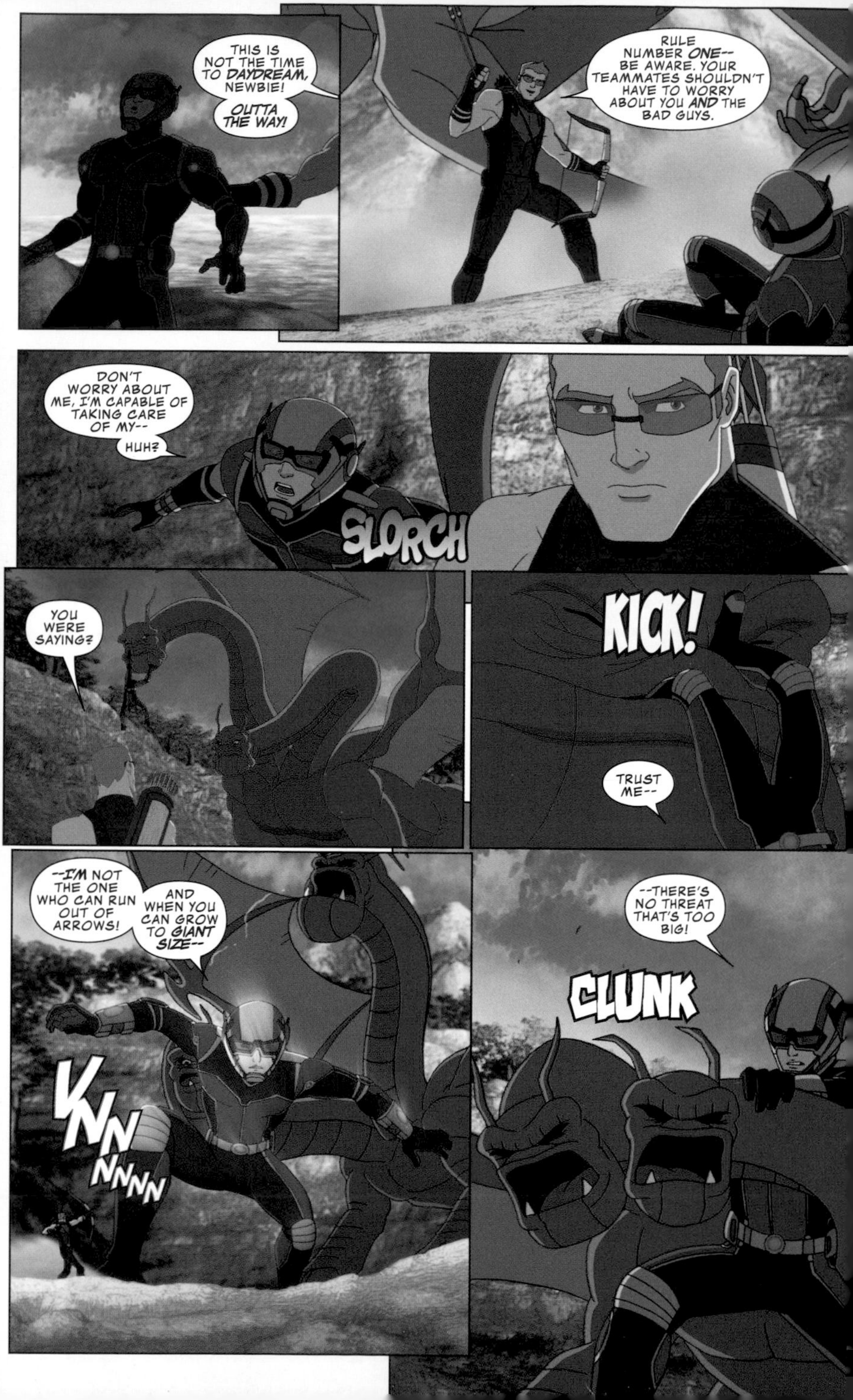

THIS IS NOT THE TIME TO DAYDREAM, NEWBIE!
OUTTA THE WAY!
RULE NUMBER ONE-- BE AWARE. YOUR TEAMMATES SHOULDN'T HAVE TO WORRY ABOUT YOU AND THE BAD GUYS.
DON'T WORRY ABOUT ME, I'M CAPABLE OF TAKING CARE OF MY--
HUH?
SLORCH
YOU WERE SAYING?
KICK!
TRUST ME--
--I'M NOT THE ONE WHO CAN RUN OUT OF ARROWS!
AND WHEN YOU CAN GROW TO GIANT SIZE--
VNNNNNN
--THERE'S NO THREAT THAT'S TOO BIG!
CLUNK

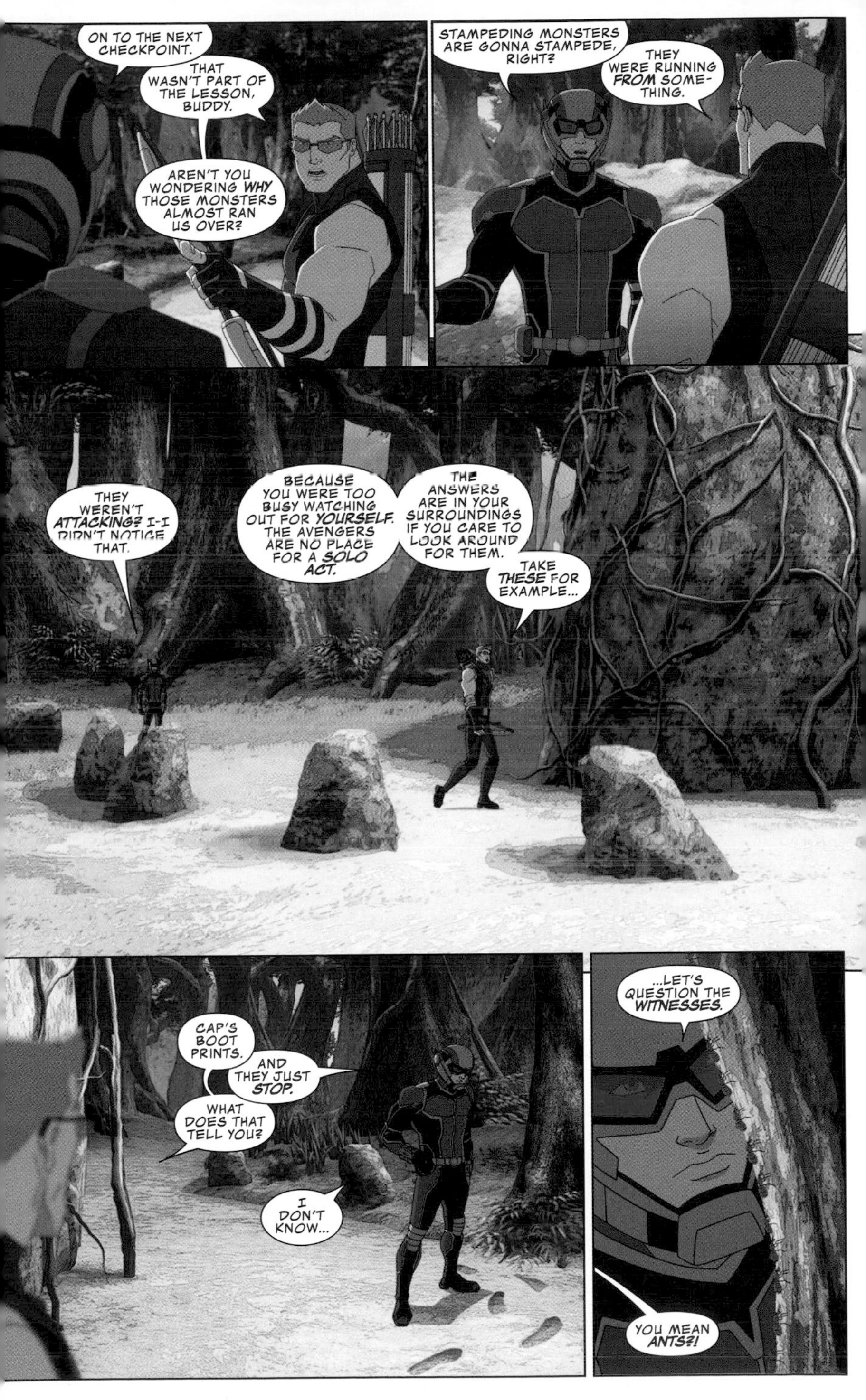
ON TO THE NEXT CHECKPOINT.
THAT WASN'T PART OF THE LESSON, BUDDY.
AREN'T YOU WONDERING WHY THOSE MONSTERS ALMOST RAN US OVER?
STAMPEDING MONSTERS ARE GONNA STAMPEDE, RIGHT?
THEY WERE RUNNING FROM SOME-THING.
THEY WEREN'T ATTACKING? I-I DIDN'T NOTICE THAT.
BECAUSE YOU WERE TOO BUSY WATCHING OUT FOR YOURSELF. THE AVENGERS ARE NO PLACE FOR A SOLO ACT.
THE ANSWERS ARE IN YOUR SURROUNDINGS IF YOU CARE TO LOOK AROUND FOR THEM.
TAKE THESE FOR EXAMPLE...
CAP'S BOOT PRINTS.
AND THEY JUST STOP.
WHAT DOES THAT TELL YOU?
I DON'T KNOW...
...LET'S QUESTION THE WITNESSES.
YOU MEAN ANTS?!

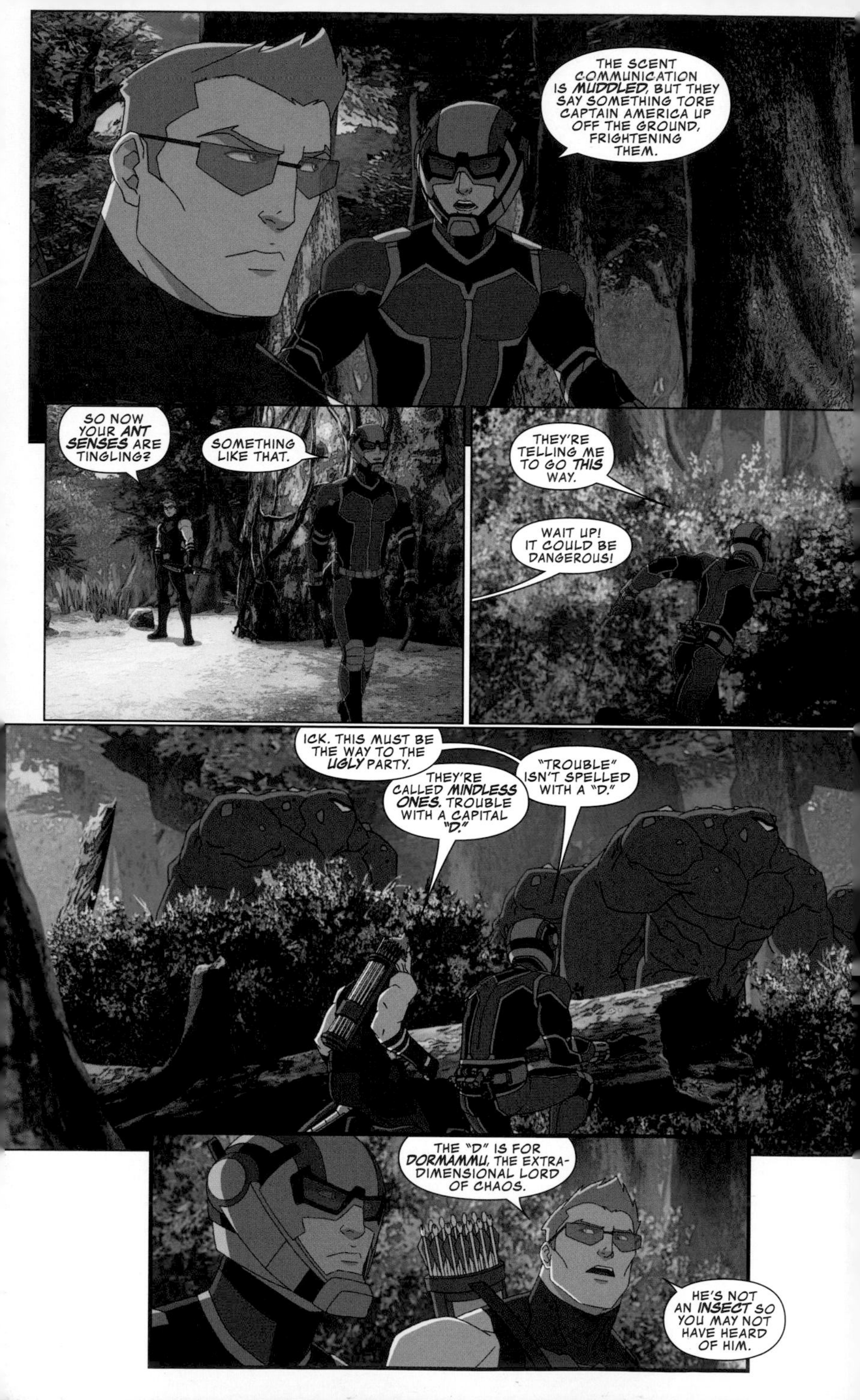
THE SCENT COMMUNICATION IS MUDDLED, BUT THEY SAY SOMETHING TORE CAPTAIN AMERICA UP OFF THE GROUND, FRIGHTENING THEM.
SO NOW YOUR ANT SENSES ARE TINGLING?
SOMETHING LIKE THAT.
THEY'RE TELLING ME TO GO THIS WAY.
WAIT UP! IT COULD BE DANGEROUS!
ICK. THIS MUST BE THE WAY TO THE UGLY PARTY.
THEY'RE CALLED MINDLESS ONES. TROUBLE WITH A CAPITAL "D."
"TROUBLE" ISN'T SPELLED WITH A "D."
THE "D" IS FOR DORMAMMU, THE EXTRA-DIMENSIONAL LORD OF CHAOS.
HE'S NOT AN INSECT SO YOU MAY NOT HAVE HEARD OF HIM.

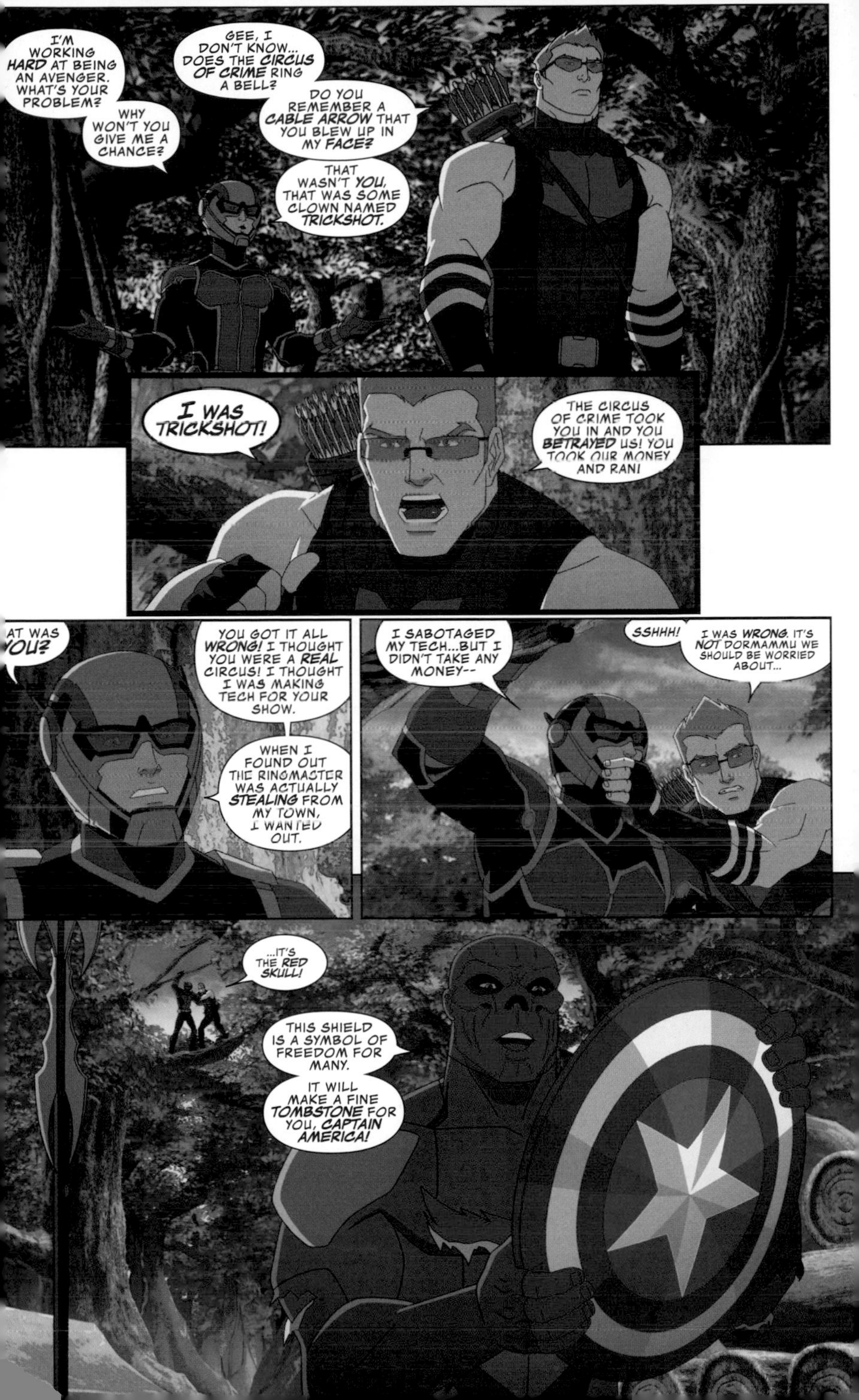
I'M WORKING HARD AT BEING AN AVENGER. WHAT'S YOUR PROBLEM?
WHY WON'T YOU GIVE ME A CHANCE?
GEE, I DON'T KNOW... DOES THE CIRCUS OF CRIME RING A BELL?
DO YOU REMEMBER A CABLE ARROW THAT YOU BLEW UP IN MY FACE?
THAT WASN'T YOU, THAT WAS SOME CLOWN NAMED TRICKSHOT.
I WAS TRICKSHOT!
THE CIRCUS OF CRIME TOOK YOU IN AND YOU BETRAYED US! YOU TOOK OUR MONEY AND RAN!
AT WAS YOU?
YOU GOT IT ALL WRONG! I THOUGHT YOU WERE A REAL CIRCUS! I THOUGHT I WAS MAKING TECH FOR YOUR SHOW.
WHEN I FOUND OUT THE RINGMASTER WAS ACTUALLY STEALING FROM MY TOWN, I WANTED OUT.
I SABOTAGED MY TECH...BUT I DIDN'T TAKE ANY MONEY--
SSHHH!
I WAS WRONG. IT'S NOT DORMAMMU WE SHOULD BE WORRIED ABOUT...
...IT'S THE RED SKULL!
THIS SHIELD IS A SYMBOL OF FREEDOM FOR MANY.
IT WILL MAKE A FINE TOMBSTONE FOR YOU, CAPTAIN AMERICA!

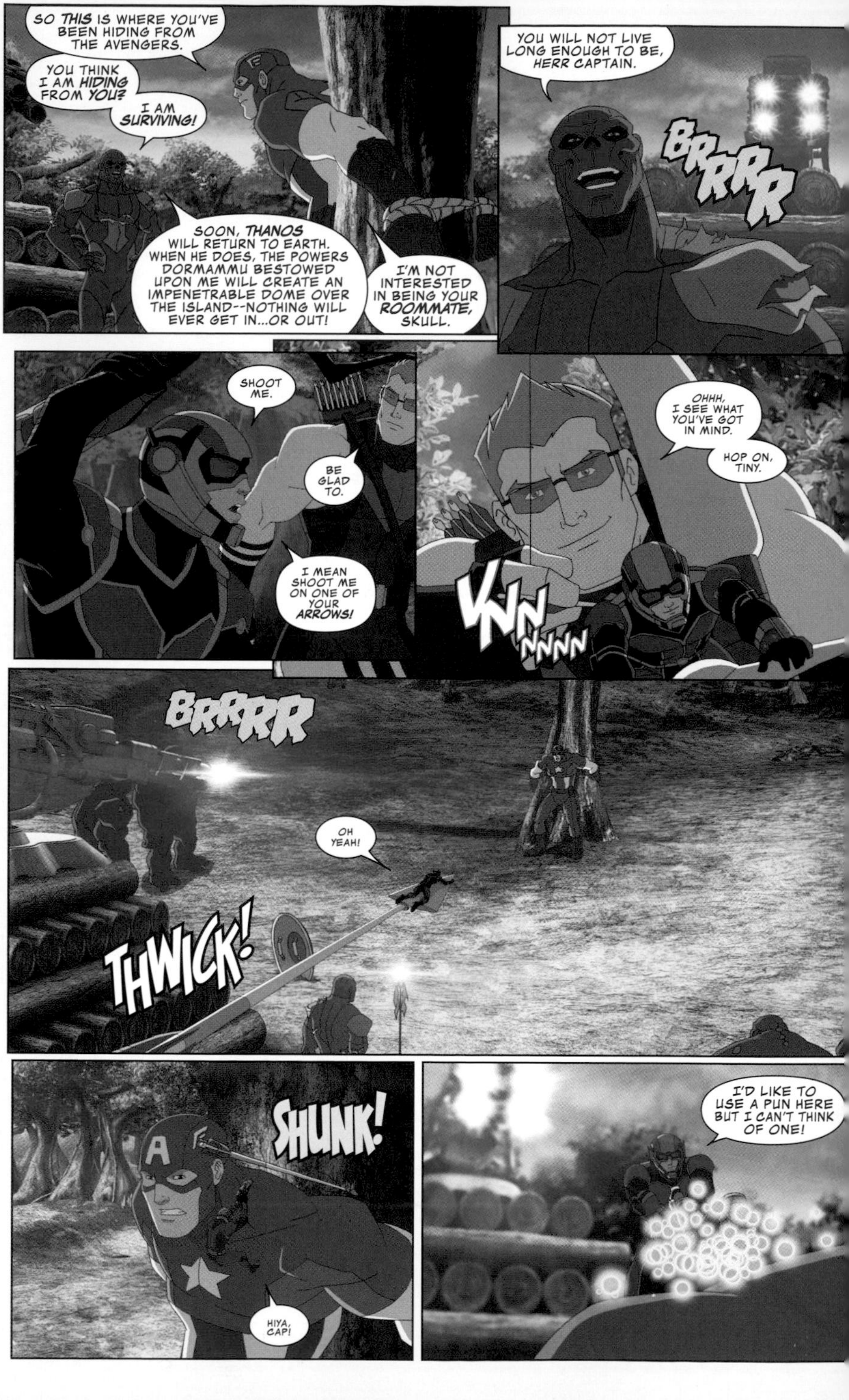
SO THIS IS WHERE YOU'VE BEEN HIDING FROM THE AVENGERS.
YOU THINK I AM HIDING FROM YOU?
I AM SURVIVING!
SOON, THANOS WILL RETURN TO EARTH. WHEN HE DOES, THE POWERS DORMAMMU BESTOWED UPON ME WILL CREATE AN IMPENETRABLE DOME OVER THE ISLAND--NOTHING WILL EVER GET IN...OR OUT!
I'M NOT INTERESTED IN BEING YOUR ROOMMATE, SKULL.
YOU WILL NOT LIVE LONG ENOUGH TO BE, HERR CAPTAIN.
BRRRR
SHOOT ME.
BE GLAD TO.
I MEAN SHOOT ME ON ONE OF YOUR ARROWS!
OHHH, I SEE WHAT YOU'VE GOT IN MIND.
HOP ON, TINY.
VNNNNNN
BRRRR
OH YEAH!
THWICK!
SHUNK!
HIYA, CAP!
I'D LIKE TO USE A PUN HERE BUT I CAN'T THINK OF ONE!

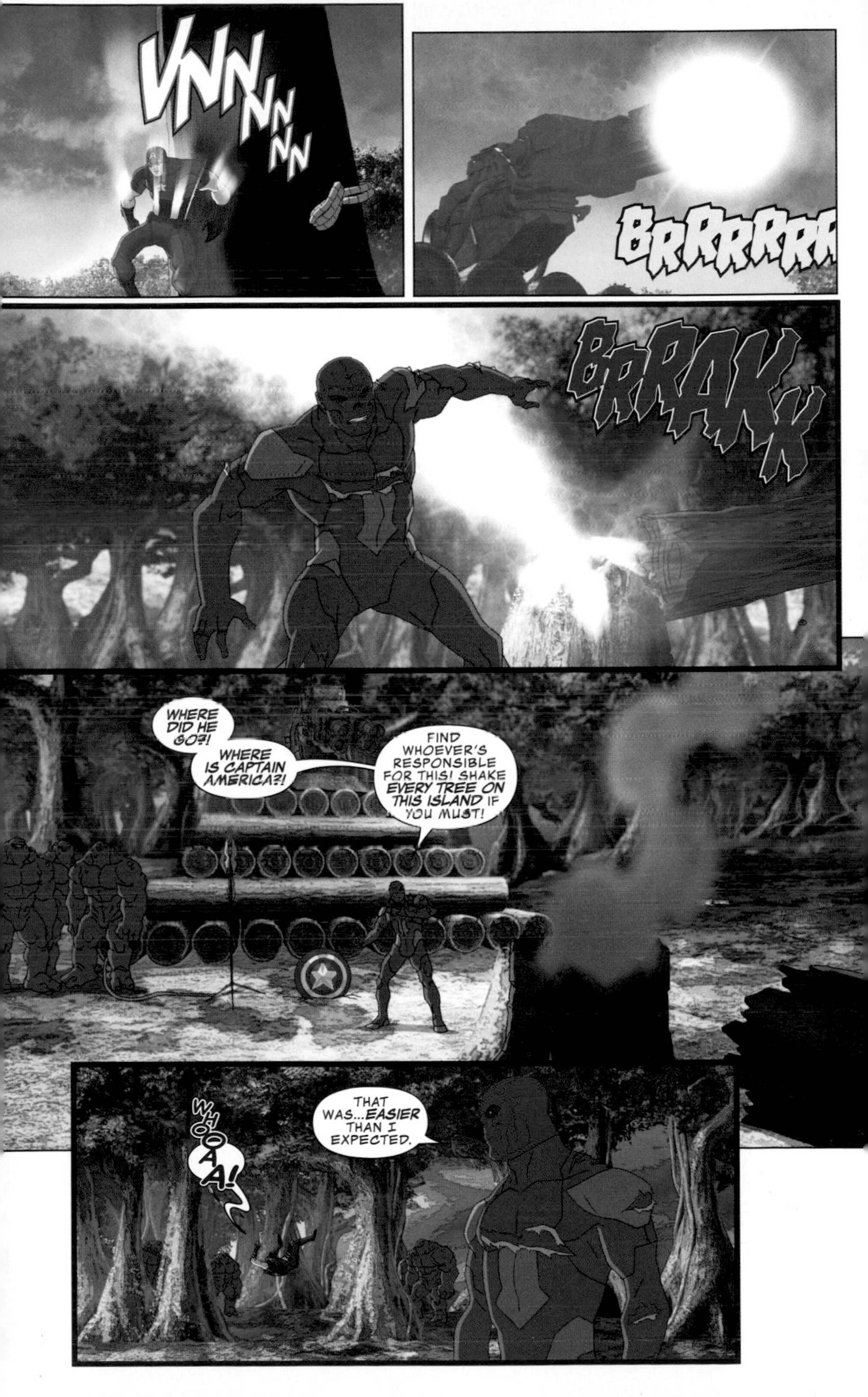
VNNNNNN
BRRRRRR
BRRAKK
WHERE DID HE GO?!
WHERE IS CAPTAIN AMERICA?!
FIND WHOEVER'S RESPONSIBLE FOR THIS! SHAKE EVERY TREE ON THIS ISLAND IF YOU MUST!
WHOOAA!
THAT WAS...EASIER THAN I EXPECTED.

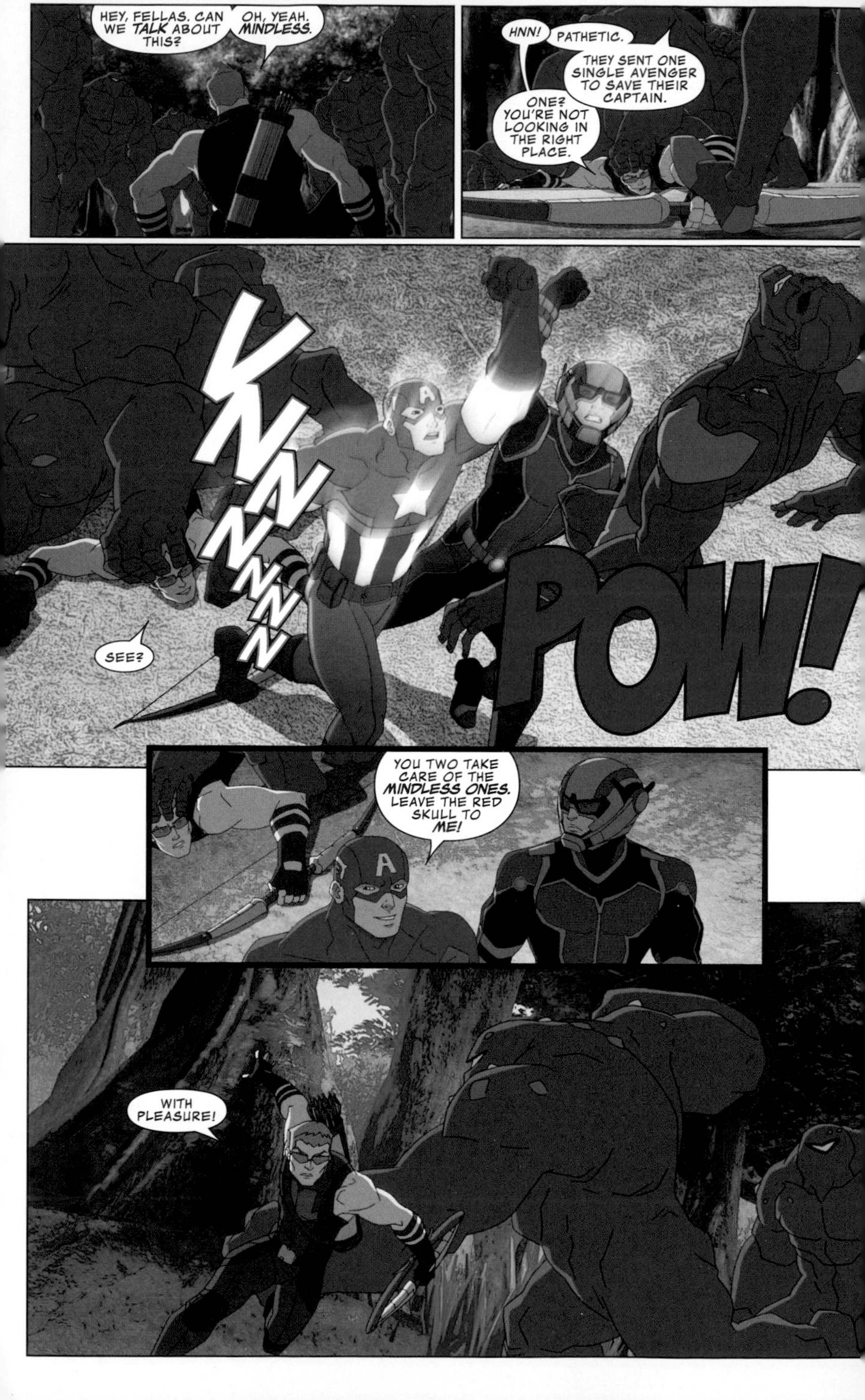
HEY, FELLAS. CAN WE TALK ABOUT THIS?
OH, YEAH. MINDLESS.
HNN!
PATHETIC.
THEY SENT ONE SINGLE AVENGER TO SAVE THEIR CAPTAIN.
ONE? YOU'RE NOT LOOKING IN THE RIGHT PLACE.
KNNNNNN
SEE?
POW!!
YOU TWO TAKE CARE OF THE MINDLESS ONES. LEAVE THE RED SKULL TO ME!
WITH PLEASURE!

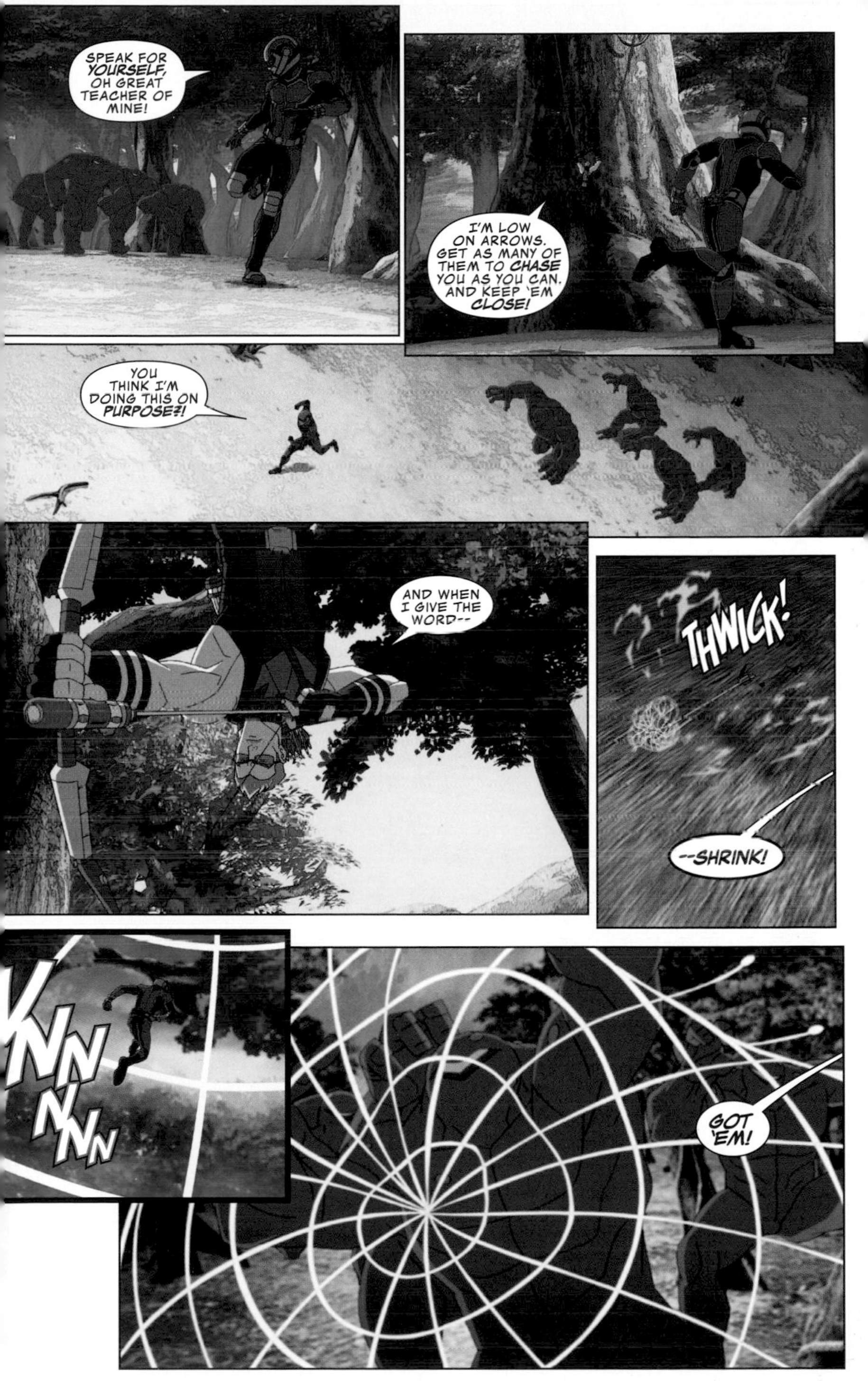
SPEAK FOR YOURSELF, OH GREAT TEACHER OF MINE!
I'M LOW ON ARROWS. GET AS MANY OF THEM TO CHASE YOU AS YOU CAN. AND KEEP 'EM CLOSE!
YOU THINK I'M DOING THIS ON PURPOSE?!
AND WHEN I GIVE THE WORD--
THWICK!
--SHRINK!
NNNNNN
GOT 'EM!

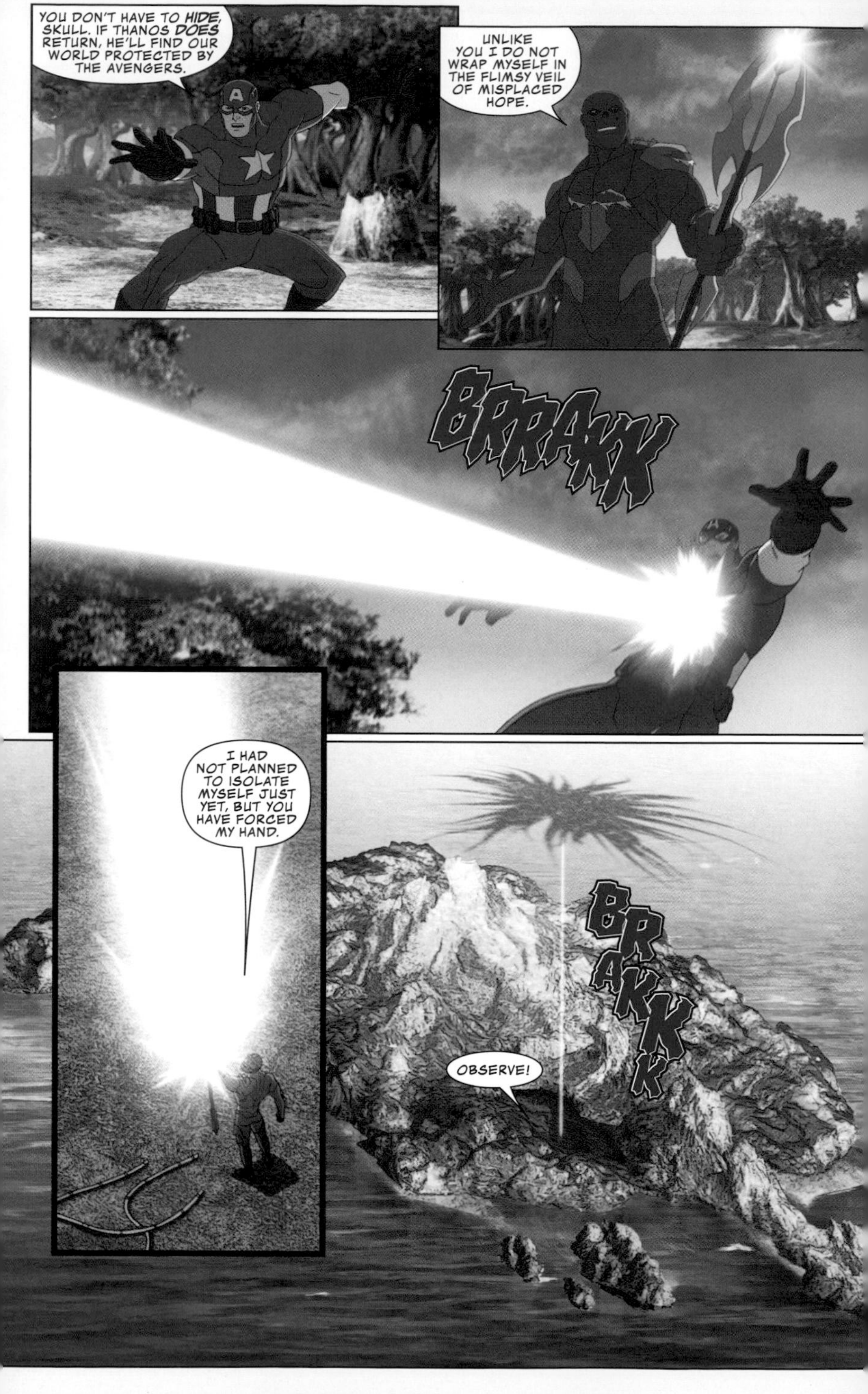
YOU DON'T HAVE TO HIDE, SKULL. IF THANOS DOES RETURN, HE'LL FIND OUR WORLD PROTECTED BY THE AVENGERS.
UNLIKE YOU I DO NOT WRAP MYSELF IN THE FLIMSY VEIL OF MISPLACED HOPE.
BRRAKK
I HAD NOT PLANNED TO ISOLATE MYSELF JUST YET, BUT YOU HAVE FORCED MY HAND.
BRAKKK
OBSERVE!

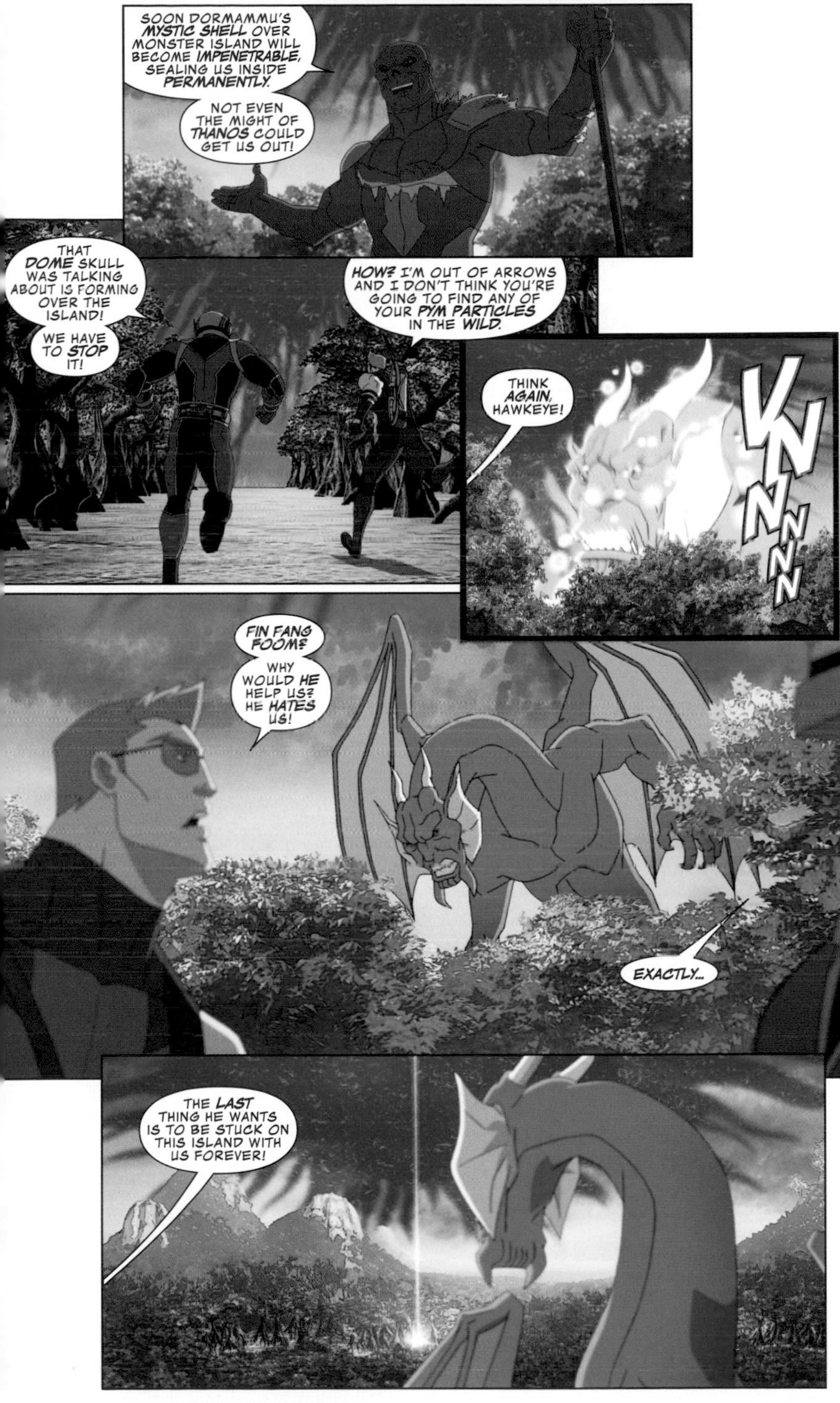
SOON DORMAMMU'S MYSTIC SHELL OVER MONSTER ISLAND WILL BECOME IMPENETRABLE, SEALING US INSIDE PERMANENTLY.
NOT EVEN THE MIGHT OF THANOS COULD GET US OUT!
THAT DOME SKULL WAS TALKING ABOUT IS FORMING OVER THE ISLAND!
WE HAVE TO STOP IT!
HOW? I'M OUT OF ARROWS AND I DON'T THINK YOU'RE GOING TO FIND ANY OF YOUR PYM PARTICLES IN THE WILD.
THINK AGAIN, HAWKEYE!
VNNNNNN
FIN FANG FOOM?
WHY WOULD HE HELP US? HE HATES US!
EXACTLY...
THE LAST THING HE WANTS IS TO BE STUCK ON THIS ISLAND WITH US FOREVER!

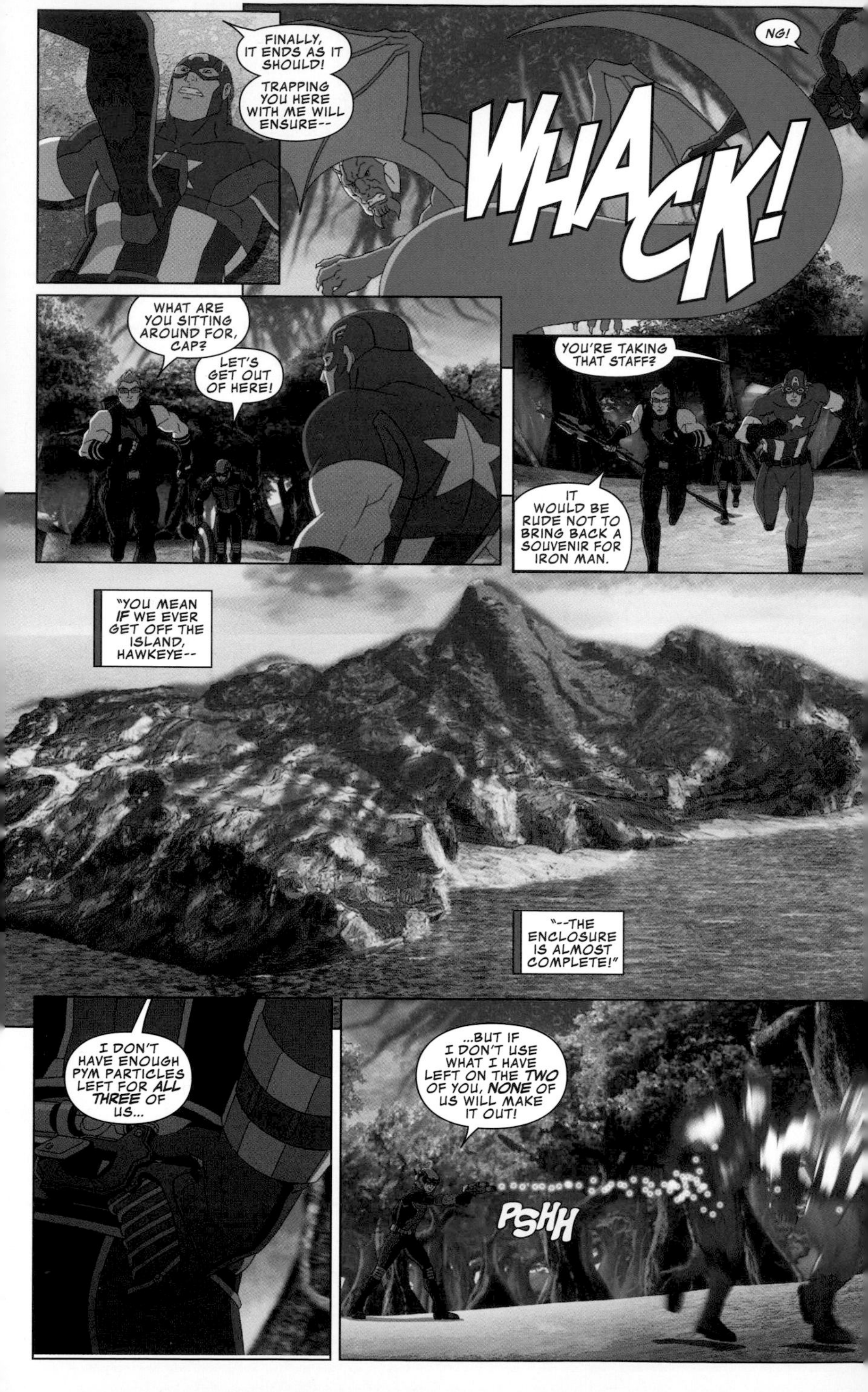
FINALLY, IT ENDS AS IT SHOULD!
TRAPPING YOU HERE WITH ME WILL ENSURE--
WHACK!
NG!
WHAT ARE YOU SITTING AROUND FOR, CAP?
LET'S GET OUT OF HERE!
YOU'RE TAKING THAT STAFF?
IT WOULD BE RUDE NOT TO BRING BACK A SOUVENIR FOR IRON MAN.
"YOU MEAN IF WE EVER GET OFF THE ISLAND, HAWKEYE--
"--THE ENCLOSURE IS ALMOST COMPLETE!"
I DON'T HAVE ENOUGH PYM PARTICLES LEFT FOR ALL THREE OF US...
...BUT IF I DON'T USE WHAT I HAVE LEFT ON THE TWO OF YOU, NONE OF US WILL MAKE IT OUT!
PSHH

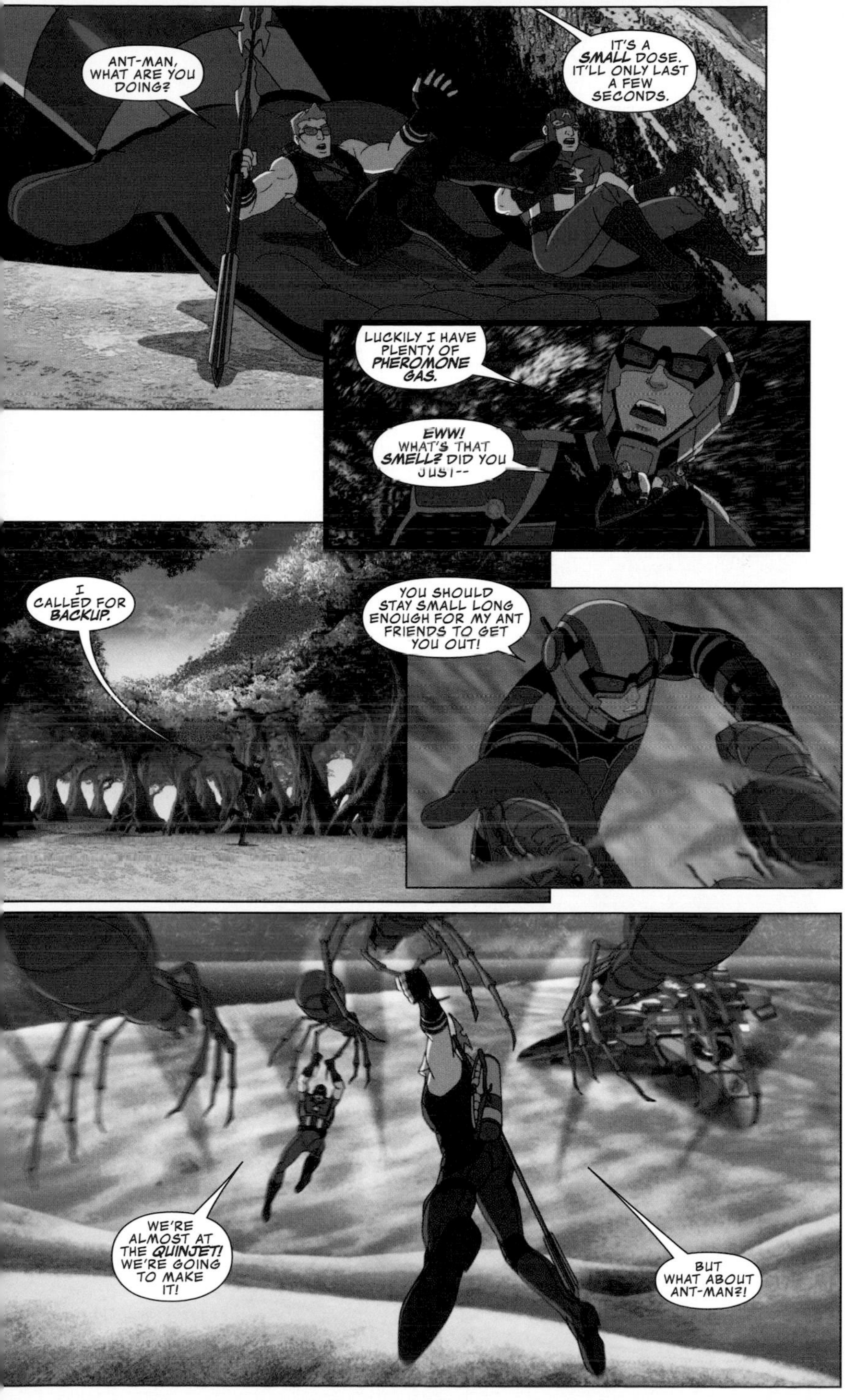
ANT-MAN, WHAT ARE YOU DOING?
IT'S A SMALL DOSE. IT'LL ONLY LAST A FEW SECONDS.
LUCKILY I HAVE PLENTY OF PHEROMONE GAS.
EWW! WHAT'S THAT SMELL? DID YOU JUST--
I CALLED FOR BACKUP.
YOU SHOULD STAY SMALL LONG ENOUGH FOR MY ANT FRIENDS TO GET YOU OUT!
WE'RE ALMOST AT THE QUINJET! WE'RE GOING TO MAKE IT!
BUT WHAT ABOUT ANT-MAN?!

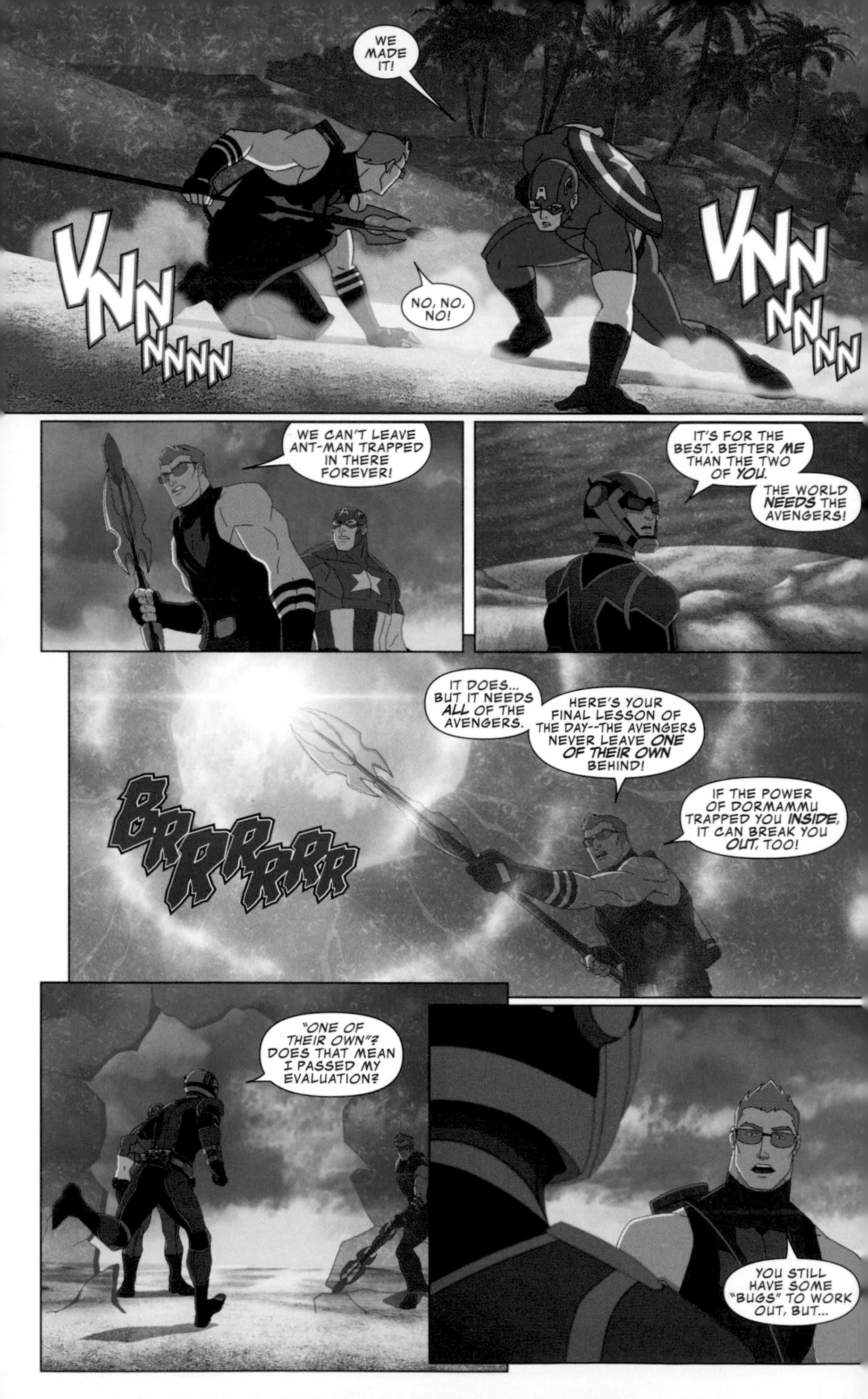
WE MADE IT!
VNNNNNN
NO, NO, NO!
VNNNNNNN
WE CAN'T LEAVE ANT-MAN TRAPPED IN THERE FOREVER!
IT'S FOR THE BEST. BETTER ME THAN THE TWO OF YOU.
THE WORLD NEEDS THE AVENGERS!
IT DOES... BUT IT NEEDS ALL OF THE AVENGERS.
HERE'S YOUR FINAL LESSON OF THE DAY--THE AVENGERS NEVER LEAVE ONE OF THEIR OWN BEHIND!
BRRRRRR
IF THE POWER OF DORMAMMU TRAPPED YOU INSIDE, IT CAN BREAK YOU OUT, TOO!
"ONE OF THEIR OWN"? DOES THAT MEAN I PASSED MY EVALUATION?
YOU STILL HAVE SOME "BUGS" TO WORK OUT, BUT...

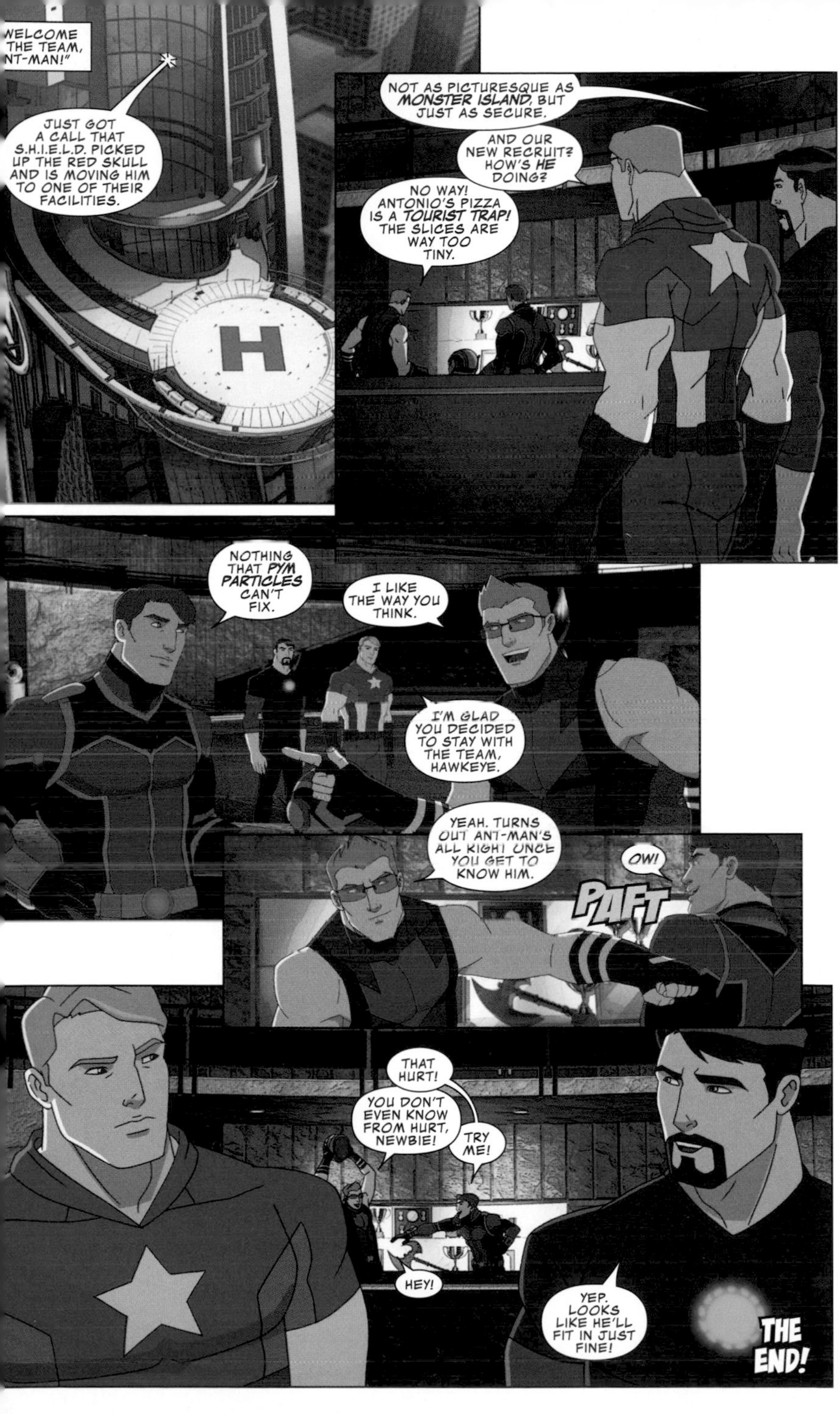

"WELCOME
THE TEAM,
NT-MAN!"
JUST GOT A CALL THAT S.H.I.E.L.D. PICKED UP THE RED SKULL AND IS MOVING HIM TO ONE OF THEIR FACILITIES.
NOT AS PICTURESQUE AS MONSTER ISLAND, BUT JUST AS SECURE.
AND OUR NEW RECRUIT? HOW'S HE DOING?
NO WAY! ANTONIO'S PIZZA IS A TOURIST TRAP! THE SLICES ARE WAY TOO TINY.
NOTHING THAT PYM PARTICLES CAN'T FIX.
I LIKE THE WAY YOU THINK.
I'M GLAD YOU DECIDED TO STAY WITH THE TEAM, HAWKEYE.
YEAH. TURNS OUT ANT-MAN'S ALL RIGHT ONCE YOU GET TO KNOW HIM.
PAFT
OW!
THAT HURT!
YOU DON'T EVEN KNOW FROM HURT, NEWBIE!
TRY ME!
HEY!
YEP. LOOKS LIKE HE'LL FIT IN JUST FINE!
THE END!

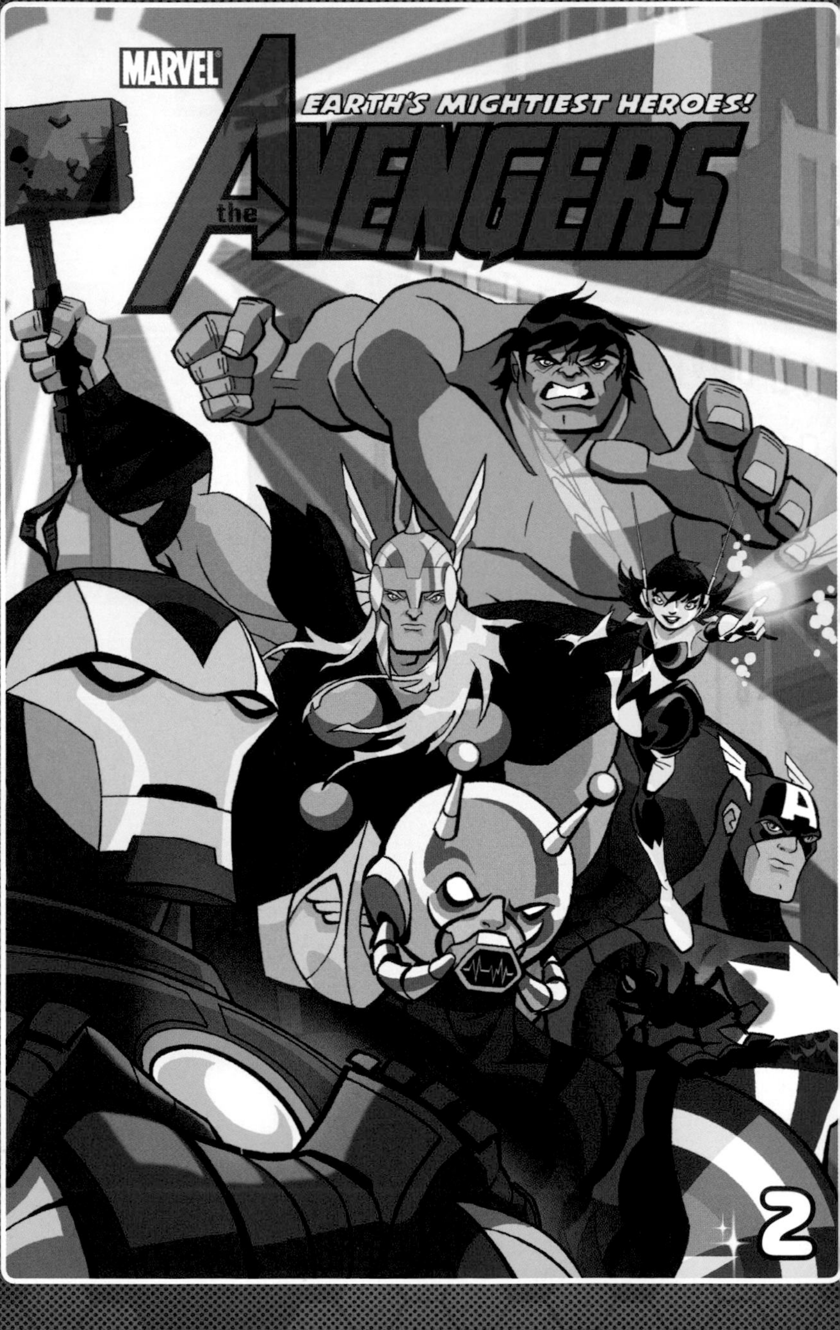
MARVEL
EARTH'S MIGHTIEST HEROES!
the AVENGERS
2

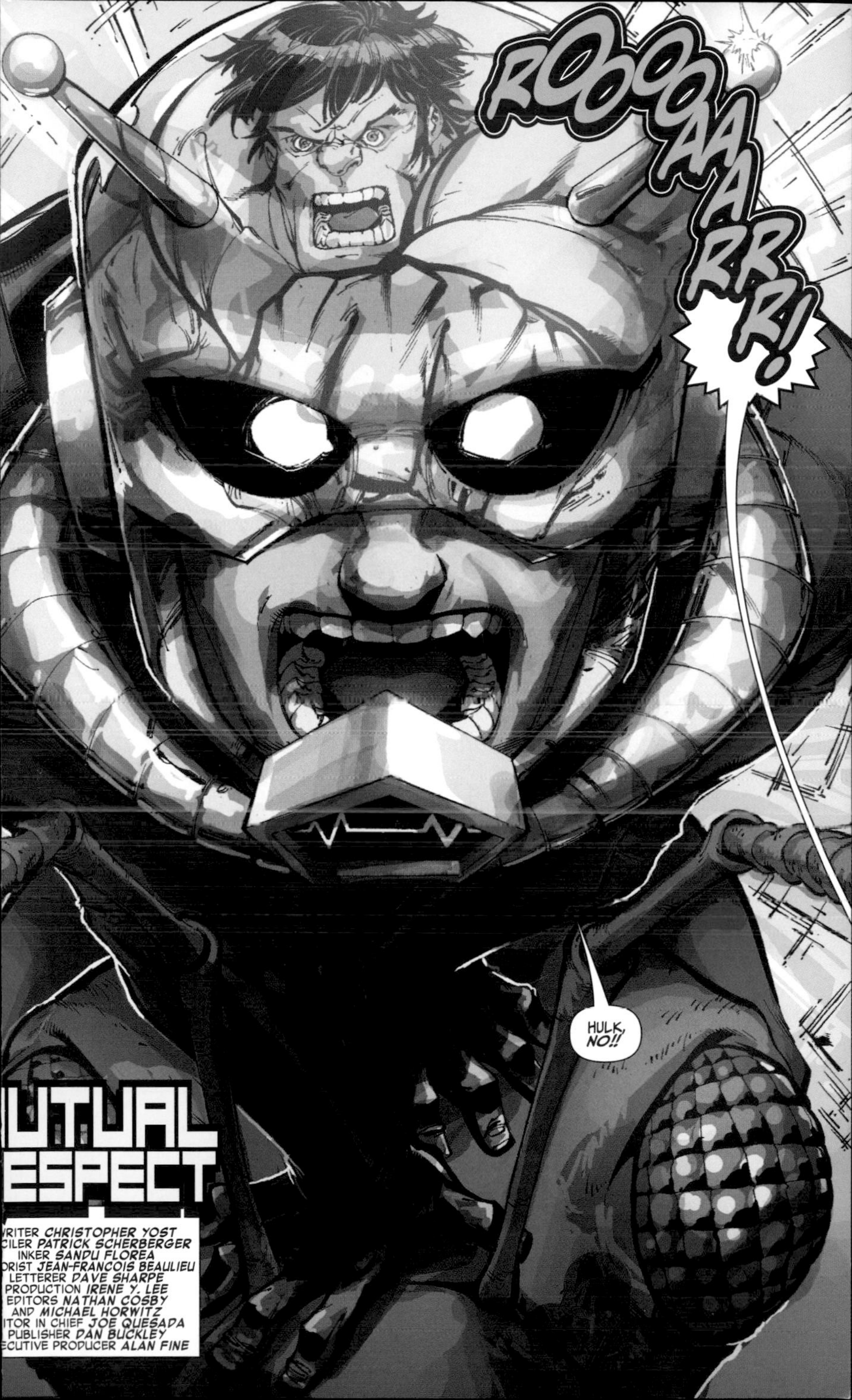
ROOOOAAARRR!
HULK, NO!!
UTUAL
ESPECT
RITER CHRISTOPHER YOST
CILER PATRICK SCHERBERGER
INKER SANDU FLOREA
ORIST JEAN-FRANCOIS BEAULIEU
LETTERER DAVE SHARPE
PRODUCTION IRENE Y. LEE
EDITORS NATHAN COSBY
AND MICHAEL HORWITZ
ITOR IN CHIEF JOE QUESADA
PUBLISHER DAN BUCKLEY
ECUTIVE PRODUCER ALAN FINE

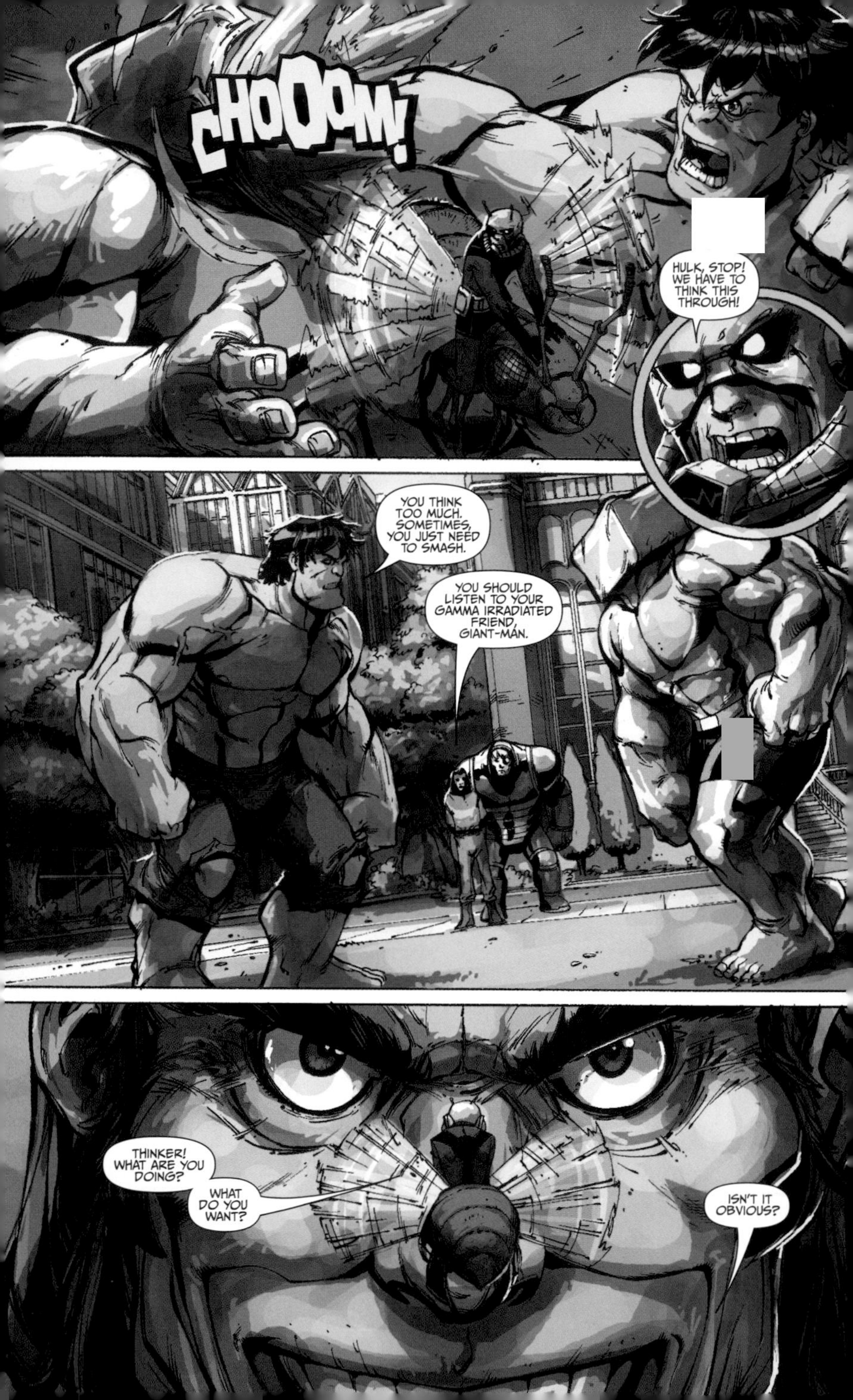
CHOOOM!
HULK, STOP! WE HAVE TO THINK THIS THROUGH!
YOU THINK TOO MUCH. SOMETIMES, YOU JUST NEED TO SMASH.
YOU SHOULD LISTEN TO YOUR GAMMA IRRADIATED FRIEND, GIANT-MAN.
THINKER! WHAT ARE YOU DOING?
WHAT DO YOU WANT?
ISN'T IT OBVIOUS?

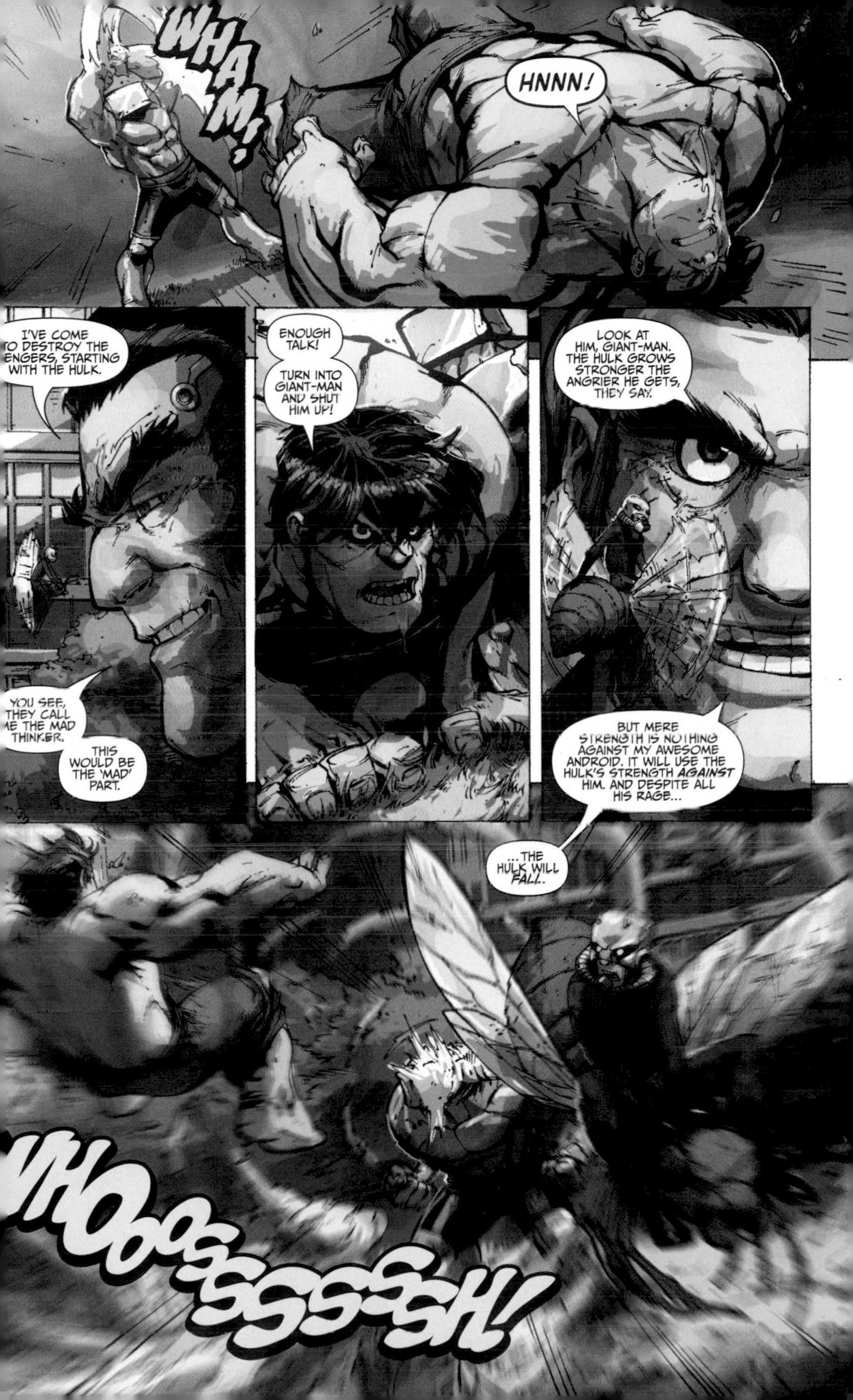
WHAM!
HNNN!
I'VE COME TO DESTROY THE ENGERS, STARTING WITH THE HULK.
YOU SEE, THEY CALL ME THE MAD THINKER.
THIS WOULD BE THE 'MAD' PART.
ENOUGH TALK!
TURN INTO GIANT-MAN AND SHUT HIM UP!
LOOK AT HIM, GIANT-MAN. THE HULK GROWS STRONGER THE ANGRIER HE GETS, THEY SAY.
BUT MERE STRENGTH IS NOTHING AGAINST MY AWESOME ANDROID. IT WILL USE THE HULK'S STRENGTH AGAINST HIM. AND DESPITE ALL HIS RAGE...
...THE HULK WILL FALL.
WHOOSSSSSSH!

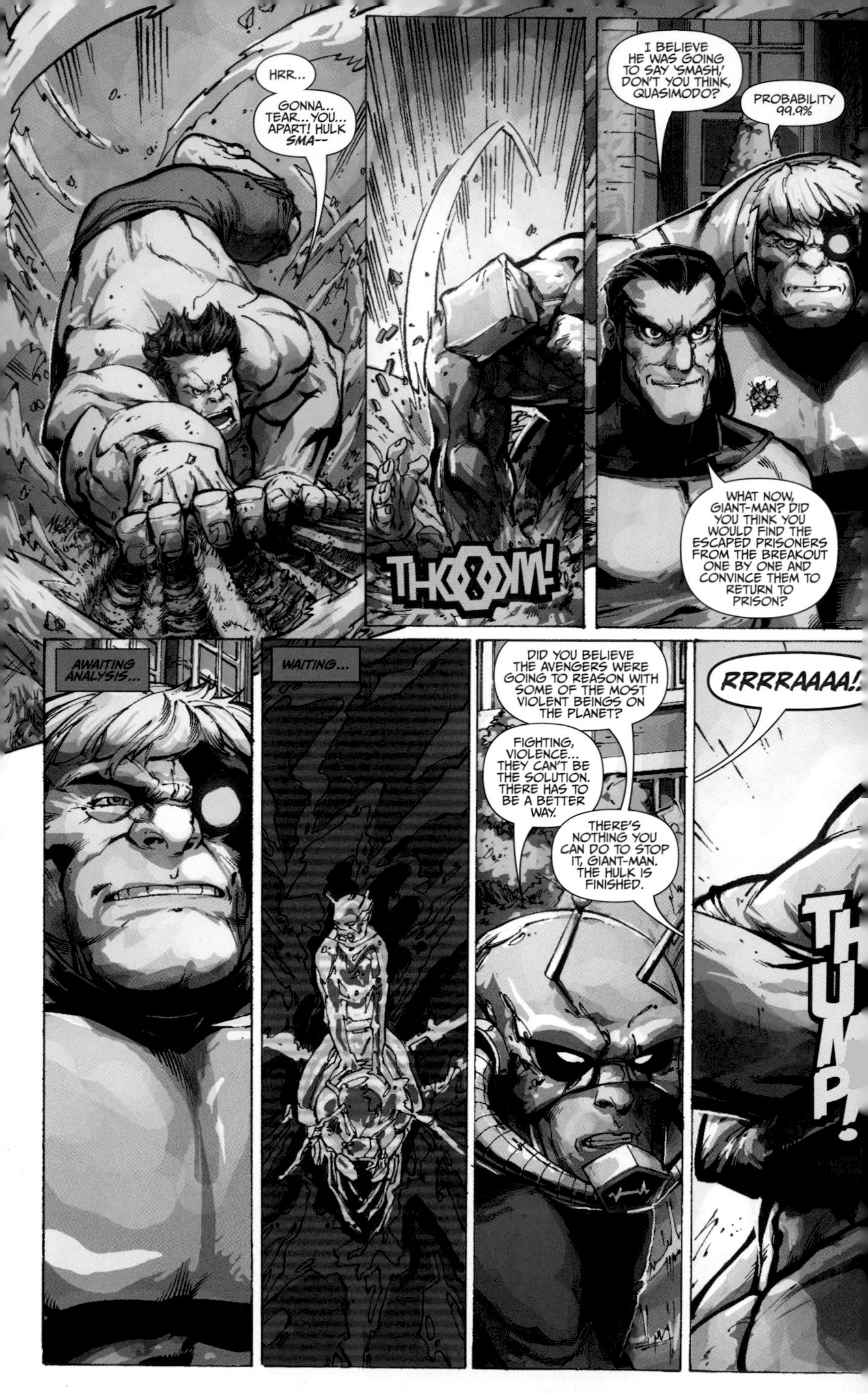

HRR...
GONNA... TEAR... YOU... APART! HULK SMA--
THOOOM!
I BELIEVE HE WAS GOING TO SAY 'SMASH,' DON'T YOU THINK, QUASIMODO?
PROBABILITY 99.9%
WHAT NOW, GIANT-MAN? DID YOU THINK YOU WOULD FIND THE ESCAPED PRISONERS FROM THE BREAKOUT ONE BY ONE AND CONVINCE THEM TO RETURN TO PRISON?
AWAITING ANALYSIS...
WAITING...
DID YOU BELIEVE THE AVENGERS WERE GOING TO REASON WITH SOME OF THE MOST VIOLENT BEINGS ON THE PLANET?
FIGHTING, VIOLENCE... THEY CAN'T BE THE SOLUTION. THERE HAS TO BE A BETTER WAY.
THERE'S NOTHING YOU CAN DO TO STOP IT, GIANT-MAN. THE HULK IS FINISHED.
RRRRAAAA!!
THUMP!

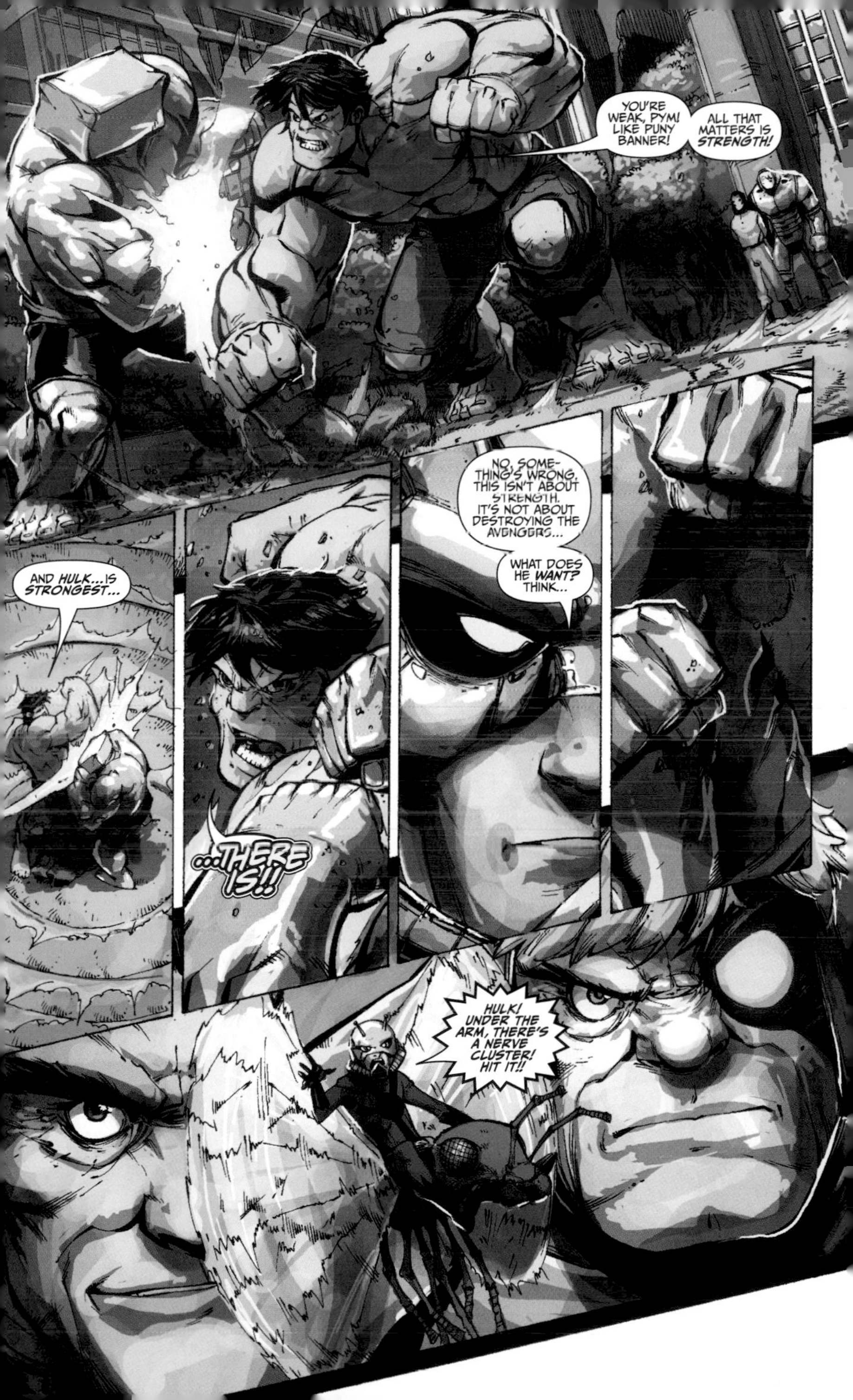
YOU'RE WEAK, PYM! LIKE PUNY BANNER!
ALL THAT MATTERS IS STRENGTH!
AND HULK...IS STRONGEST...
...THERE IS!!
NO, SOMETHING'S WRONG. THIS ISN'T ABOUT STRENGTH. IT'S NOT ABOUT DESTROYING THE AVENGERS...
WHAT DOES HE WANT? THINK...
HULK! UNDER THE ARM, THERE'S A NERVE CLUSTER! HIT IT!!

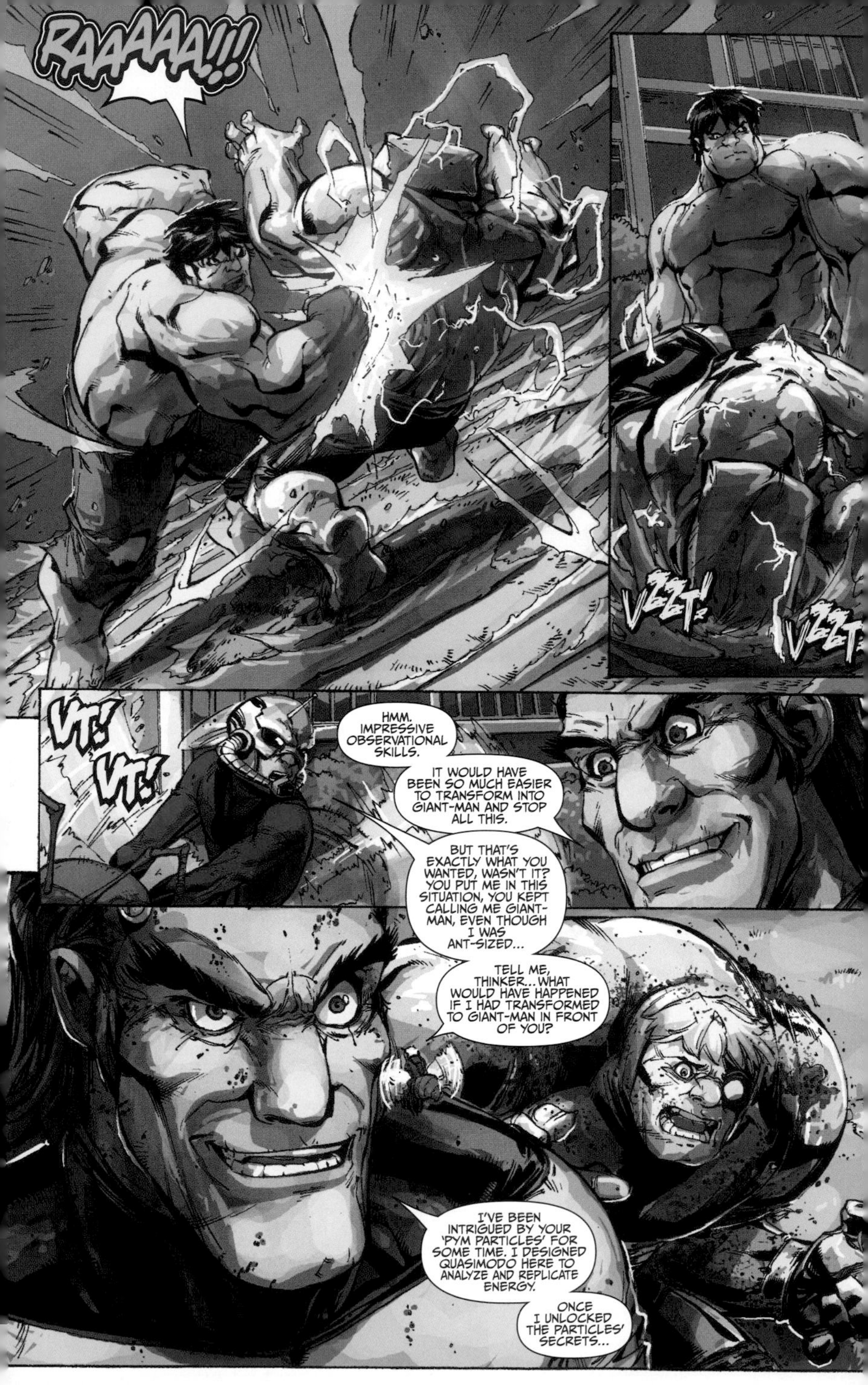
RAAAAA!!!
VZZZT!
VZZZT!
VT! VT!
HMM. IMPRESSIVE OBSERVATIONAL SKILLS.
IT WOULD HAVE BEEN SO MUCH EASIER TO TRANSFORM INTO GIANT-MAN AND STOP ALL THIS.
BUT THAT'S EXACTLY WHAT YOU WANTED, WASN'T IT? YOU PUT ME IN THIS SITUATION, YOU KEPT CALLING ME GIANT-MAN, EVEN THOUGH I WAS ANT-SIZED...
TELL ME, THINKER... WHAT WOULD HAVE HAPPENED IF I HAD TRANSFORMED TO GIANT-MAN IN FRONT OF YOU?
I'VE BEEN INTRIGUED BY YOUR 'PYM PARTICLES' FOR SOME TIME. I DESIGNED QUASIMODO HERE TO ANALYZE AND REPLICATE ENERGY.
ONCE I UNLOCKED THE PARTICLES' SECRETS...

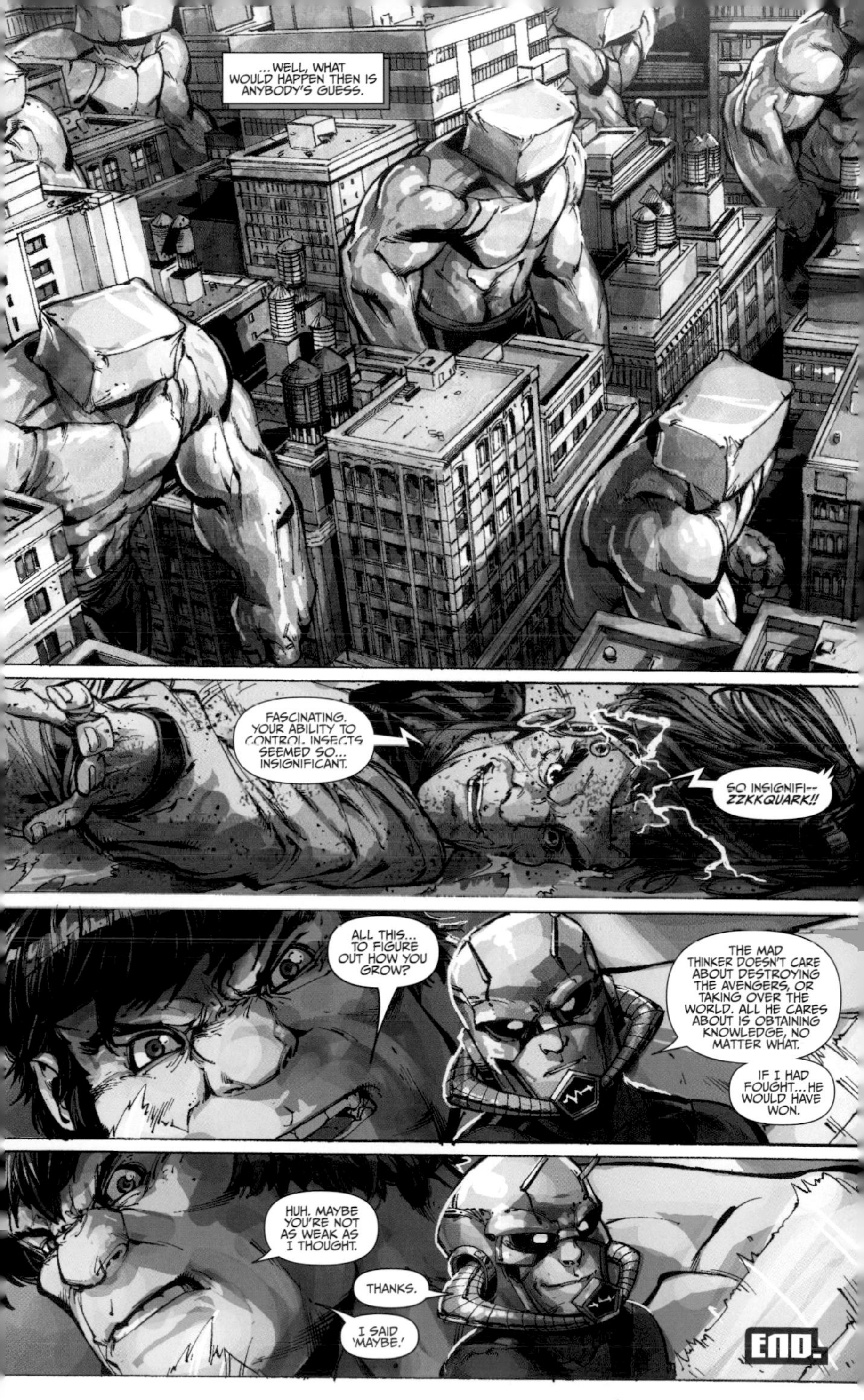
...WELL, WHAT WOULD HAPPEN THEN IS ANYBODY'S GUESS.
FASCINATING. YOUR ABILITY TO CONTROL INSECTS SEEMED SO... INSIGNIFICANT.
SO INSIGNIFI-- ZZKKQUARK!!
ALL THIS... TO FIGURE OUT HOW YOU GROW?
THE MAD THINKER DOESN'T CARE ABOUT DESTROYING THE AVENGERS, OR TAKING OVER THE WORLD. ALL HE CARES ABOUT IS OBTAINING KNOWLEDGE, NO MATTER WHAT.
IF I HAD FOUGHT... HE WOULD HAVE WON.
HUH. MAYBE YOU'RE NOT AS WEAK AS I THOUGHT.
THANKS.
I SAID 'MAYBE.'
END.

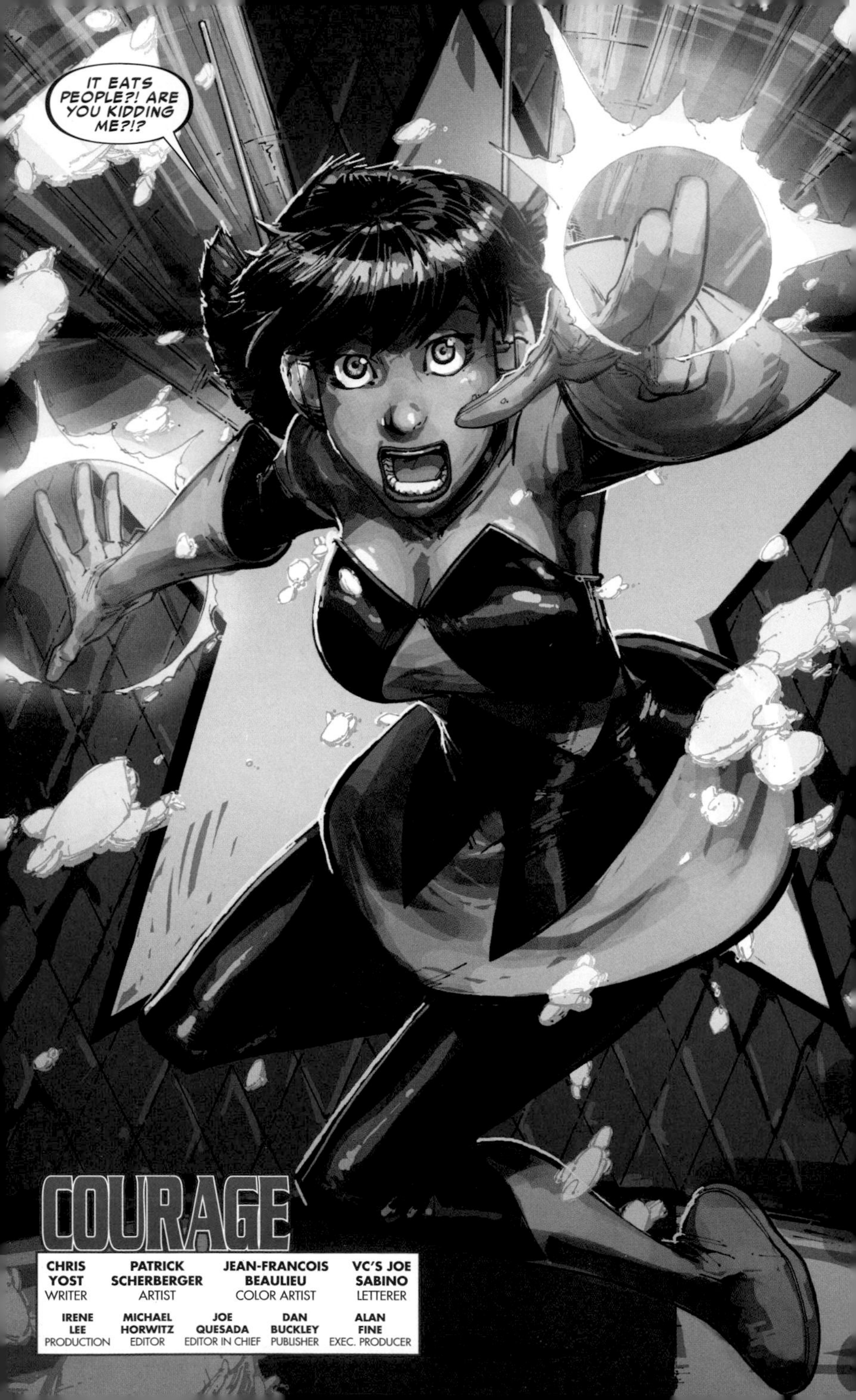
IT EATS PEOPLE?! ARE YOU KIDDING ME?!?
COURAGE
CHRIS YOST WRITER
PATRICK SCHERBERGER ARTIST
JEAN-FRANCOIS BEAULIEU COLOR ARTIST
VC'S JOE SABINO LETTERER
IRENE LEE PRODUCTION
MICHAEL HORWITZ EDITOR
JOE QUESADA EDITOR IN CHIEF
DAN BUCKLEY PUBLISHER
ALAN FINE EXEC. PRODUCER

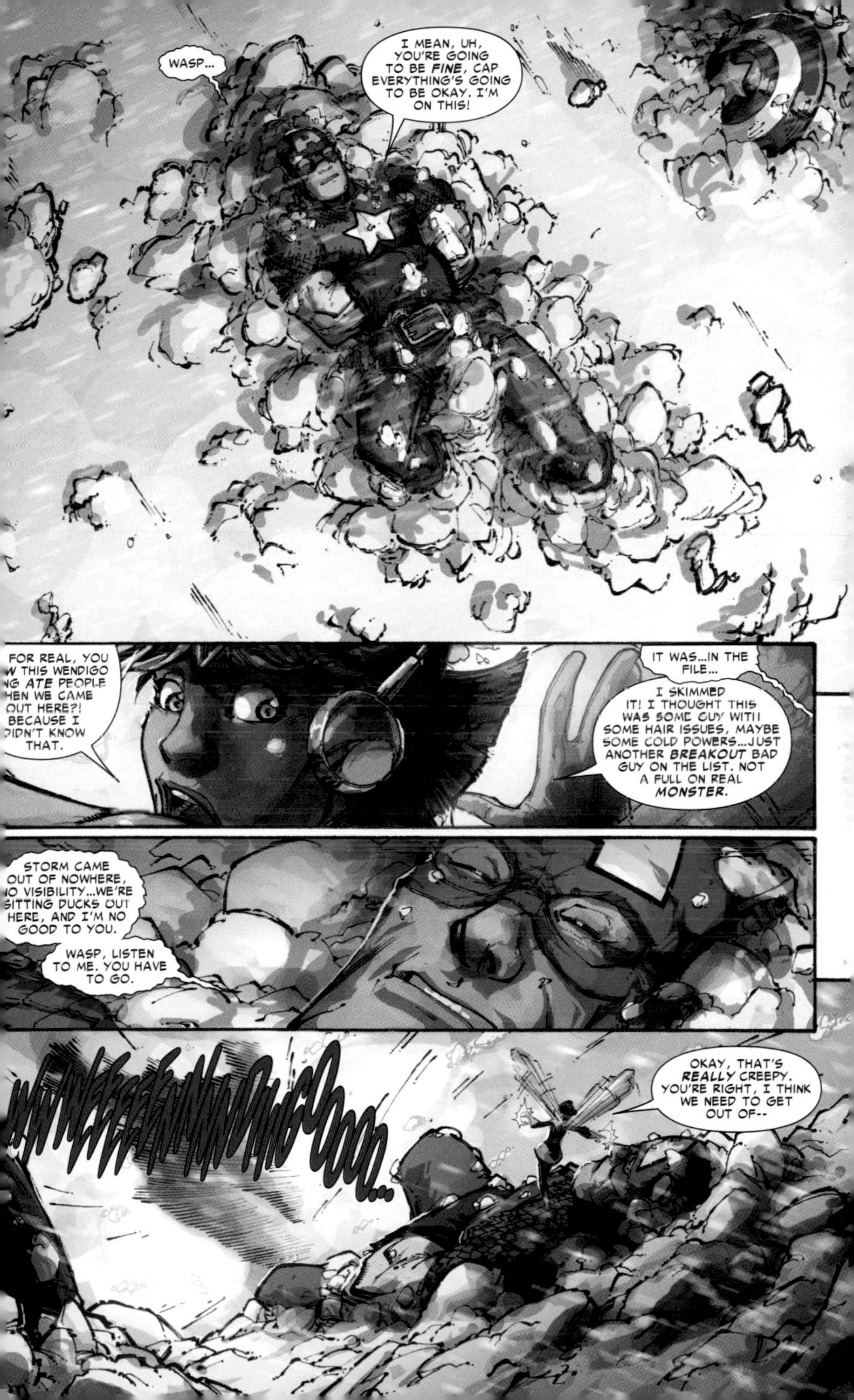
WASP...
I MEAN, UH, YOU'RE GOING TO BE FINE, CAP EVERYTHING'S GOING TO BE OKAY. I'M ON THIS!
FOR REAL, YOU W THIS WENDIGO NG ATE PEOPLE HEN WE CAME OUT HERE?! BECAUSE I DIDN'T KNOW THAT.
IT WAS...IN THE FILE...
I SKIMMED IT! I THOUGHT THIS WAS SOME GUY WITH SOME HAIR ISSUES, MAYBE SOME COLD POWERS...JUST ANOTHER BREAKOUT BAD GUY ON THE LIST. NOT A FULL ON REAL MONSTER.
STORM CAME OUT OF NOWHERE, NO VISIBILITY...WE'RE SITTING DUCKS OUT HERE, AND I'M NO GOOD TO YOU.
WASP, LISTEN TO ME. YOU HAVE TO GO.
OKAY, THAT'S REALLY CREEPY. YOU'RE RIGHT, I THINK WE NEED TO GET OUT OF--

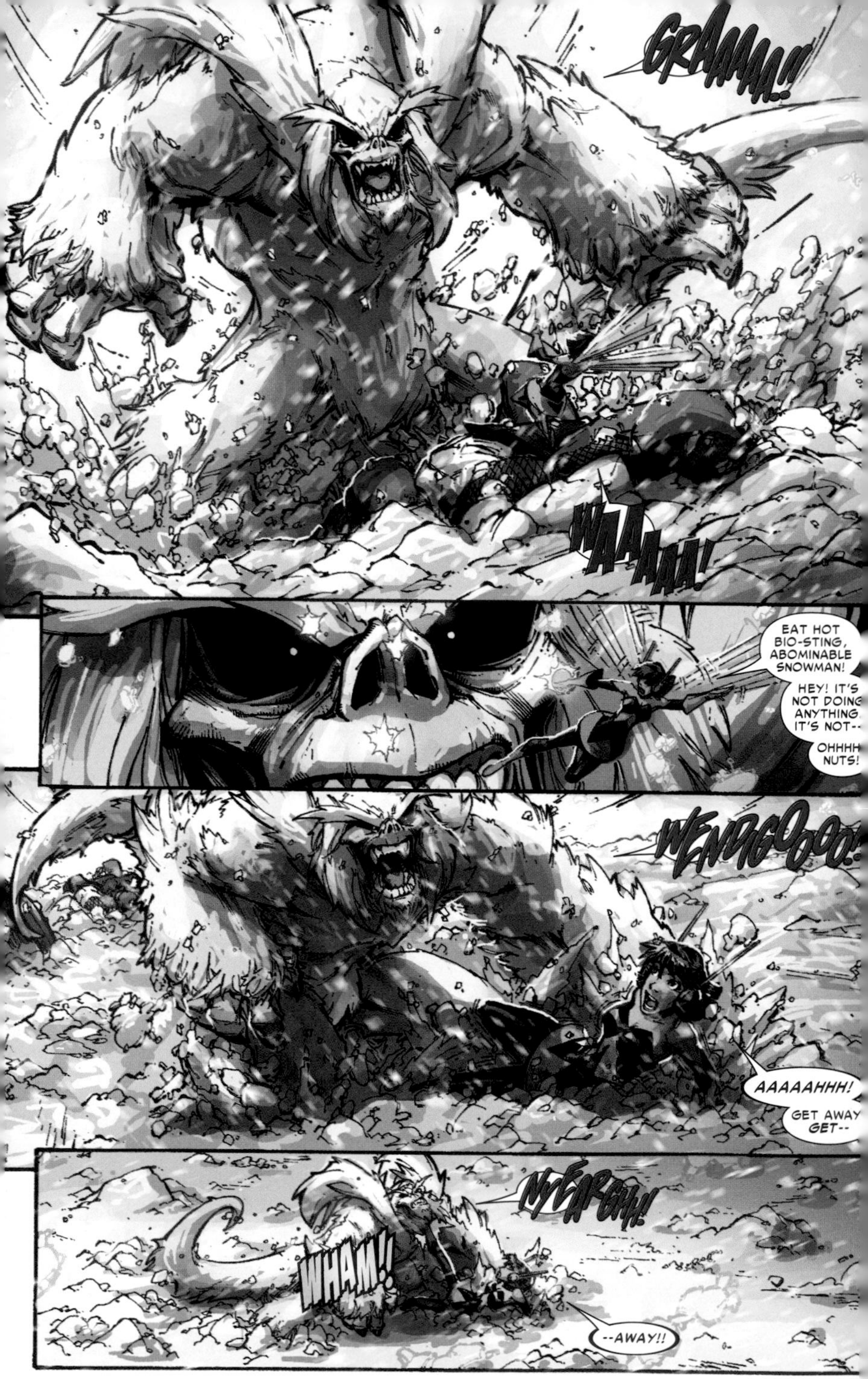
GRAAAAAA!!
WAAAAAA!
EAT HOT BIO-STING, ABOMINABLE SNOWMAN!
HEY! IT'S NOT DOING ANYTHING. IT'S NOT--
OHHHH NUTS!
WENDIGOOOOO!
AAAAAHHH!
GET AWAY GET--
NYEARGHH!
WHAM!!
--AWAY!!

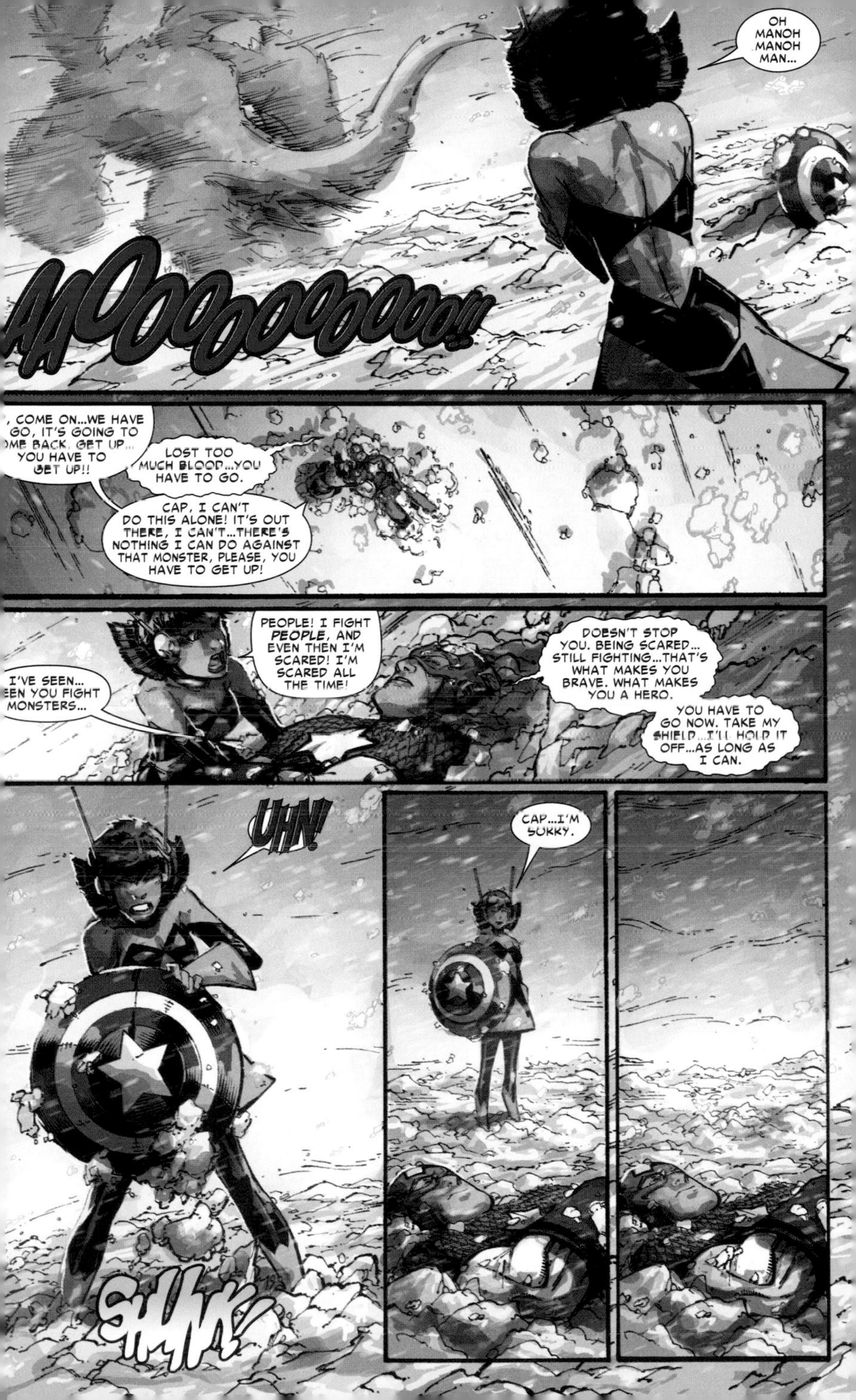
OH MANOH MANOH MAN...
AAOOOOOOOOOOO!!
, COME ON...WE HAVE GO, IT'S GOING TO OME BACK. GET UP... YOU HAVE TO GET UP!!
LOST TOO MUCH BLOOD...YOU HAVE TO GO.
CAP, I CAN'T DO THIS ALONE! IT'S OUT THERE, I CAN'T...THERE'S NOTHING I CAN DO AGAINST THAT MONSTER, PLEASE, YOU HAVE TO GET UP!
I'VE SEEN... EEN YOU FIGHT MONSTERS...
PEOPLE! I FIGHT *PEOPLE*, AND EVEN THEN I'M SCARED! I'M SCARED ALL THE TIME!
DOESN'T STOP YOU. BEING SCARED... STILL FIGHTING...THAT'S WHAT MAKES YOU BRAVE. WHAT MAKES YOU A HERO.
YOU HAVE TO GO NOW. TAKE MY SHIELD...I'LL HOLD IT OFF...AS LONG AS I CAN.
UHN!
SHUK!
CAP...I'M SORRY.

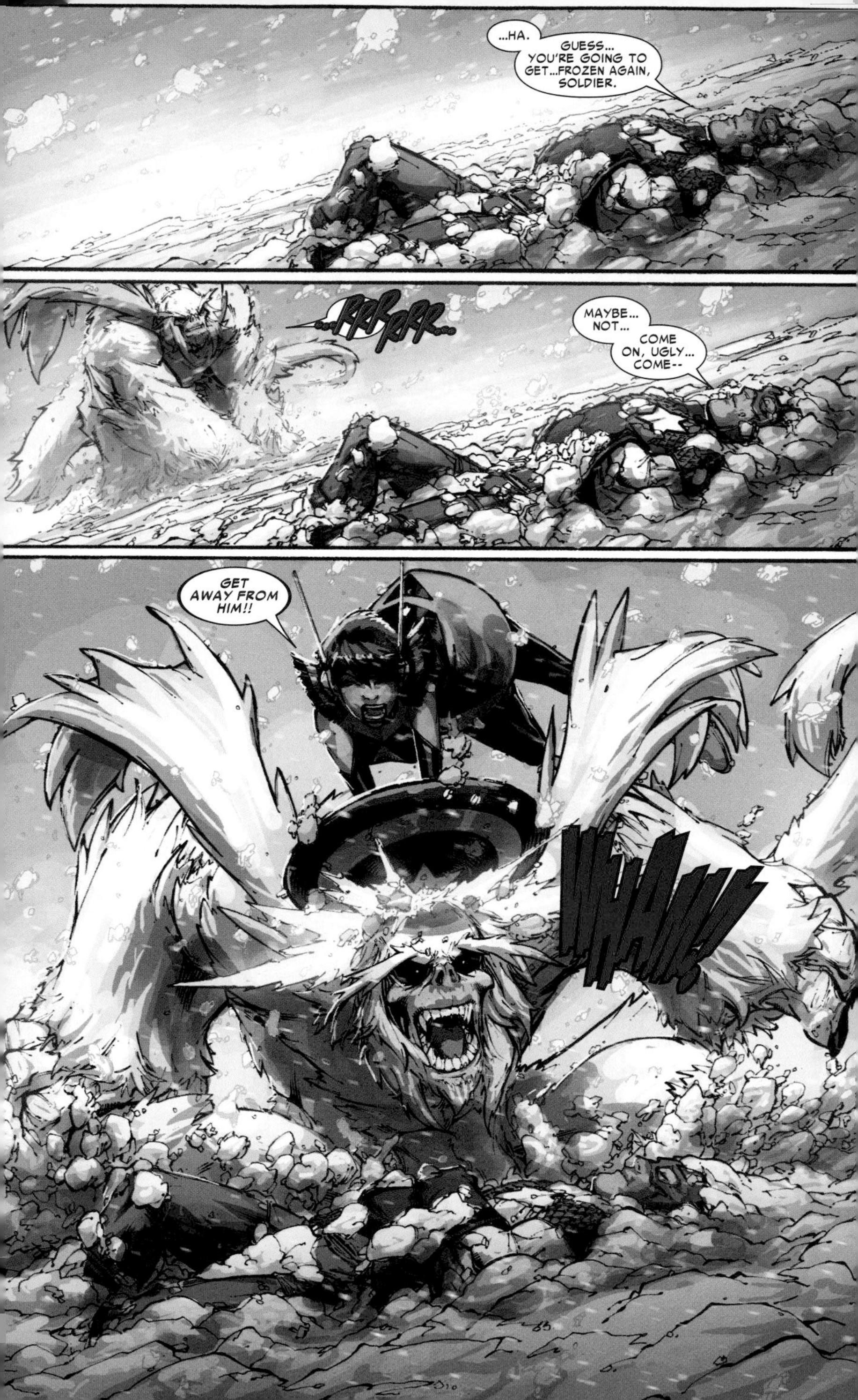
...HA.
GUESS... YOU'RE GOING TO GET...FROZEN AGAIN, SOLDIER.
...RRRRRRR...
MAYBE... NOT...
COME ON, UGLY... COME--
GET AWAY FROM HIM!!
WHANK!

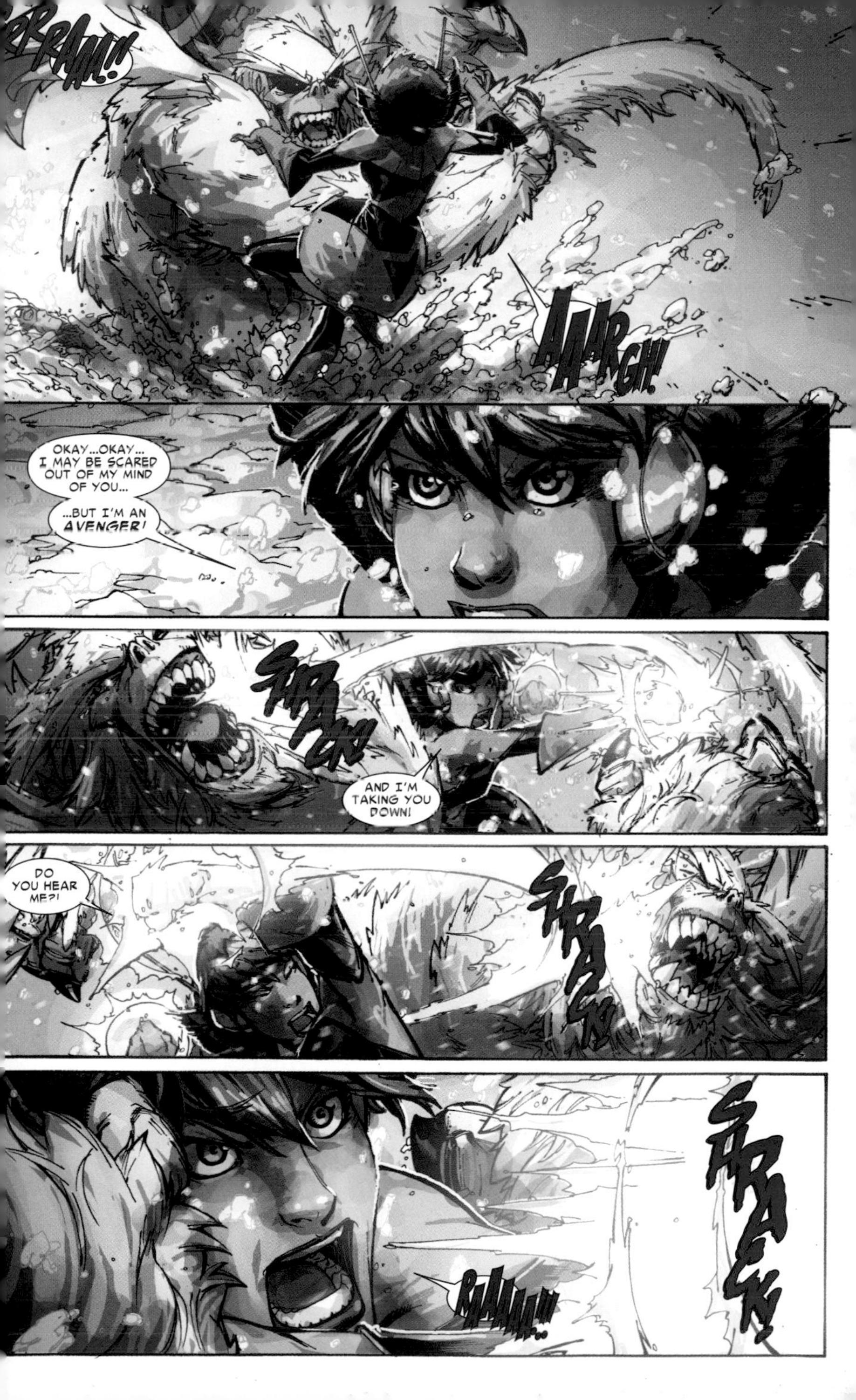
RRAAA!!
AAAARGH!
OKAY...OKAY... I MAY BE SCARED OUT OF MY MIND OF YOU...
...BUT I'M AN AVENGER!
AND I'M TAKING YOU DOWN!
DO YOU HEAR ME?!
RAAAAAA!!

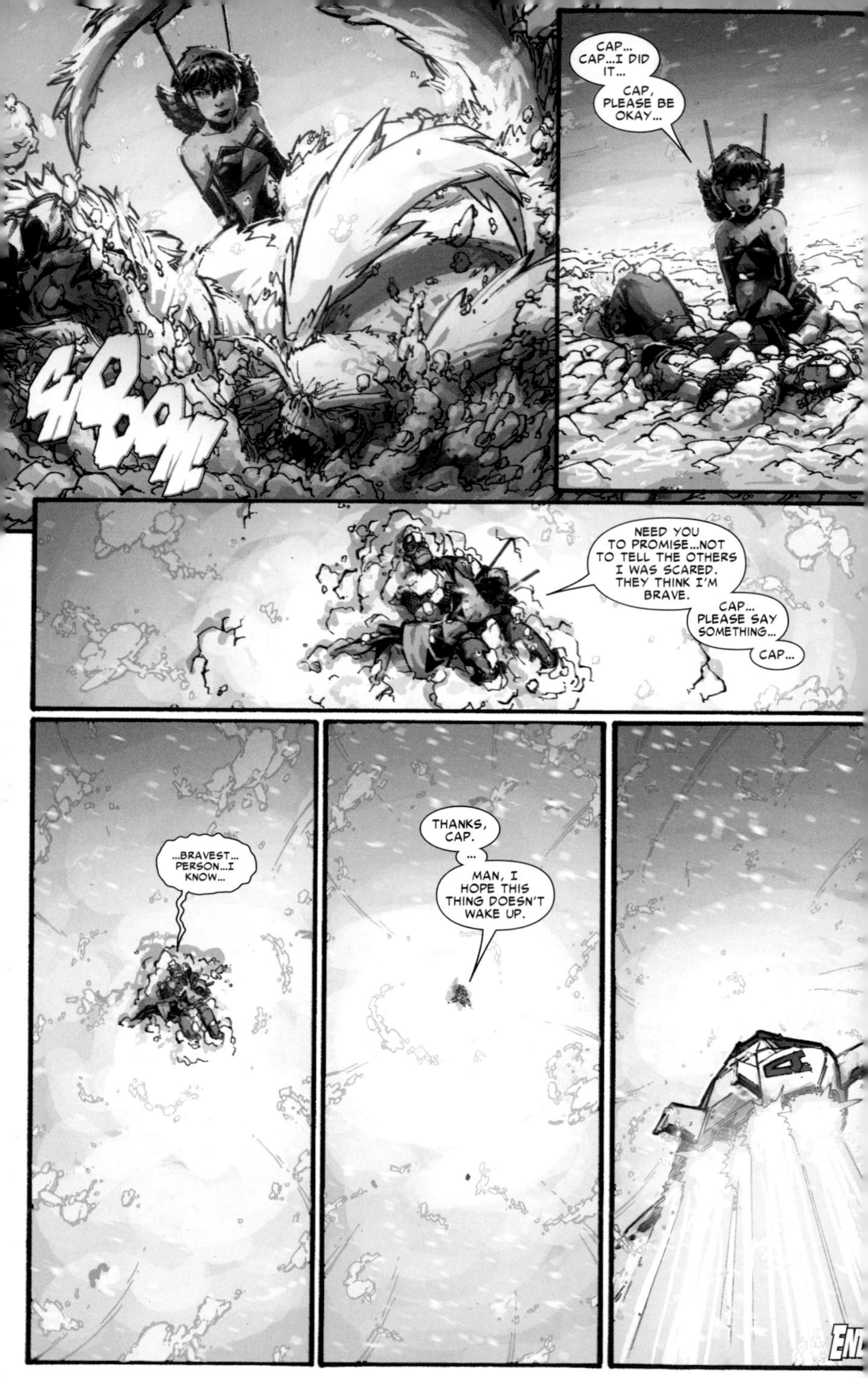
SHBOOM
CAP... CAP...I DID IT...
CAP, PLEASE BE OKAY...
NEED YOU TO PROMISE...NOT TO TELL THE OTHERS I WAS SCARED. THEY THINK I'M BRAVE.
CAP... PLEASE SAY SOMETHING...
CAP...
...BRAVEST... PERSON...I KNOW...
THANKS, CAP.
...
MAN, I HOPE THIS THING DOESN'T WAKE UP.

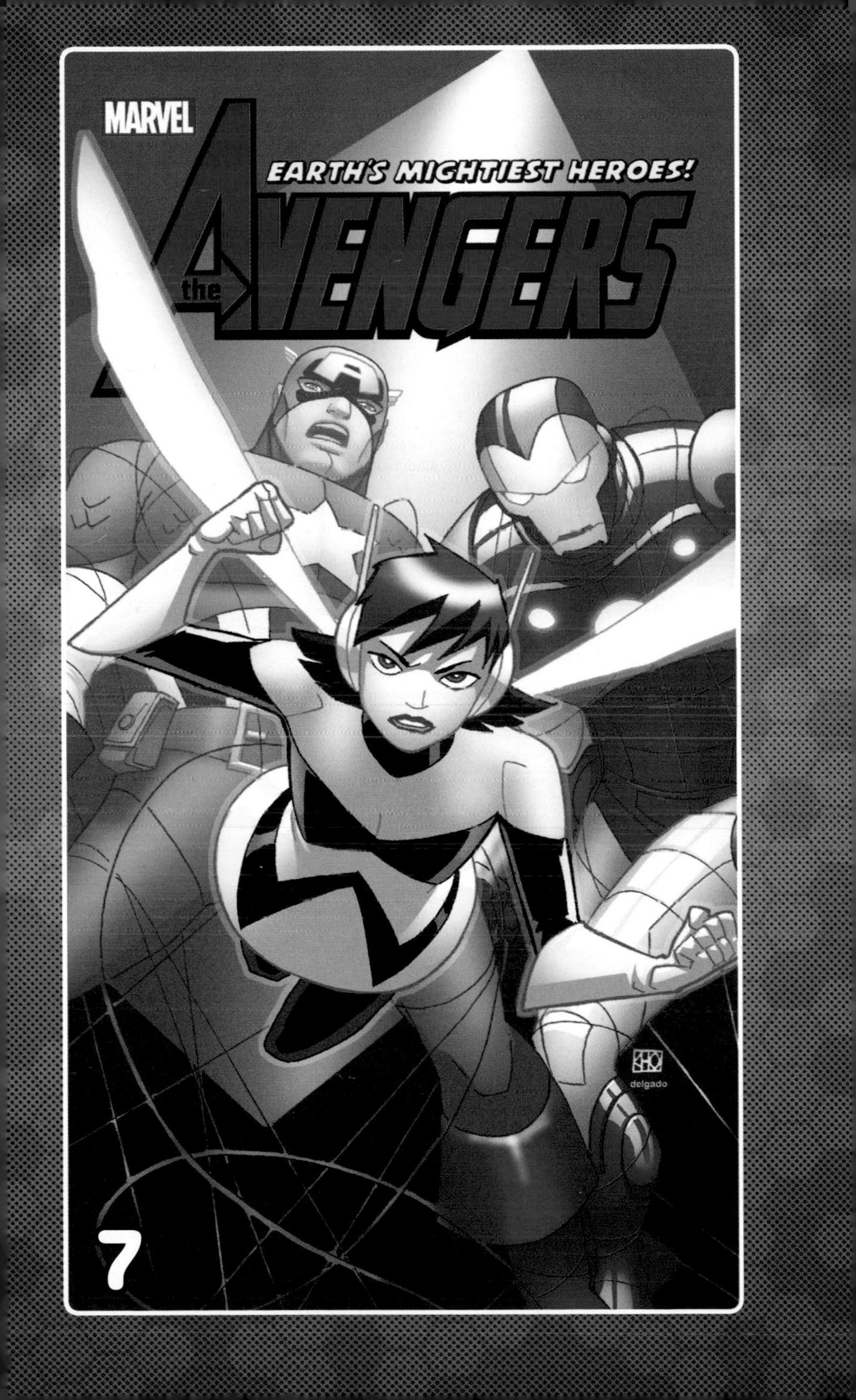
MARVEL
EARTH'S MIGHTIEST HEROES!
the AVENGERS
delgado
7

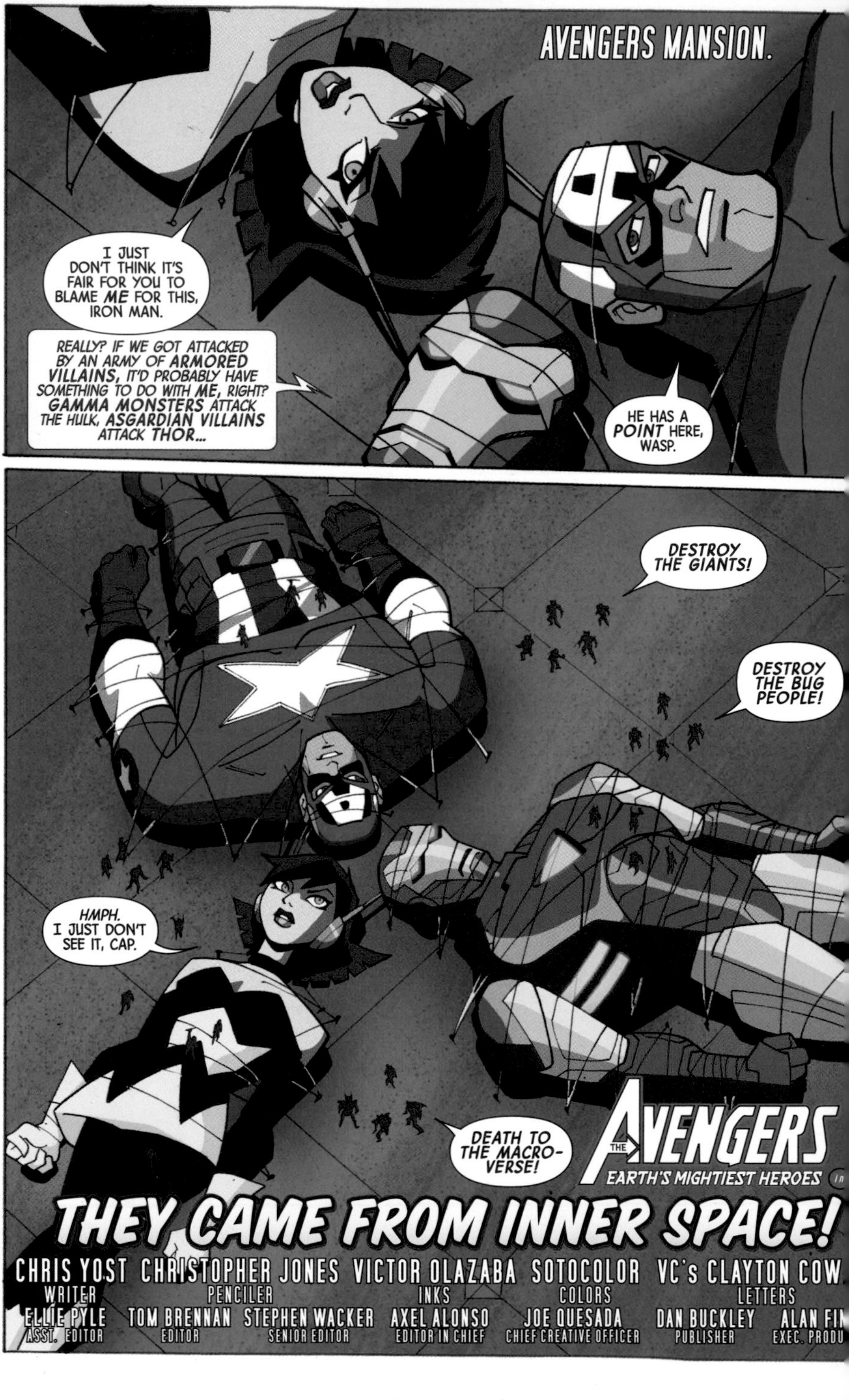
AVENGERS MANSION.
I JUST DON'T THINK IT'S FAIR FOR YOU TO BLAME ME FOR THIS, IRON MAN.
REALLY? IF WE GOT ATTACKED BY AN ARMY OF ARMORED VILLAINS, IT'D PROBABLY HAVE SOMETHING TO DO WITH ME, RIGHT? GAMMA MONSTERS ATTACK THE HULK, ASGARDIAN VILLAINS ATTACK THOR...
HE HAS A POINT HERE, WASP.
DESTROY THE GIANTS!
DESTROY THE BUG PEOPLE!
HMPH. I JUST DON'T SEE IT, CAP.
DEATH TO THE MACRO-VERSE!
THE AVENGERS
EARTH'S MIGHTIEST HEROES
THEY CAME FROM INNER SPACE!
CHRIS YOST WRITER
CHRISTOPHER JONES PENCILER
VICTOR OLAZABA INKS
SOTOCOLOR COLORS
VC's CLAYTON COW LETTERS
ELLIE PYLE ASST. EDITOR
TOM BRENNAN EDITOR
STEPHEN WACKER SENIOR EDITOR
AXEL ALONSO EDITOR IN CHIEF
JOE QUESADA CHIEF CREATIVE OFFICER
DAN BUCKLEY PUBLISHER
ALAN FI EXEC. PRODU

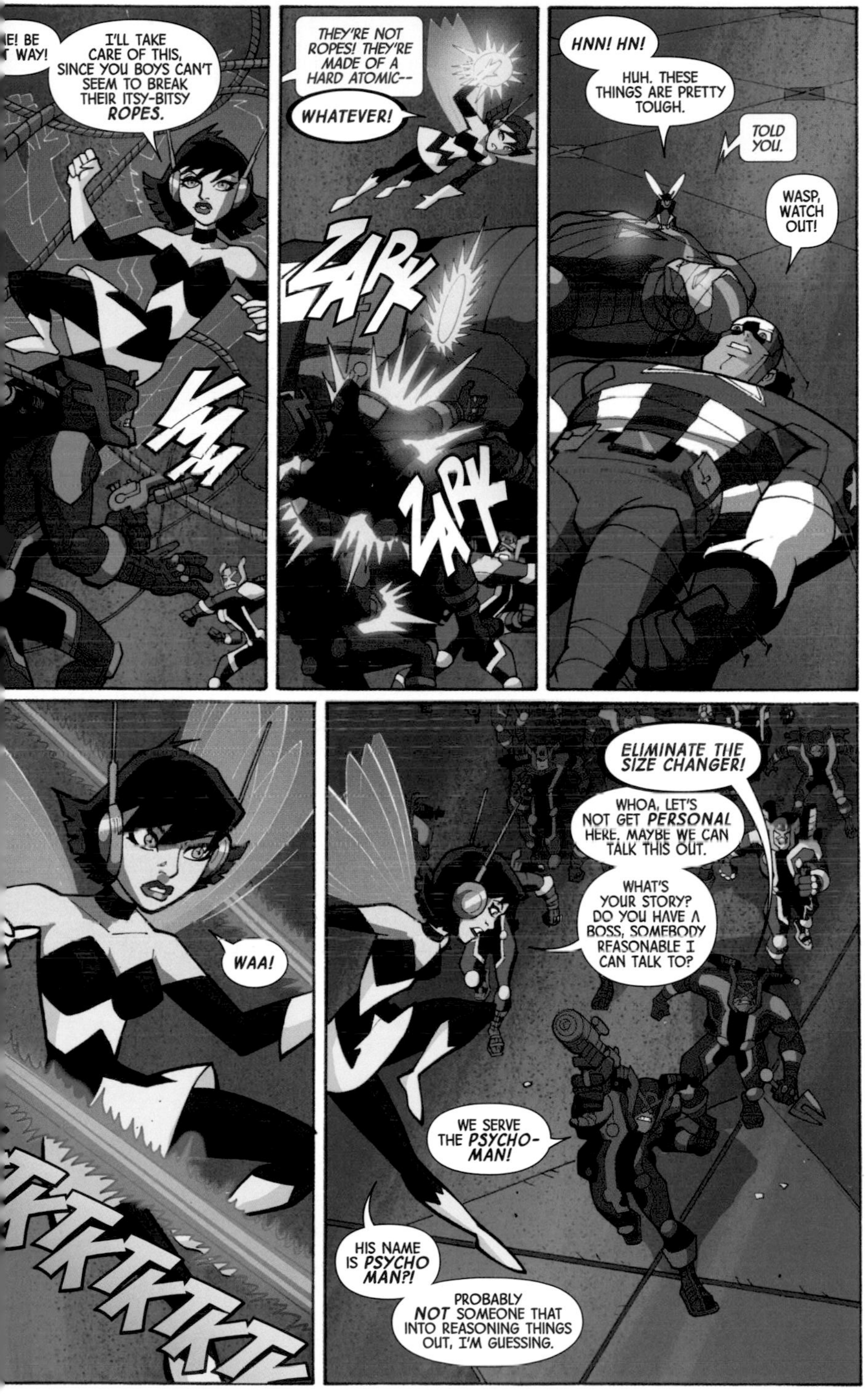

E! BE
T WAY!
I'LL TAKE CARE OF THIS, SINCE YOU BOYS CAN'T SEEM TO BREAK THEIR ITSY-BITSY *ROPES.*
VMM
THEY'RE NOT ROPES! THEY'RE MADE OF A HARD ATOMIC--
WHATEVER!
ZARK
ZARK
HNN! HN!
HUH. THESE THINGS ARE PRETTY TOUGH.
TOLD YOU.
WASP, WATCH OUT!
WAA!
TKTKTKTKT
ELIMINATE THE SIZE CHANGER!
WHOA, LET'S NOT GET *PERSONAL* HERE. MAYBE WE CAN TALK THIS OUT.
WHAT'S YOUR STORY? DO YOU HAVE A BOSS, SOMEBODY REASONABLE I CAN TALK TO?
WE SERVE THE *PSYCHO-MAN!*
HIS NAME IS *PSYCHO MAN?!*
PROBABLY *NOT* SOMEONE THAT INTO REASONING THINGS OUT, I'M GUESSING.

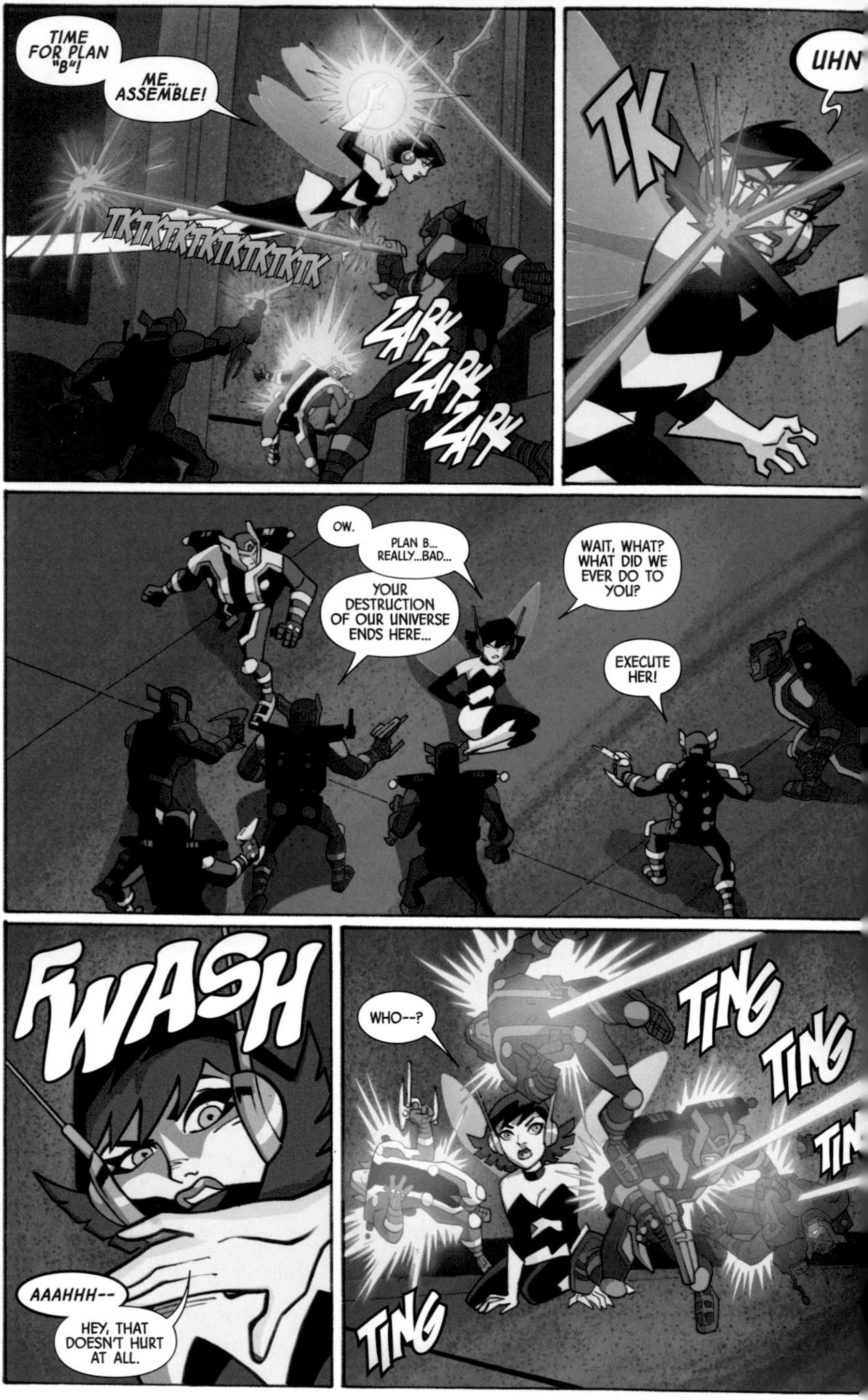

TIME FOR PLAN "B"!
ME... ASSEMBLE!
TKTKTKTKTKTKTKTKTKTK
ZARK ZARK ZARK
TK
UHN
OW.
PLAN B... REALLY...BAD...
YOUR DESTRUCTION OF OUR UNIVERSE ENDS HERE...
WAIT, WHAT? WHAT DID WE EVER DO TO YOU?
EXECUTE HER!
FWASH
AAAHHH--
HEY, THAT DOESN'T HURT AT ALL.
WHO--?
TING
TING
TING

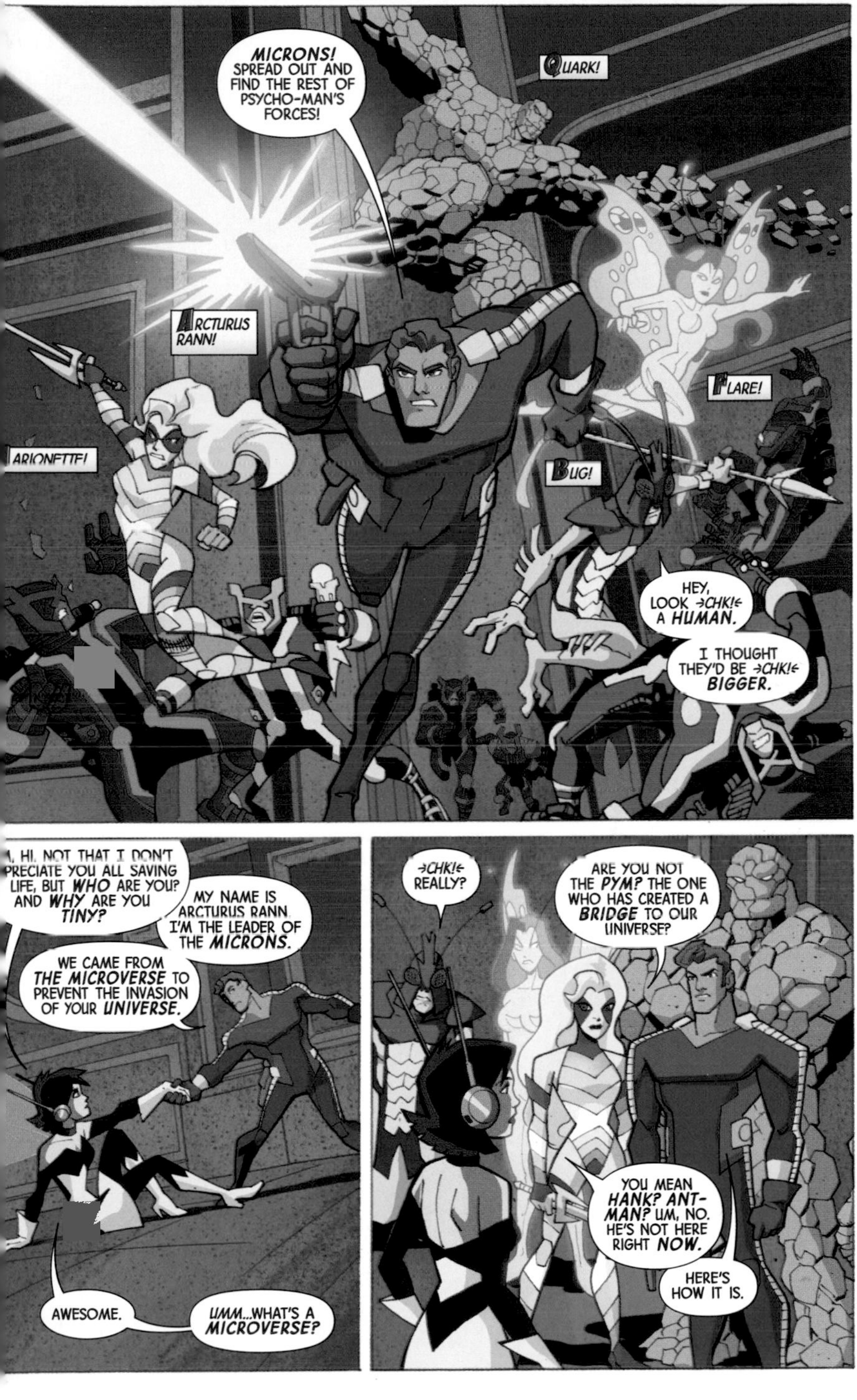
MICRONS! SPREAD OUT AND FIND THE REST OF PSYCHO-MAN'S FORCES!
QUARK!
ARCTURUS RANN!
FLARE!
ARIONETTE!
BUG!
HEY, LOOK →CHK!← A HUMAN.
I THOUGHT THEY'D BE →CHK!← BIGGER.
M, HI. NOT THAT I DON'T PRECIATE YOU ALL SAVING LIFE, BUT WHO ARE YOU? AND WHY ARE YOU TINY?
MY NAME IS ARCTURUS RANN. I'M THE LEADER OF THE MICRONS.
WE CAME FROM THE MICROVERSE TO PREVENT THE INVASION OF YOUR UNIVERSE.
AWESOME.
UMM...WHAT'S A MICROVERSE?
→CHK!← REALLY?
ARE YOU NOT THE PYM? THE ONE WHO HAS CREATED A BRIDGE TO OUR UNIVERSE?
YOU MEAN HANK? ANT-MAN? UM, NO. HE'S NOT HERE RIGHT NOW.
HERE'S HOW IT IS.

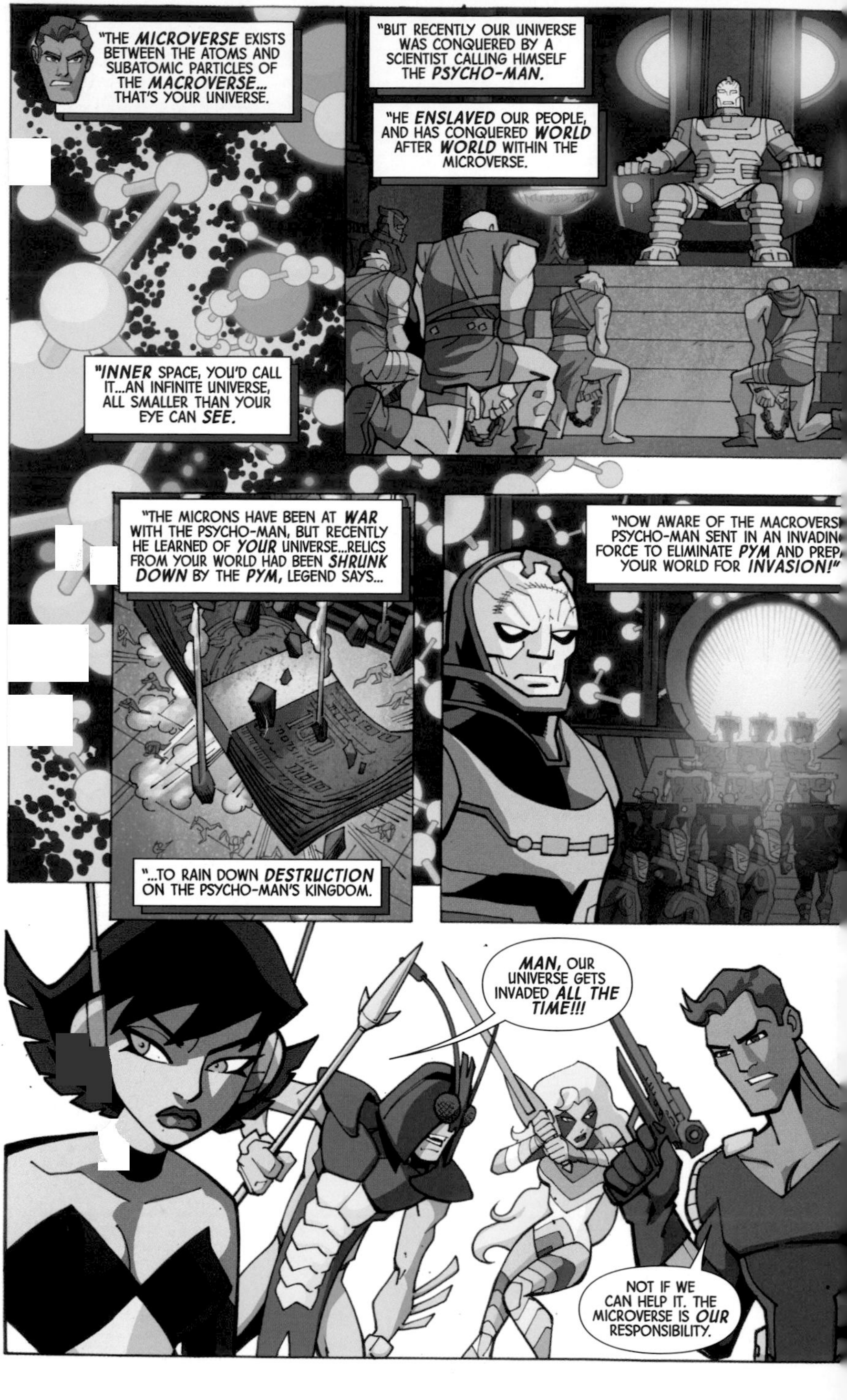
"THE MICROVERSE EXISTS BETWEEN THE ATOMS AND SUBATOMIC PARTICLES OF THE MACROVERSE... THAT'S YOUR UNIVERSE.
"INNER SPACE, YOU'D CALL IT...AN INFINITE UNIVERSE, ALL SMALLER THAN YOUR EYE CAN SEE.
"BUT RECENTLY OUR UNIVERSE WAS CONQUERED BY A SCIENTIST CALLING HIMSELF THE PSYCHO-MAN.
"HE ENSLAVED OUR PEOPLE, AND HAS CONQUERED WORLD AFTER WORLD WITHIN THE MICROVERSE.
"THE MICRONS HAVE BEEN AT WAR WITH THE PSYCHO-MAN, BUT RECENTLY HE LEARNED OF YOUR UNIVERSE...RELICS FROM YOUR WORLD HAD BEEN SHRUNK DOWN BY THE PYM, LEGEND SAYS...
"...TO RAIN DOWN DESTRUCTION ON THE PSYCHO-MAN'S KINGDOM.
"NOW AWARE OF THE MACROVERS PSYCHO-MAN SENT IN AN INVADIN FORCE TO ELIMINATE PYM AND PREP YOUR WORLD FOR INVASION!"
MAN, OUR UNIVERSE GETS INVADED ALL THE TIME!!!
NOT IF WE CAN HELP IT. THE MICROVERSE IS OUR RESPONSIBILITY.

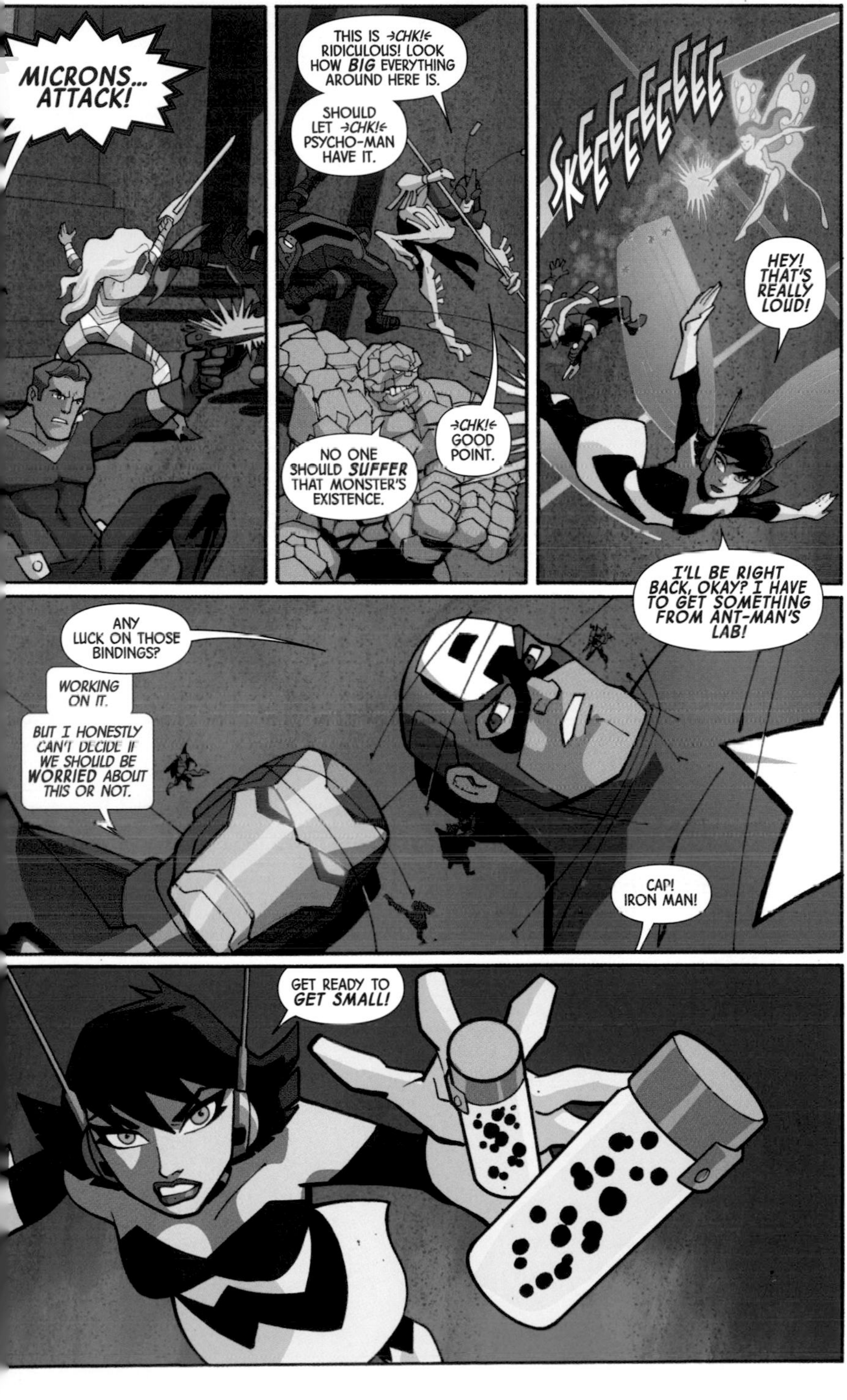
MICRONS... ATTACK!
THIS IS →CHK!← RIDICULOUS! LOOK HOW BIG EVERYTHING AROUND HERE IS.
SHOULD LET →CHK!← PSYCHO-MAN HAVE IT.
NO ONE SHOULD SUFFER THAT MONSTER'S EXISTENCE.
→CHK!← GOOD POINT.
SKEEEEEEEEEE
HEY! THAT'S REALLY LOUD!
I'LL BE RIGHT BACK, OKAY? I HAVE TO GET SOMETHING FROM ANT-MAN'S LAB!
ANY LUCK ON THOSE BINDINGS?
WORKING ON IT.
BUT I HONESTLY CAN'T DECIDE IF WE SHOULD BE WORRIED ABOUT THIS OR NOT.
CAP! IRON MAN!
GET READY TO GET SMALL!

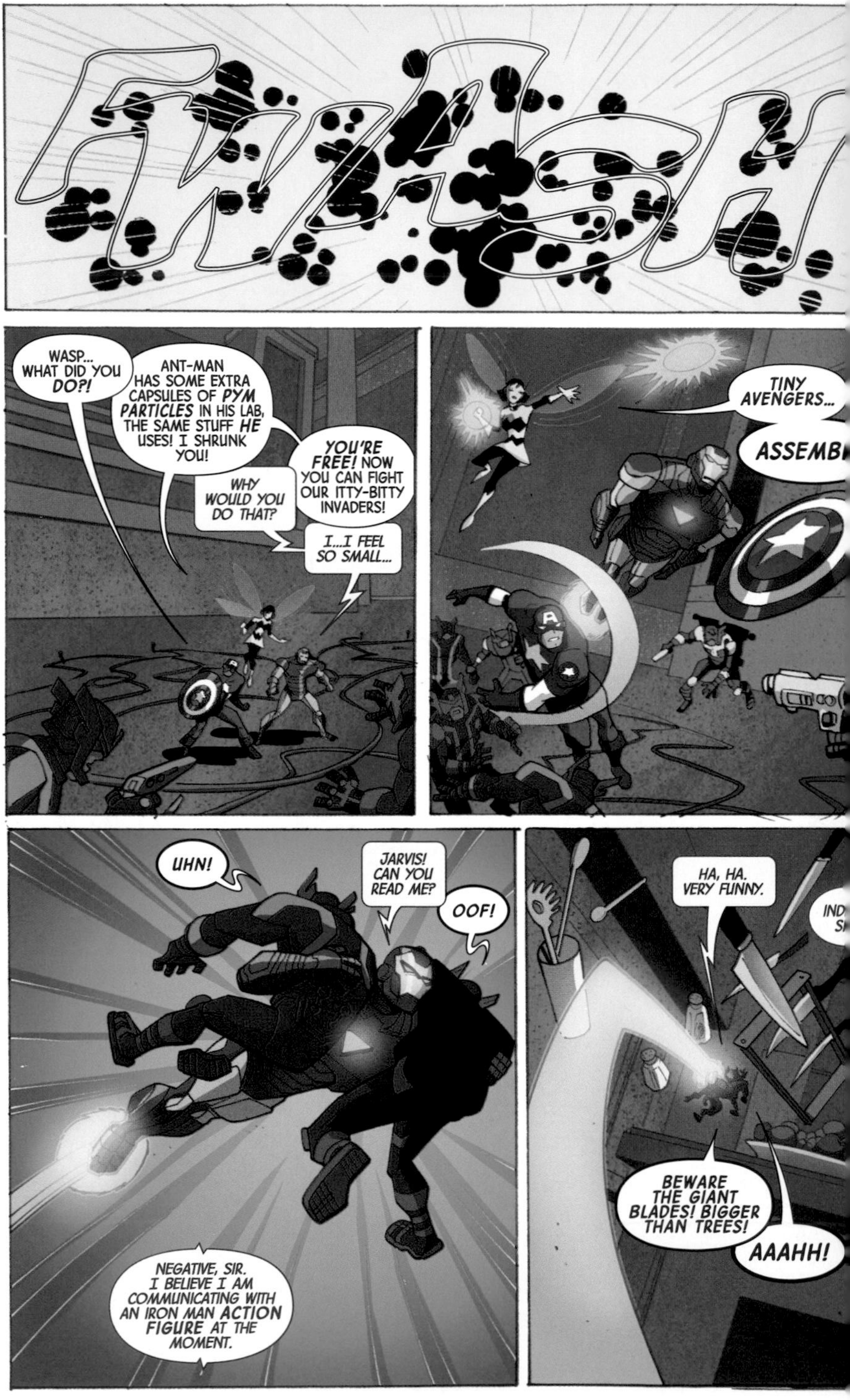
FWASH!
WASP... WHAT DID YOU DO?!
ANT-MAN HAS SOME EXTRA CAPSULES OF PYM PARTICLES IN HIS LAB, THE SAME STUFF HE USES! I SHRUNK YOU!
YOU'RE FREE! NOW YOU CAN FIGHT OUR ITTY-BITTY INVADERS!
WHY WOULD YOU DO THAT?
I...I FEEL SO SMALL...
TINY AVENGERS...
ASSEMB
UHN!
JARVIS! CAN YOU READ ME?
OOF!
NEGATIVE, SIR. I BELIEVE I AM COMMUNICATING WITH AN IRON MAN ACTION FIGURE AT THE MOMENT.
HA, HA. VERY FUNNY.
BEWARE THE GIANT BLADES! BIGGER THAN TREES!
AAAHH!

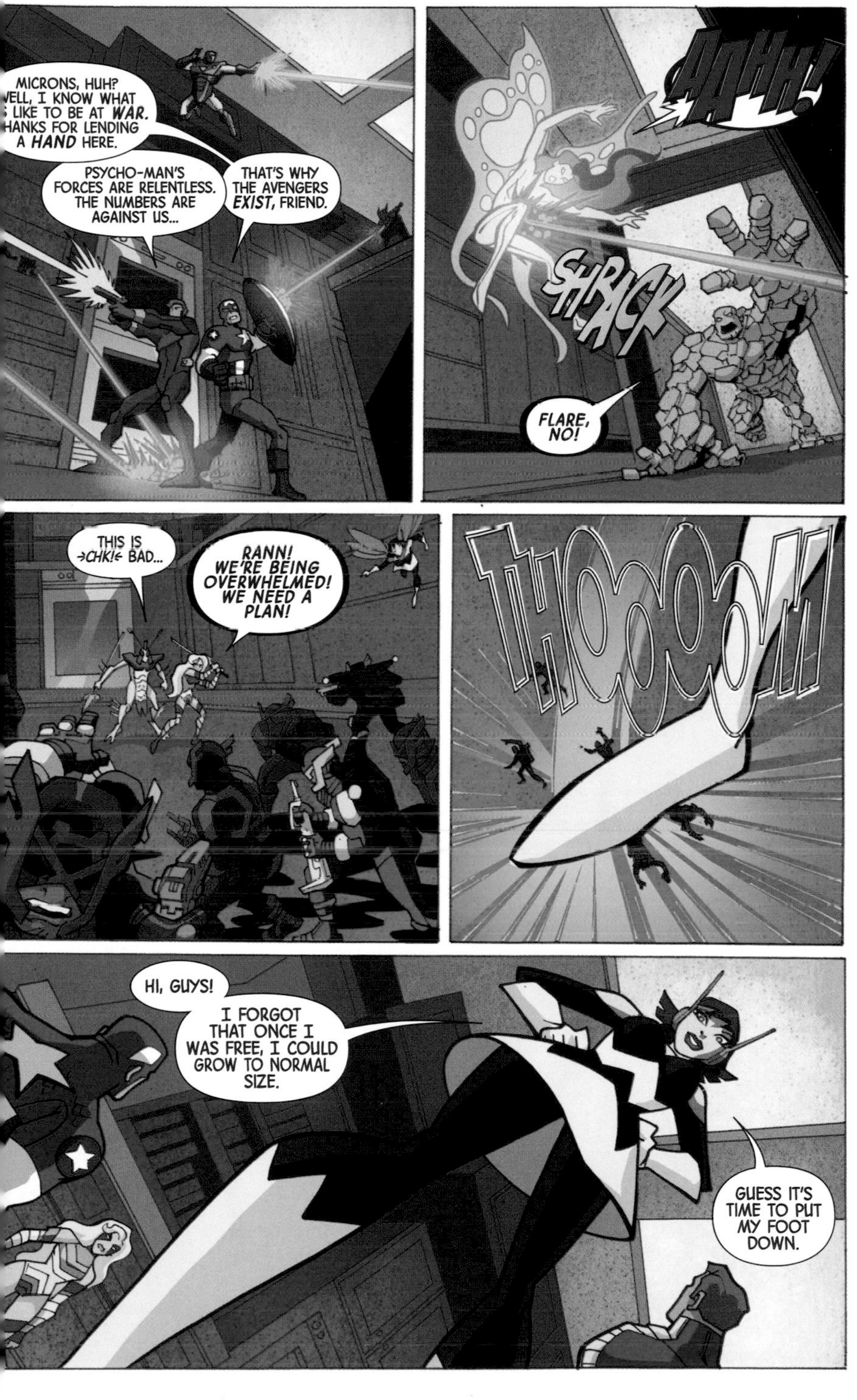
MICRONS, HUH? WELL, I KNOW WHAT 'S LIKE TO BE AT WAR. THANKS FOR LENDING A HAND HERE.
PSYCHO-MAN'S FORCES ARE RELENTLESS. THE NUMBERS ARE AGAINST US...
THAT'S WHY THE AVENGERS EXIST, FRIEND.
AAHH!
SHRACK
FLARE, NO!
THIS IS →CHK!← BAD...
RANN! WE'RE BEING OVERWHELMED! WE NEED A PLAN!
THOOOOM
HI, GUYS!
I FORGOT THAT ONCE I WAS FREE, I COULD GROW TO NORMAL SIZE.
GUESS IT'S TIME TO PUT MY FOOT DOWN.

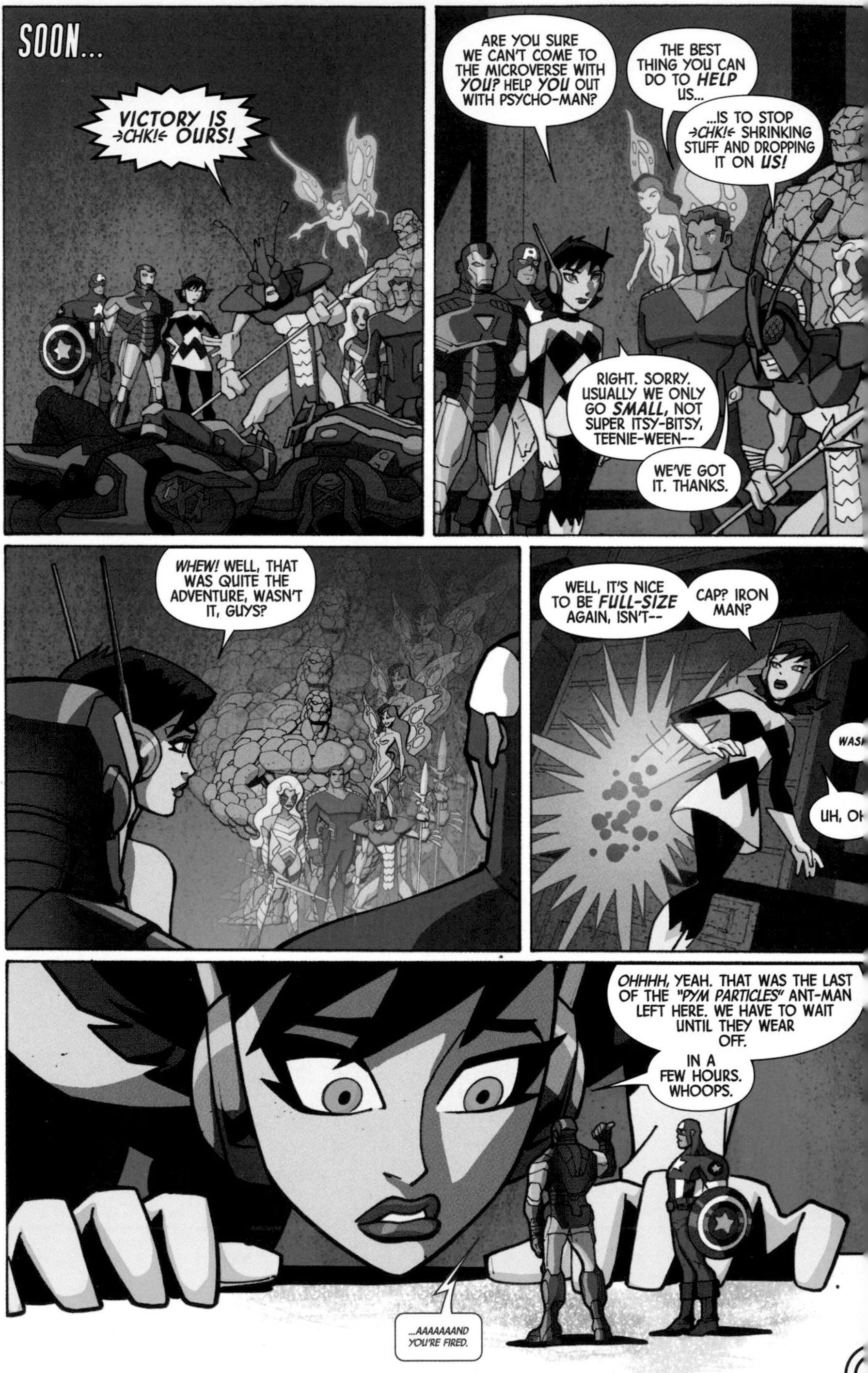
SOON...
VICTORY IS ➔CHK!⬅ OURS!
ARE YOU SURE WE CAN'T COME TO THE MICROVERSE WITH YOU? HELP YOU OUT WITH PSYCHO-MAN?
THE BEST THING YOU CAN DO TO HELP US...
...IS TO STOP ➔CHK!⬅ SHRINKING STUFF AND DROPPING IT ON US!
RIGHT. SORRY. USUALLY WE ONLY GO SMALL, NOT SUPER ITSY-BITSY, TEENIE-WEEN--
WE'VE GOT IT. THANKS.
WHEW! WELL, THAT WAS QUITE THE ADVENTURE, WASN'T IT, GUYS?
WELL, IT'S NICE TO BE FULL-SIZE AGAIN, ISN'T--
CAP? IRON MAN?
OHHHH, YEAH. THAT WAS THE LAST OF THE "PYM PARTICLES" ANT-MAN LEFT HERE. WE HAVE TO WAIT UNTIL THEY WEAR OFF.
IN A FEW HOURS. WHOOPS.
...AAAAAAAND YOU'RE FIRED.

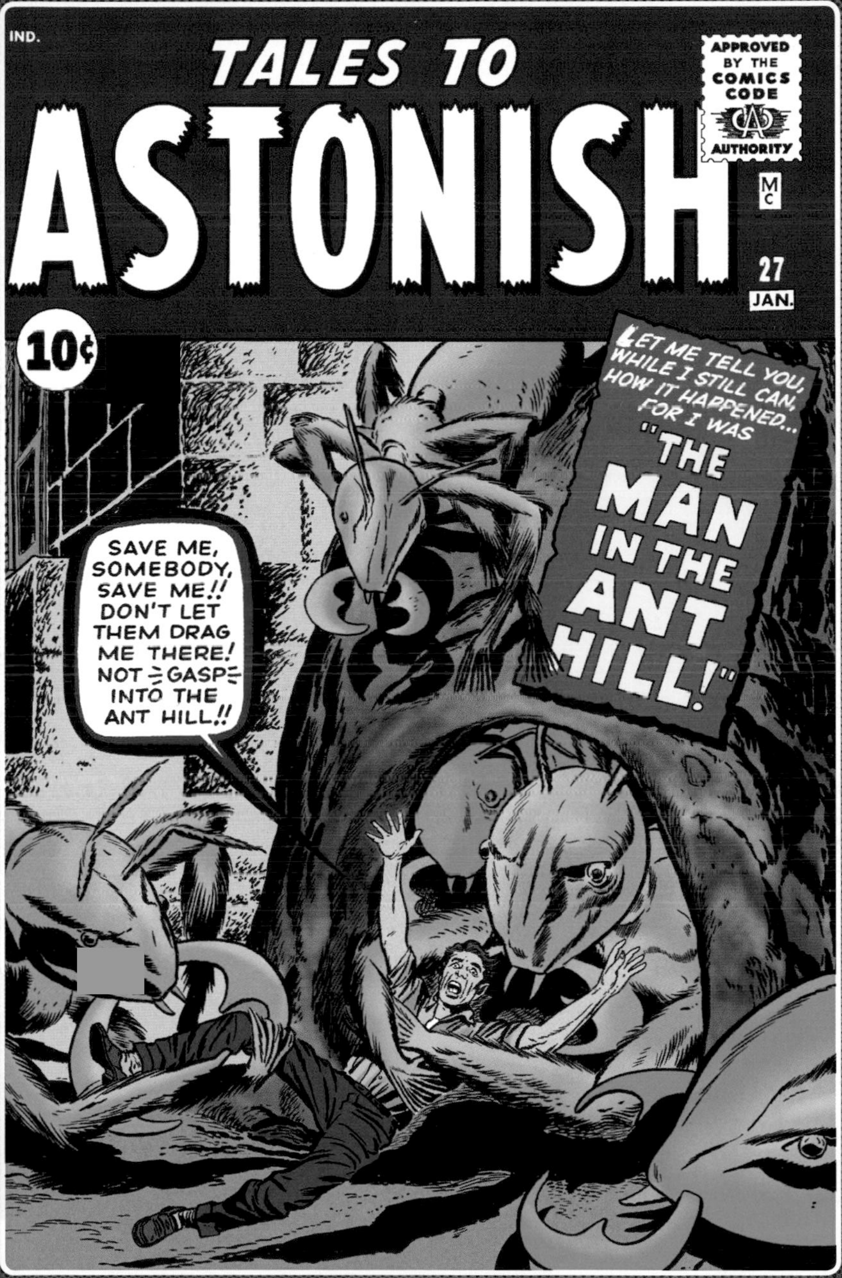
IND.
TALES TO ASTONISH
APPROVED BY THE COMICS CODE AUTHORITY
MC
27
JAN.
10¢
LET ME TELL YOU, WHILE I STILL CAN, HOW IT HAPPENED... FOR I WAS "THE MAN IN THE ANT HILL!"
SAVE ME, SOMEBODY, SAVE ME!! DON'T LET THEM DRAG ME THERE! NOT =GASP= INTO THE ANT HILL!!

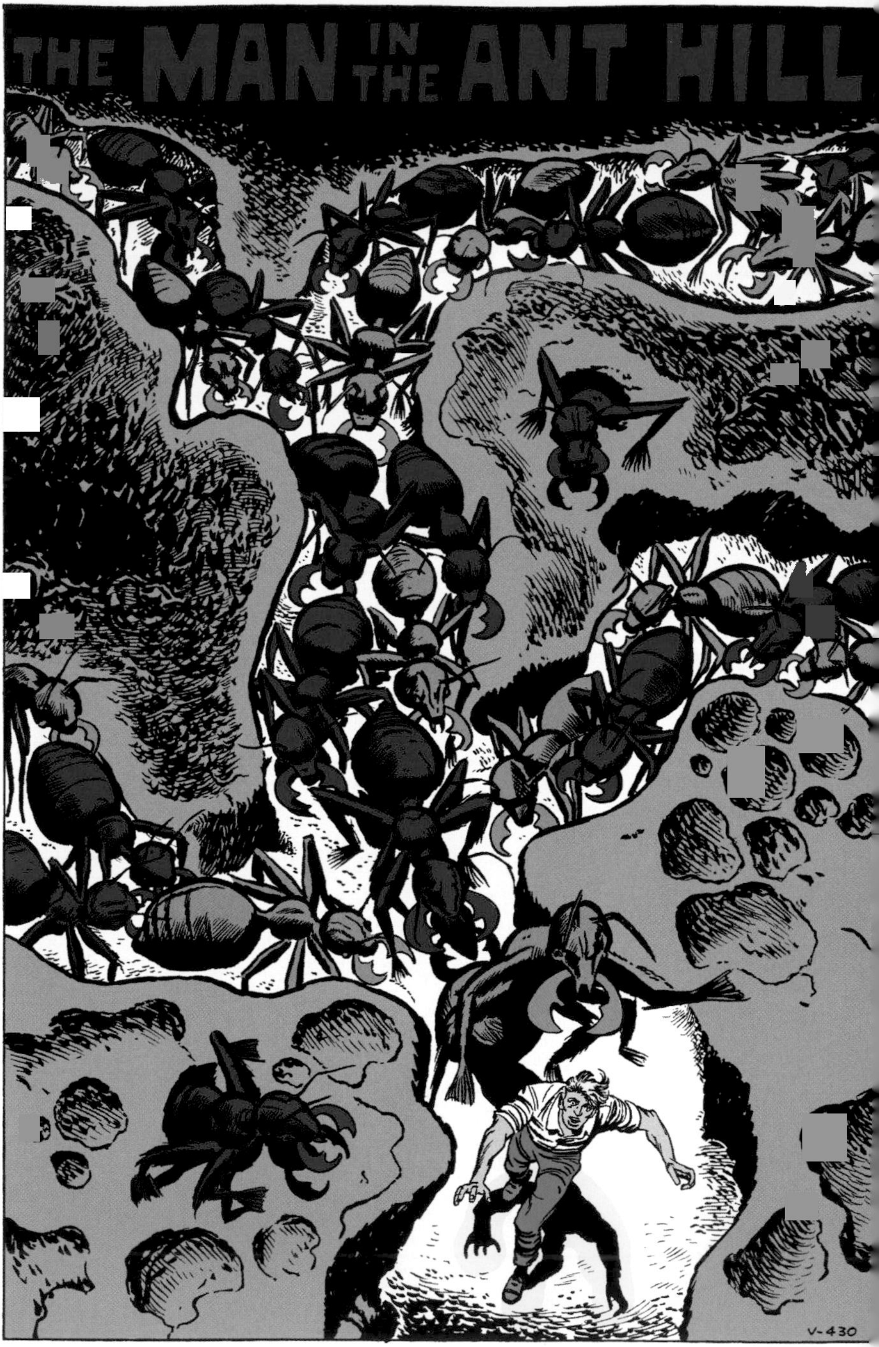
THE MAN IN THE ANT HILL
V-430

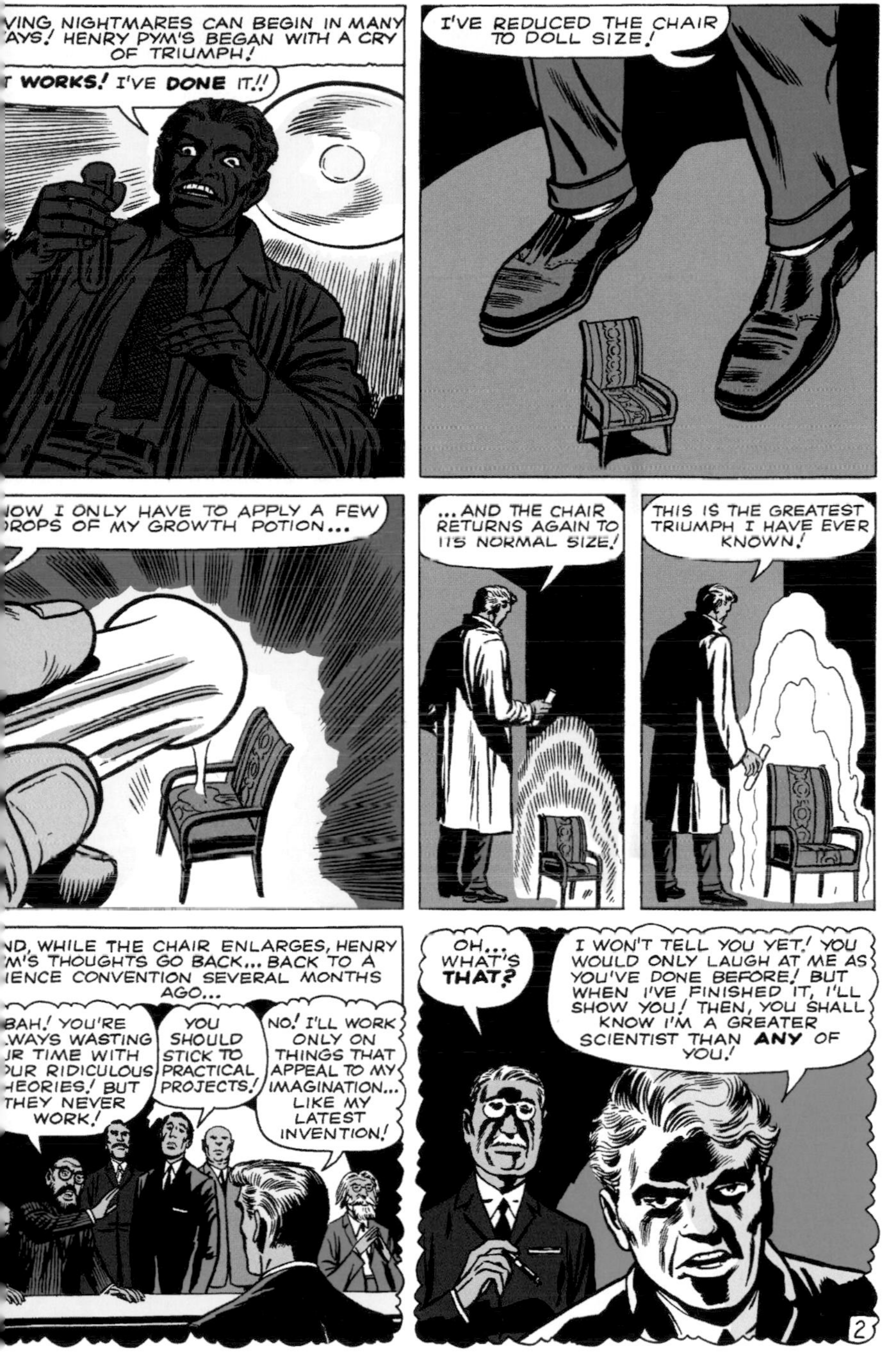

VING NIGHTMARES CAN BEGIN IN MANY
AYS! HENRY PYM'S BEGAN WITH A CRY OF TRIUMPH!
T WORKS! I'VE DONE IT!!
I'VE REDUCED THE CHAIR TO DOLL SIZE!
IOW I ONLY HAVE TO APPLY A FEW
ROPS OF MY GROWTH POTION...
...AND THE CHAIR RETURNS AGAIN TO ITS NORMAL SIZE!
THIS IS THE GREATEST TRIUMPH I HAVE EVER KNOWN!
ND, WHILE THE CHAIR ENLARGES, HENRY
M'S THOUGHTS GO BACK... BACK TO A
IENCE CONVENTION SEVERAL MONTHS AGO...
BAH! YOU'RE
WAYS WASTING
R TIME WITH
OUR RIDICULOUS
HEORIES! BUT THEY NEVER WORK!
YOU SHOULD STICK TO PRACTICAL PROJECTS!
NO! I'LL WORK ONLY ON THINGS THAT APPEAL TO MY IMAGINATION... LIKE MY LATEST INVENTION!
OH... WHAT'S THAT?
I WON'T TELL YOU YET! YOU WOULD ONLY LAUGH AT ME AS YOU'VE DONE BEFORE! BUT WHEN I'VE FINISHED IT, I'LL SHOW YOU! THEN, YOU SHALL KNOW I'M A GREATER SCIENTIST THAN ANY OF YOU!
2

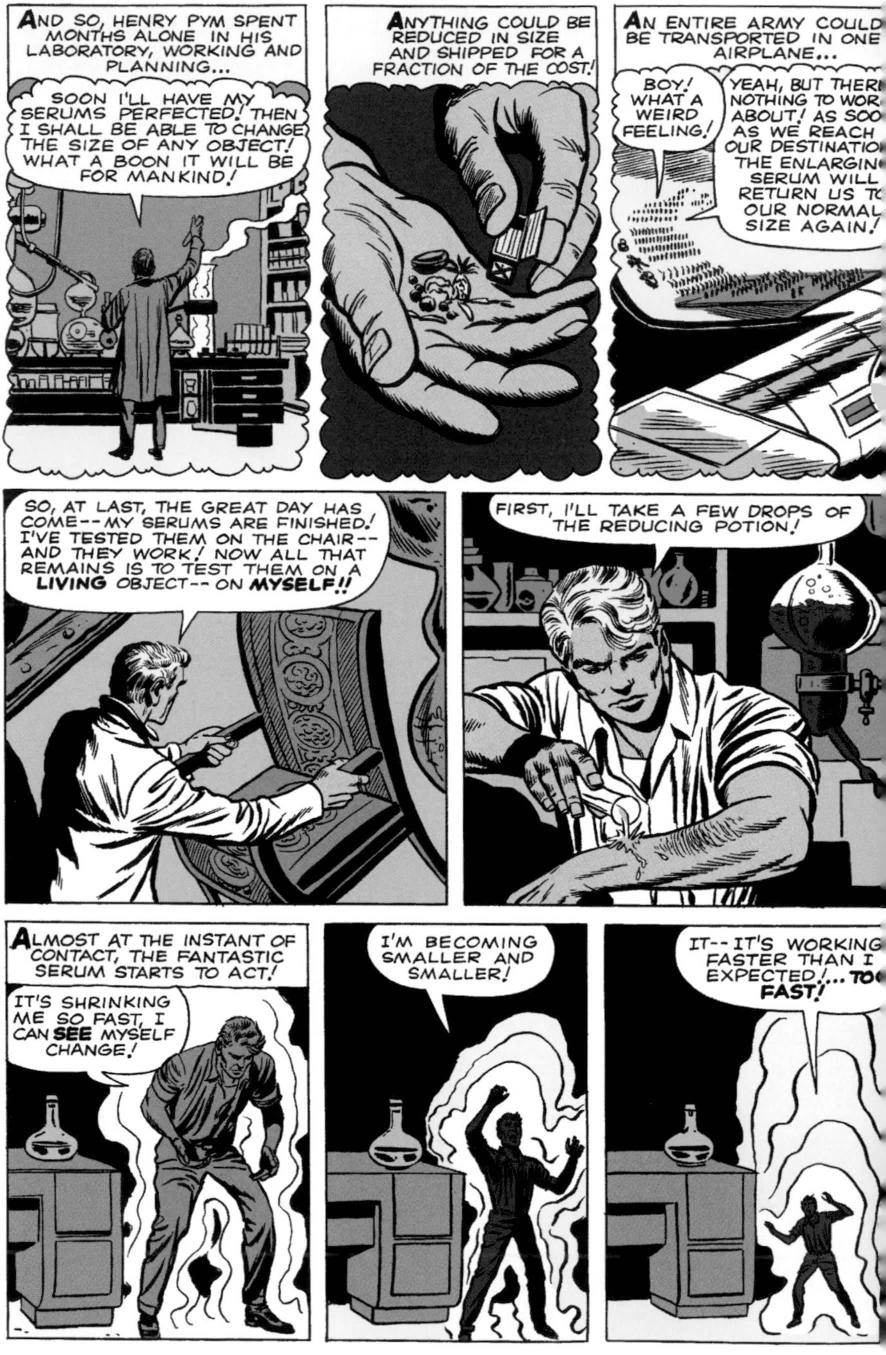

AND SO, HENRY PYM SPENT MONTHS ALONE IN HIS LABORATORY, WORKING AND PLANNING...
SOON I'LL HAVE MY SERUMS PERFECTED! THEN I SHALL BE ABLE TO CHANGE THE SIZE OF ANY OBJECT! WHAT A BOON IT WILL BE FOR MANKIND!
ANYTHING COULD BE REDUCED IN SIZE AND SHIPPED FOR A FRACTION OF THE COST!
AN ENTIRE ARMY COULD BE TRANSPORTED IN ONE AIRPLANE...
BOY! WHAT A WEIRD FEELING!
SO, AT LAST, THE GREAT DAY HAS COME--MY SERUMS ARE FINISHED! I'VE TESTED THEM ON THE CHAIR--AND THEY WORK! NOW ALL THAT REMAINS IS TO TEST THEM ON A LIVING OBJECT--ON MYSELF!!
FIRST, I'LL TAKE A FEW DROPS OF THE REDUCING POTION!
ALMOST AT THE INSTANT OF CONTACT, THE FANTASTIC SERUM STARTS TO ACT!
IT'S SHRINKING ME SO FAST, I CAN SEE MYSELF CHANGE!
I'M BECOMING SMALLER AND SMALLER!

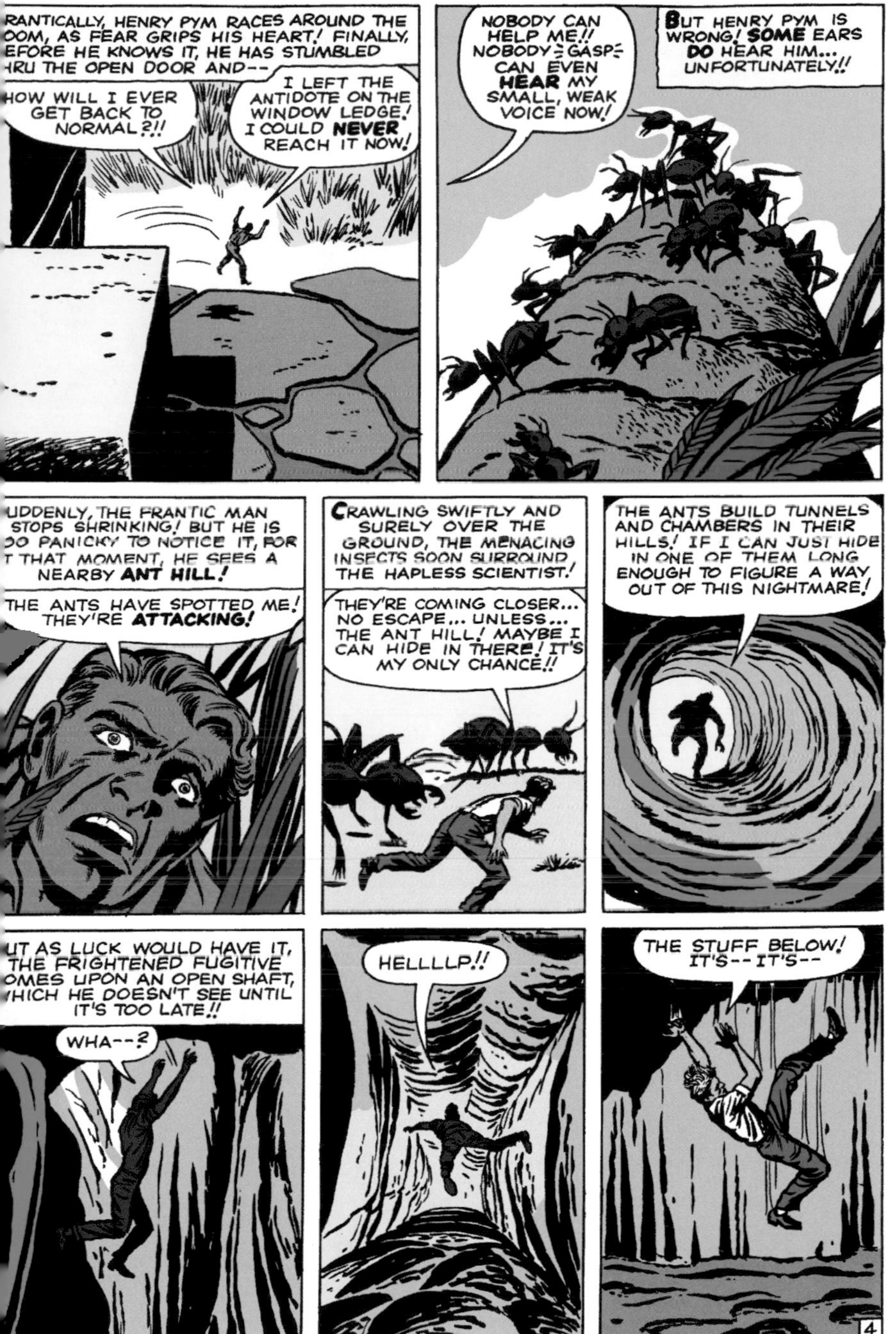

RANTICALLY, HENRY PYM RACES AROUND THE OOM, AS FEAR GRIPS HIS HEART! FINALLY, EFORE HE KNOWS IT, HE HAS STUMBLED HRU THE OPEN DOOR AND--
HOW WILL I EVER GET BACK TO NORMAL?!!
I LEFT THE ANTIDOTE ON THE WINDOW LEDGE! I COULD NEVER REACH IT NOW!
NOBODY CAN HELP ME!! NOBODY-GASP-CAN EVEN HEAR MY SMALL, WEAK VOICE NOW!
BUT HENRY PYM IS WRONG! SOME EARS DO HEAR HIM... UNFORTUNATELY!!
UDDENLY, THE FRANTIC MAN STOPS SHRINKING! BUT HE IS OO PANICKY TO NOTICE IT, FOR T THAT MOMENT, HE SEES A NEARBY ANT HILL!
THE ANTS HAVE SPOTTED ME! THEY'RE ATTACKING!
CRAWLING SWIFTLY AND SURELY OVER THE GROUND, THE MENACING INSECTS SOON SURROUND THE HAPLESS SCIENTIST!
THEY'RE COMING CLOSER... NO ESCAPE... UNLESS... THE ANT HILL! MAYBE I CAN HIDE IN THERE! IT'S MY ONLY CHANCE!!
THE ANTS BUILD TUNNELS AND CHAMBERS IN THEIR HILLS! IF I CAN JUST HIDE IN ONE OF THEM LONG ENOUGH TO FIGURE A WAY OUT OF THIS NIGHTMARE!
UT AS LUCK WOULD HAVE IT, THE FRIGHTENED FUGITIVE OMES UPON AN OPEN SHAFT, VHICH HE DOESN'T SEE UNTIL IT'S TOO LATE!!
WHA--?
HELLLLP!!
THE STUFF BELOW! IT'S--IT'S--
4

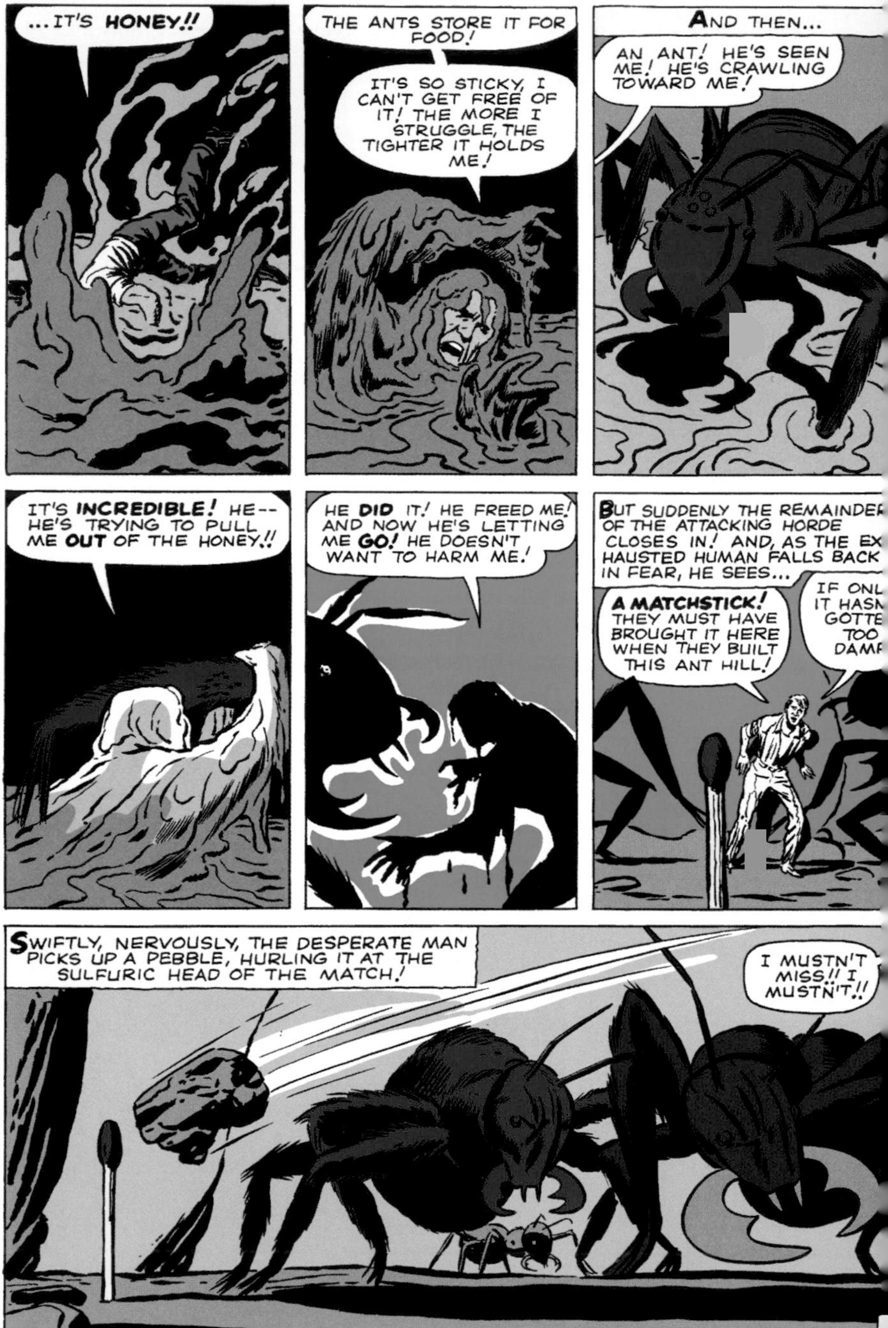
...IT'S HONEY!!
THE ANTS STORE IT FOR FOOD!
IT'S SO STICKY, I CAN'T GET FREE OF IT! THE MORE I STRUGGLE, THE TIGHTER IT HOLDS ME!
AND THEN...
AN ANT! HE'S SEEN ME! HE'S CRAWLING TOWARD ME!
IT'S INCREDIBLE! HE-- HE'S TRYING TO PULL ME OUT OF THE HONEY!!
HE DID IT! HE FREED ME! AND NOW HE'S LETTING ME GO! HE DOESN'T WANT TO HARM ME!
BUT SUDDENLY THE REMAINDEF OF THE ATTACKING HORDE CLOSES IN! AND, AS THE EX HAUSTED HUMAN FALLS BACK IN FEAR, HE SEES...
A MATCHSTICK! THEY MUST HAVE BROUGHT IT HERE WHEN THEY BUILT THIS ANT HILL!
IF ONL IT HASN GOTTE TOO DAMF
SWIFTLY, NERVOUSLY, THE DESPERATE MAN PICKS UP A PEBBLE, HURLING IT AT THE SULFURIC HEAD OF THE MATCH!
I MUSTN'T MISS!! I MUSTN'T!!

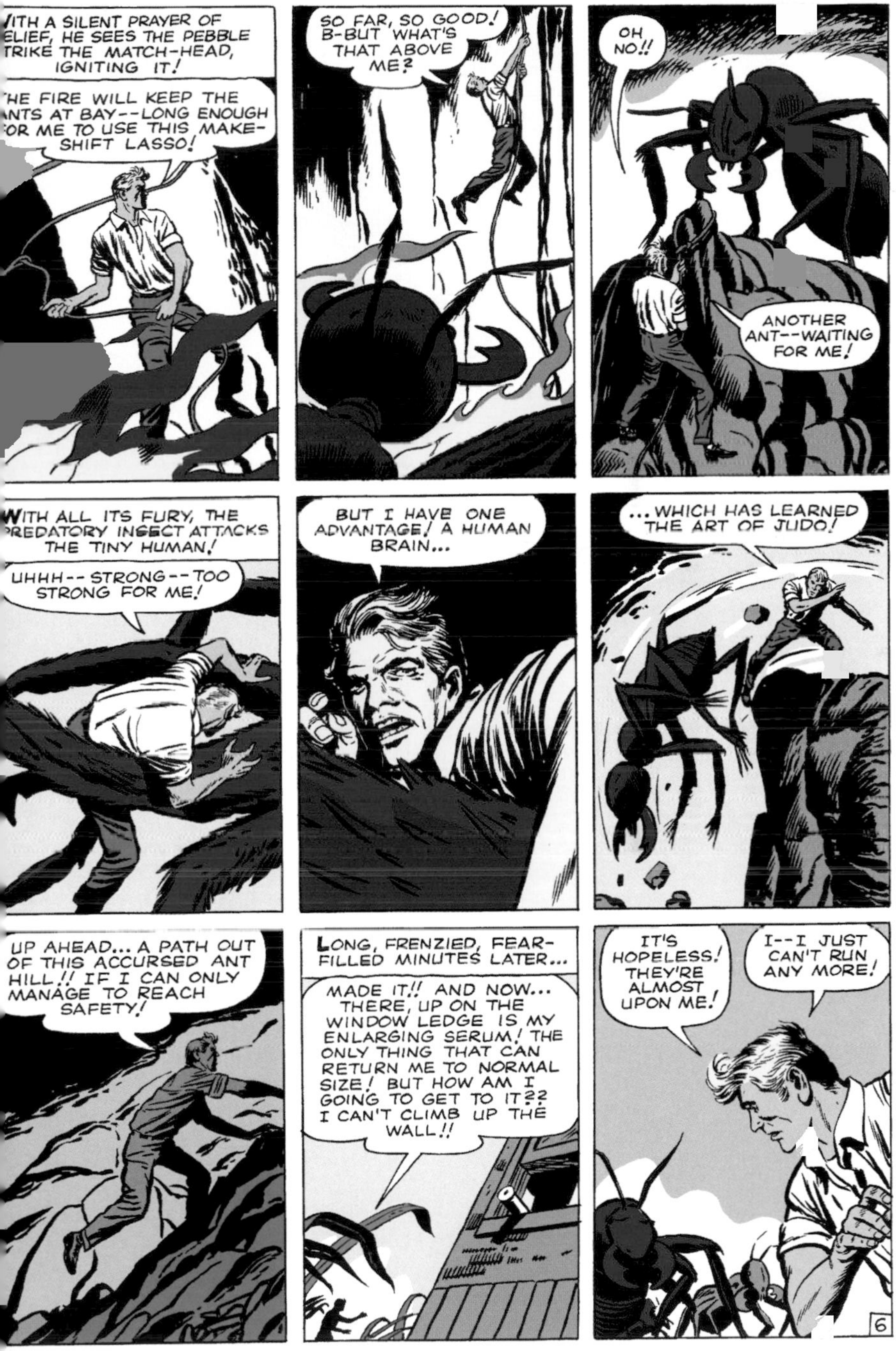

VITH A SILENT PRAYER OF
ELIEF, HE SEES THE PEBBLE
TRIKE THE MATCH-HEAD, IGNITING IT!
HE FIRE WILL KEEP THE
NTS AT BAY--LONG ENOUGH
OR ME TO USE THIS MAKE-SHIFT LASSO!
SO FAR, SO GOOD! B-BUT WHAT'S THAT ABOVE ME?
OH NO!!
ANOTHER ANT--WAITING FOR ME!
WITH ALL ITS FURY, THE
REDATORY INSECT ATTACKS THE TINY HUMAN!
UHHH--STRONG--TOO STRONG FOR ME!
BUT I HAVE ONE ADVANTAGE! A HUMAN BRAIN...
...WHICH HAS LEARNED THE ART OF JUDO!
UP AHEAD... A PATH OUT OF THIS ACCURSED ANT HILL!! IF I CAN ONLY MANAGE TO REACH SAFETY!
LONG, FRENZIED, FEAR-FILLED MINUTES LATER...
MADE IT!! AND NOW... THERE, UP ON THE WINDOW LEDGE IS MY ENLARGING SERUM! THE ONLY THING THAT CAN RETURN ME TO NORMAL SIZE! BUT HOW AM I GOING TO GET TO IT?? I CAN'T CLIMB UP THE WALL!!
IT'S HOPELESS! THEY'RE ALMOST UPON ME!
I--I JUST CAN'T RUN ANY MORE!
6

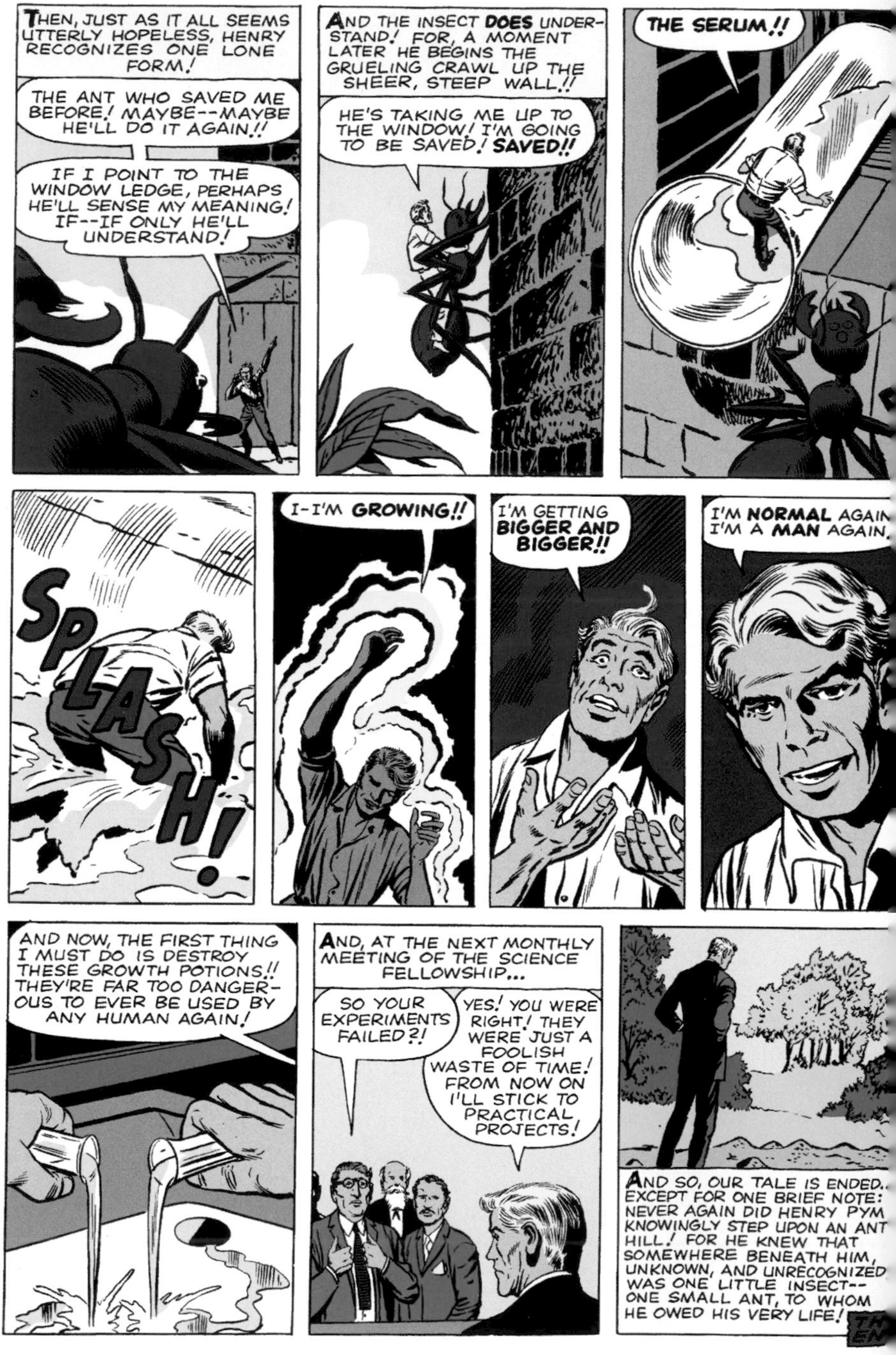
THEN, JUST AS IT ALL SEEMS UTTERLY HOPELESS, HENRY RECOGNIZES ONE LONE FORM!
THE ANT WHO SAVED ME BEFORE! MAYBE--MAYBE HE'LL DO IT AGAIN!!
IF I POINT TO THE WINDOW LEDGE, PERHAPS HE'LL SENSE MY MEANING! IF--IF ONLY HE'LL UNDERSTAND!
AND THE INSECT DOES UNDERSTAND! FOR, A MOMENT LATER HE BEGINS THE GRUELING CRAWL UP THE SHEER, STEEP WALL!!
HE'S TAKING ME UP TO THE WINDOW! I'M GOING TO BE SAVED! SAVED!!
THE SERUM!!
SPLASH!
I-I'M GROWING!!
I'M GETTING BIGGER AND BIGGER!!
I'M NORMAL AGAIN
I'M A MAN AGAIN
AND NOW, THE FIRST THING I MUST DO IS DESTROY THESE GROWTH POTIONS!! THEY'RE FAR TOO DANGEROUS TO EVER BE USED BY ANY HUMAN AGAIN!
AND, AT THE NEXT MONTHLY MEETING OF THE SCIENCE FELLOWSHIP...
SO YOUR EXPERIMENTS FAILED?!
YES! YOU WERE RIGHT! THEY WERE JUST A FOOLISH WASTE OF TIME! FROM NOW ON I'LL STICK TO PRACTICAL PROJECTS!
AND SO, OUR TALE IS ENDED.. EXCEPT FOR ONE BRIEF NOTE: NEVER AGAIN DID HENRY PYM KNOWINGLY STEP UPON AN ANT HILL! FOR HE KNEW THAT SOMEWHERE BENEATH HIM, UNKNOWN, AND UNRECOGNIZED WAS ONE LITTLE INSECT-- ONE SMALL ANT, TO WHOM HE OWED HIS VERY LIFE!

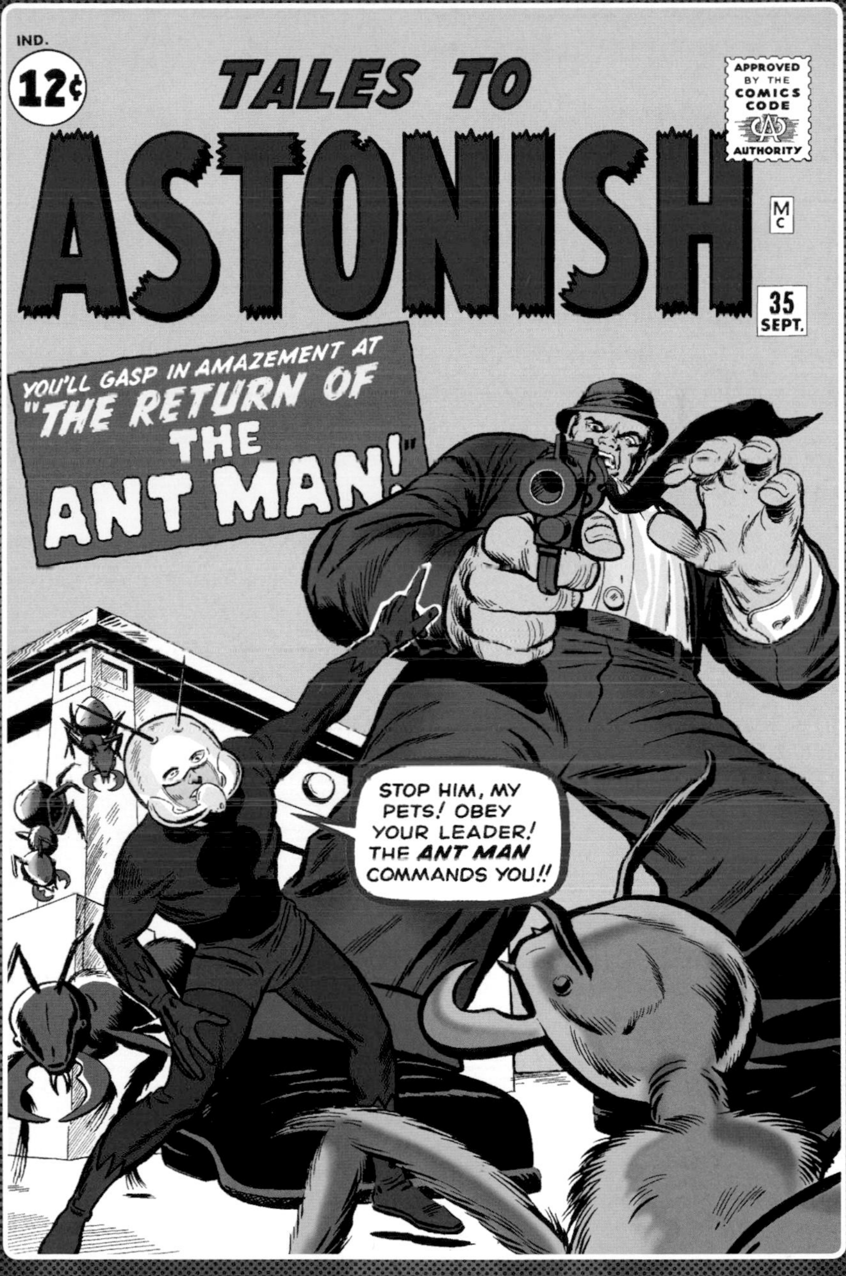
IND.
12¢
TALES TO
ASTONISH
APPROVED BY THE COMICS CODE AUTHORITY
MC
35
SEPT.
YOU'LL GASP IN AMAZEMENT AT
"THE RETURN OF
THE
ANT MAN!"
STOP HIM, MY PETS! OBEY YOUR LEADER! THE ANT MAN COMMANDS YOU!!

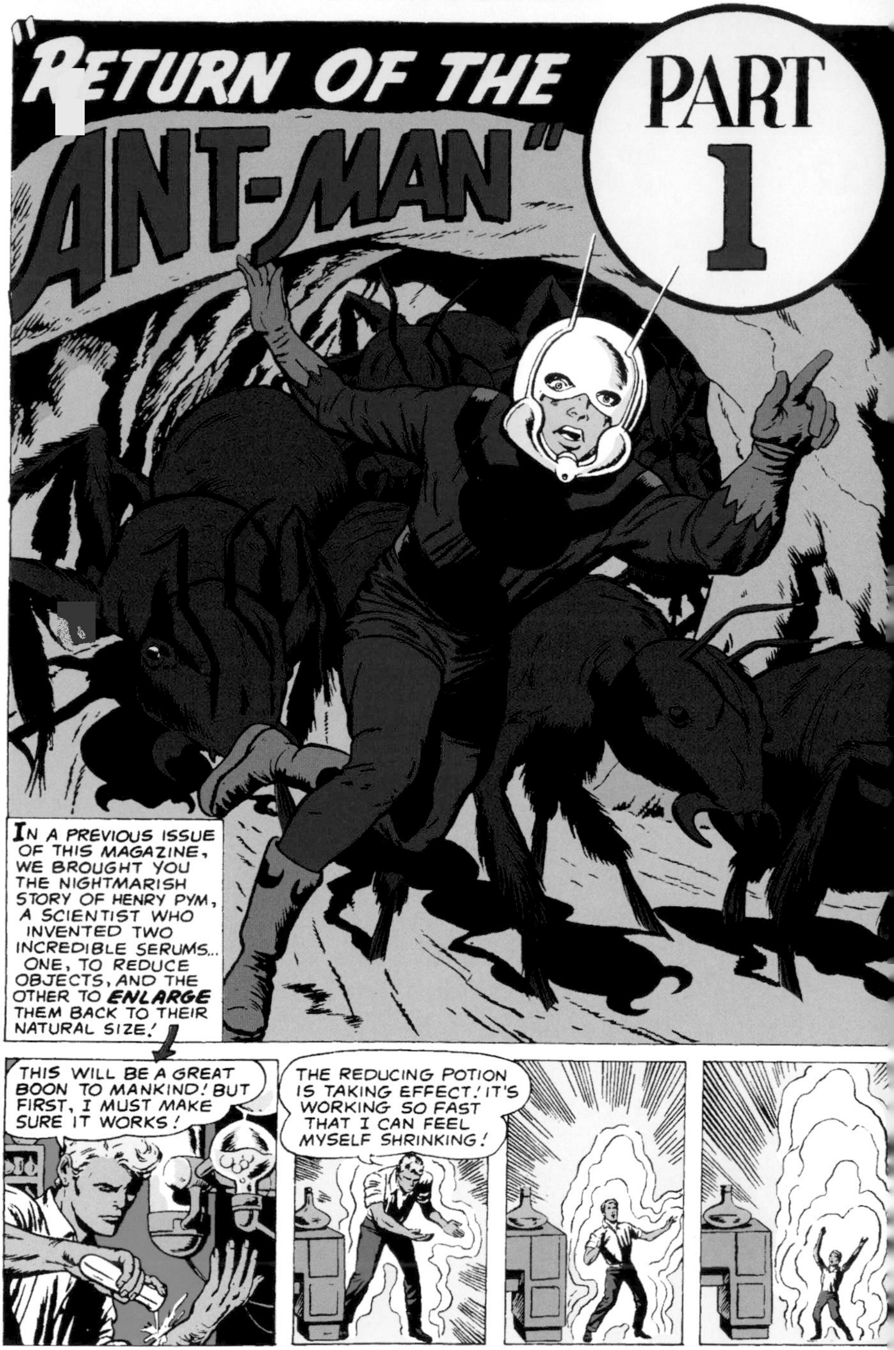
"RETURN OF THE ANT-MAN"
PART 1
IN A PREVIOUS ISSUE OF THIS MAGAZINE, WE BROUGHT YOU THE NIGHTMARISH STORY OF HENRY PYM, A SCIENTIST WHO INVENTED TWO INCREDIBLE SERUMS... ONE, TO REDUCE OBJECTS, AND THE OTHER TO ENLARGE THEM BACK TO THEIR NATURAL SIZE!
THIS WILL BE A GREAT BOON TO MANKIND! BUT FIRST, I MUST MAKE SURE IT WORKS!
THE REDUCING POTION IS TAKING EFFECT! IT'S WORKING SO FAST THAT I CAN FEEL MYSELF SHRINKING!

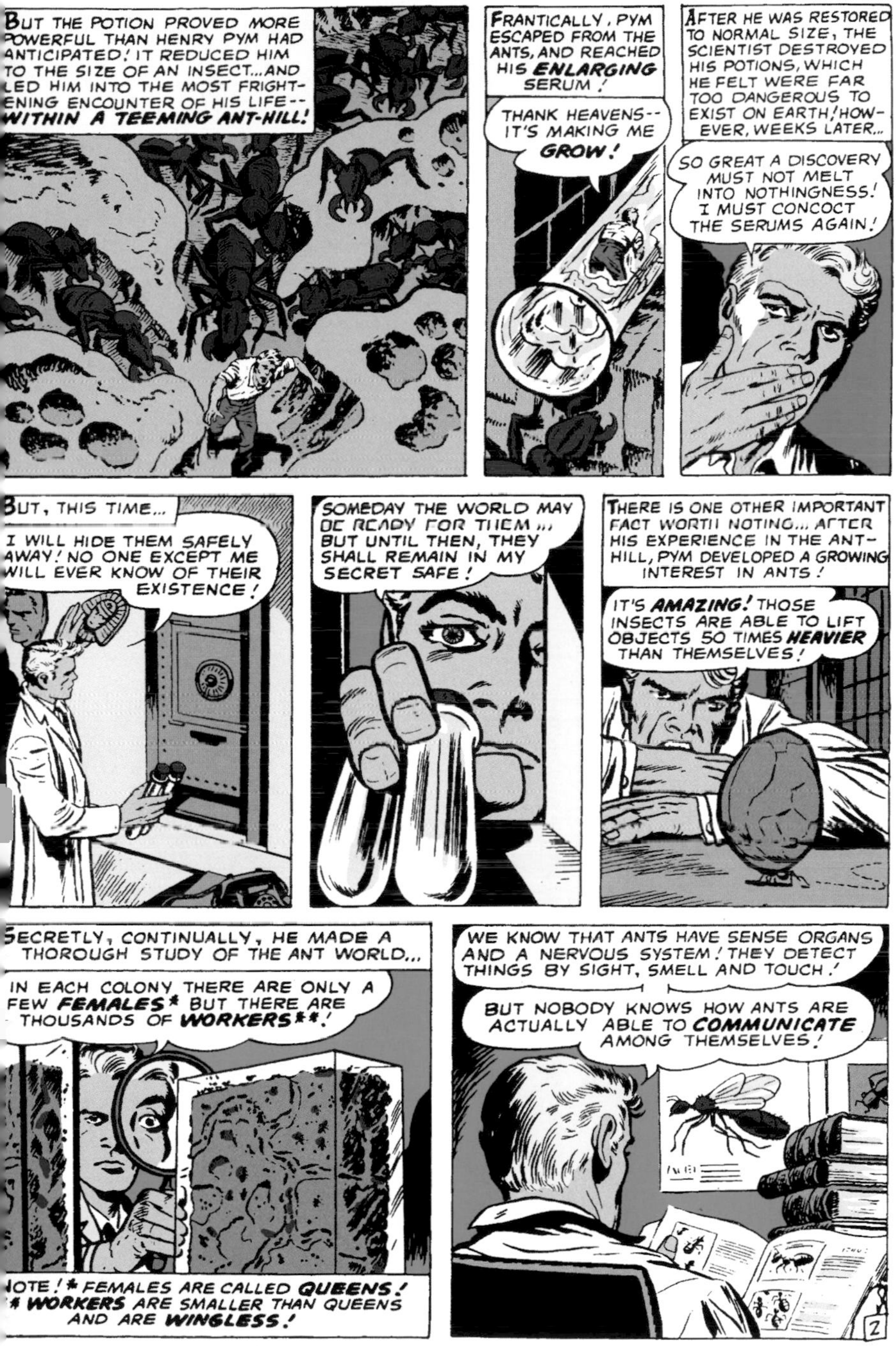

BUT THE POTION PROVED MORE POWERFUL THAN HENRY PYM HAD ANTICIPATED! IT REDUCED HIM TO THE SIZE OF AN INSECT...AND LED HIM INTO THE MOST FRIGHTENING ENCOUNTER OF HIS LIFE-- WITHIN A TEEMING ANT-HILL!
FRANTICALLY, PYM ESCAPED FROM THE ANTS, AND REACHED HIS ENLARGING SERUM!
THANK HEAVENS-- IT'S MAKING ME GROW!
AFTER HE WAS RESTORED TO NORMAL SIZE, THE SCIENTIST DESTROYED HIS POTIONS, WHICH HE FELT WERE FAR TOO DANGEROUS TO EXIST ON EARTH! HOWEVER, WEEKS LATER...
SO GREAT A DISCOVERY MUST NOT MELT INTO NOTHINGNESS! I MUST CONCOCT THE SERUMS AGAIN!
BUT, THIS TIME...
I WILL HIDE THEM SAFELY AWAY! NO ONE EXCEPT ME WILL EVER KNOW OF THEIR EXISTENCE!
SOMEDAY THE WORLD MAY BE READY FOR THEM ... BUT UNTIL THEN, THEY SHALL REMAIN IN MY SECRET SAFE!
THERE IS ONE OTHER IMPORTANT FACT WORTH NOTING... AFTER HIS EXPERIENCE IN THE ANT-HILL, PYM DEVELOPED A GROWING INTEREST IN ANTS!
IT'S AMAZING! THOSE INSECTS ARE ABLE TO LIFT OBJECTS 50 TIMES HEAVIER THAN THEMSELVES!
SECRETLY, CONTINUALLY, HE MADE A THOROUGH STUDY OF THE ANT WORLD...
IN EACH COLONY THERE ARE ONLY A FEW FEMALES* BUT THERE ARE THOUSANDS OF WORKERS**!
NOTE! * FEMALES ARE CALLED QUEENS! ** WORKERS ARE SMALLER THAN QUEENS AND ARE WINGLESS!
WE KNOW THAT ANTS HAVE SENSE ORGANS AND A NERVOUS SYSTEM! THEY DETECT THINGS BY SIGHT, SMELL AND TOUCH!
BUT NOBODY KNOWS HOW ANTS ARE ACTUALLY ABLE TO COMMUNICATE AMONG THEMSELVES!
2

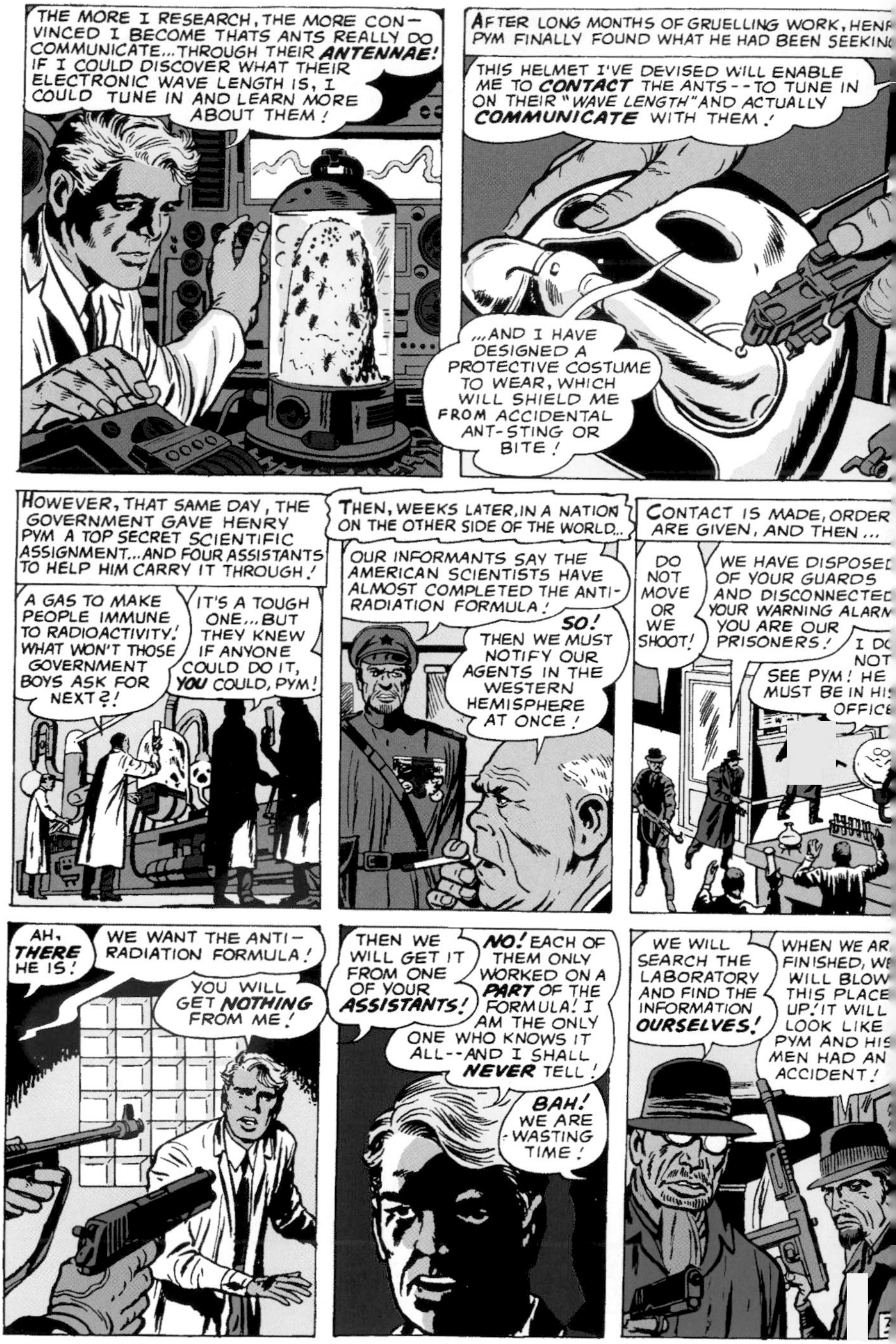
THE MORE I RESEARCH, THE MORE CONVINCED I BECOME THATS ANTS REALLY DO COMMUNICATE...THROUGH THEIR ANTENNAE! IF I COULD DISCOVER WHAT THEIR ELECTRONIC WAVE LENGTH IS, I COULD TUNE IN AND LEARN MORE ABOUT THEM!
AFTER LONG MONTHS OF GRUELLING WORK, HENR PYM FINALLY FOUND WHAT HE HAD BEEN SEEKIN
THIS HELMET I'VE DEVISED WILL ENABLE ME TO CONTACT THE ANTS--TO TUNE IN ON THEIR "WAVE LENGTH" AND ACTUALLY COMMUNICATE WITH THEM!
...AND I HAVE DESIGNED A PROTECTIVE COSTUME TO WEAR, WHICH WILL SHIELD ME FROM ACCIDENTAL ANT-STING OR BITE!
HOWEVER, THAT SAME DAY, THE GOVERNMENT GAVE HENRY PYM A TOP SECRET SCIENTIFIC ASSIGNMENT...AND FOUR ASSISTANTS TO HELP HIM CARRY IT THROUGH!
A GAS TO MAKE PEOPLE IMMUNE TO RADIOACTIVITY! WHAT WON'T THOSE GOVERNMENT BOYS ASK FOR NEXT?!
IT'S A TOUGH ONE...BUT THEY KNEW IF ANYONE COULD DO IT, YOU COULD, PYM!
THEN, WEEKS LATER, IN A NATION ON THE OTHER SIDE OF THE WORLD...
OUR INFORMANTS SAY THE AMERICAN SCIENTISTS HAVE ALMOST COMPLETED THE ANTI-RADIATION FORMULA!
SO! THEN WE MUST NOTIFY OUR AGENTS IN THE WESTERN HEMISPHERE AT ONCE!
CONTACT IS MADE, ORDER ARE GIVEN, AND THEN...
DO NOT MOVE OR WE SHOOT!
WE HAVE DISPOSE OF YOUR GUARDS AND DISCONNECTE YOUR WARNING ALARM YOU ARE OUR PRISONERS!
I DO NOT SEE PYM! HE MUST BE IN HI OFFIC
AH, THERE HE IS!
WE WANT THE ANTI-RADIATION FORMULA!
YOU WILL GET NOTHING FROM ME!
THEN WE WILL GET IT FROM ONE OF YOUR ASSISTANTS!
NO! EACH OF THEM ONLY WORKED ON A PART OF THE FORMULA! I AM THE ONLY ONE WHO KNOWS IT ALL--AND I SHALL NEVER TELL!
BAH! WE ARE WASTING TIME!
WE WILL SEARCH THE LABORATORY AND FIND THE INFORMATION OURSELVES!
WHEN WE AR FINISHED, W WILL BLOW THIS PLACE UP! IT WILL LOOK LIKE PYM AND HIS MEN HAD AN ACCIDENT!

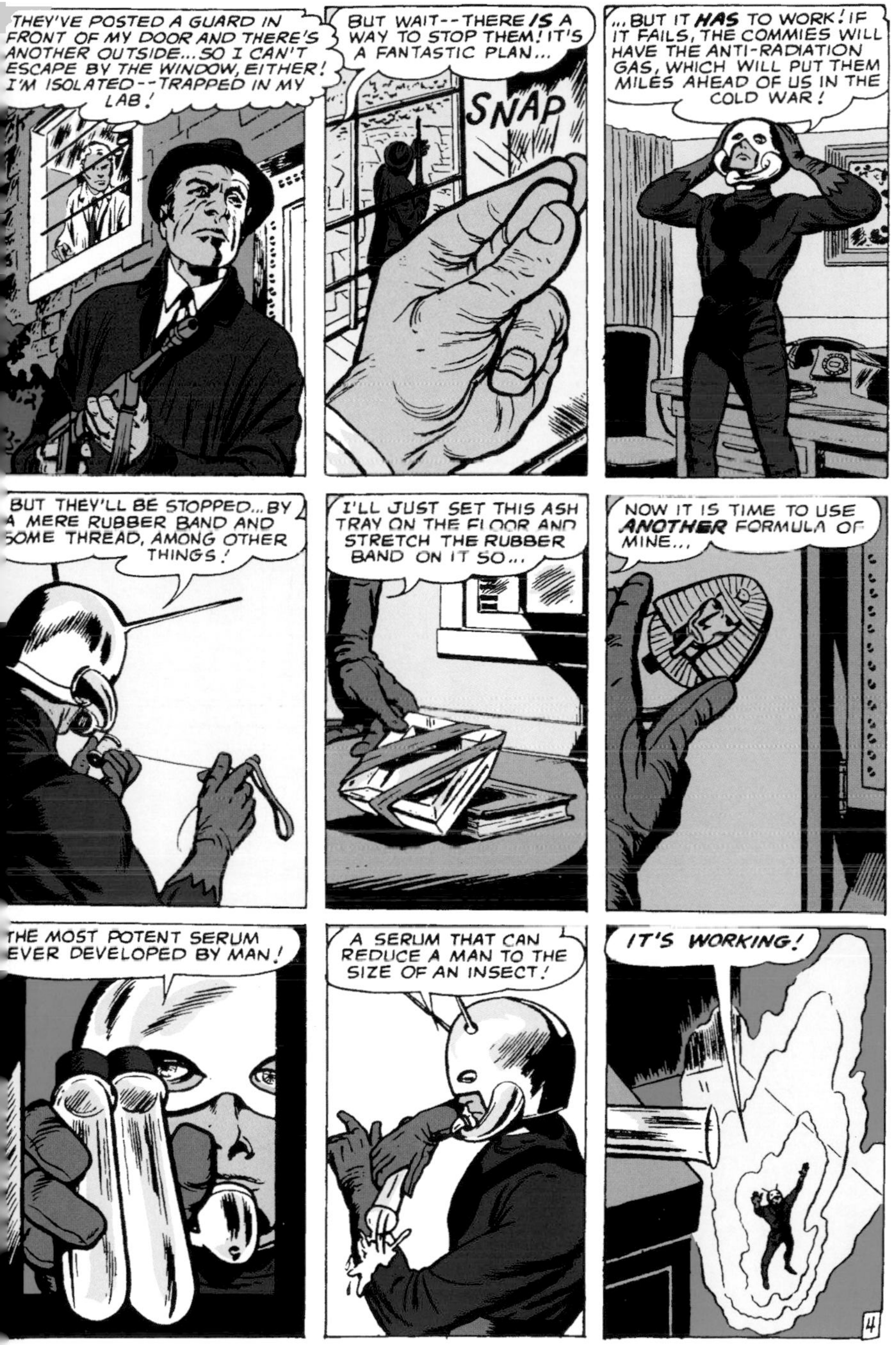
THEY'VE POSTED A GUARD IN FRONT OF MY DOOR AND THERE'S ANOTHER OUTSIDE... SO I CAN'T ESCAPE BY THE WINDOW, EITHER! I'M ISOLATED--TRAPPED IN MY LAB!
BUT WAIT--THERE IS A WAY TO STOP THEM! IT'S A FANTASTIC PLAN...
SNAP
...BUT IT HAS TO WORK! IF IT FAILS, THE COMMIES WILL HAVE THE ANTI-RADIATION GAS, WHICH WILL PUT THEM MILES AHEAD OF US IN THE COLD WAR!
BUT THEY'LL BE STOPPED... BY A MERE RUBBER BAND AND SOME THREAD, AMONG OTHER THINGS!
I'LL JUST SET THIS ASH TRAY ON THE FLOOR AND STRETCH THE RUBBER BAND ON IT SO...
NOW IT IS TIME TO USE ANOTHER FORMULA OF MINE...
THE MOST POTENT SERUM EVER DEVELOPED BY MAN!
A SERUM THAT CAN REDUCE A MAN TO THE SIZE OF AN INSECT!
IT'S WORKING!
4

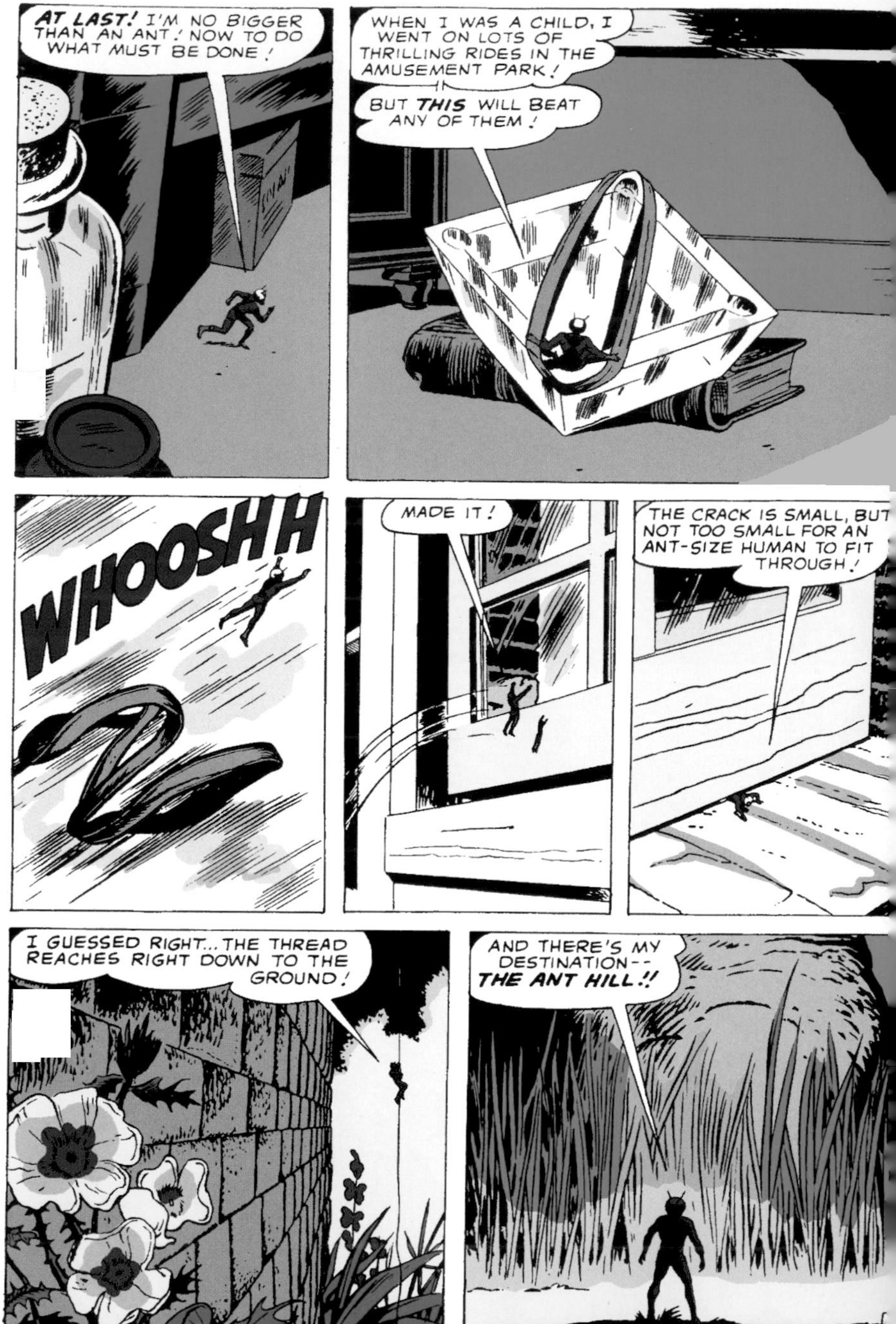
AT LAST! I'M NO BIGGER THAN AN ANT! NOW TO DO WHAT MUST BE DONE!
WHEN I WAS A CHILD, I WENT ON LOTS OF THRILLING RIDES IN THE AMUSEMENT PARK!
BUT THIS WILL BEAT ANY OF THEM!
WHOOSHH
MADE IT!
THE CRACK IS SMALL, BUT NOT TOO SMALL FOR AN ANT-SIZE HUMAN TO FIT THROUGH!
I GUESSED RIGHT... THE THREAD REACHES RIGHT DOWN TO THE GROUND!
AND THERE'S MY DESTINATION-- THE ANT HILL!!

PART 2

"AN ARMY OF ANTS!"

MUST BE CAREFUL! I DON'T WANT THE ANTS TO SEE ME YET!

WAIT-- I FEEL VIBRATIONS AGAINST MY HELMET!

VIBRATIONS--JUST AS I SUSPECTED! THE ANTS' ANTENNAE **DO** GIVE OFF ELECTRONIC IMPULSES! **THAT'S** HOW THEY COMMUNICATE WITH EACH OTHER!

TWOINNN'GG

BUT, SUDDENLY...

THEY'RE TURNING AROUND! THEY'RE COMING THIS WAY! B-BUT HOW DID THEY ?? OH, NO, I **FORGOT**--

I FORGOT THAT THEY HAVE A HIGHLY DEVELOPED SENSE OF **SMELL!** THEY'RE ABLE TO DETECT ANY ALIEN CREATURE NEAR THEM!

6

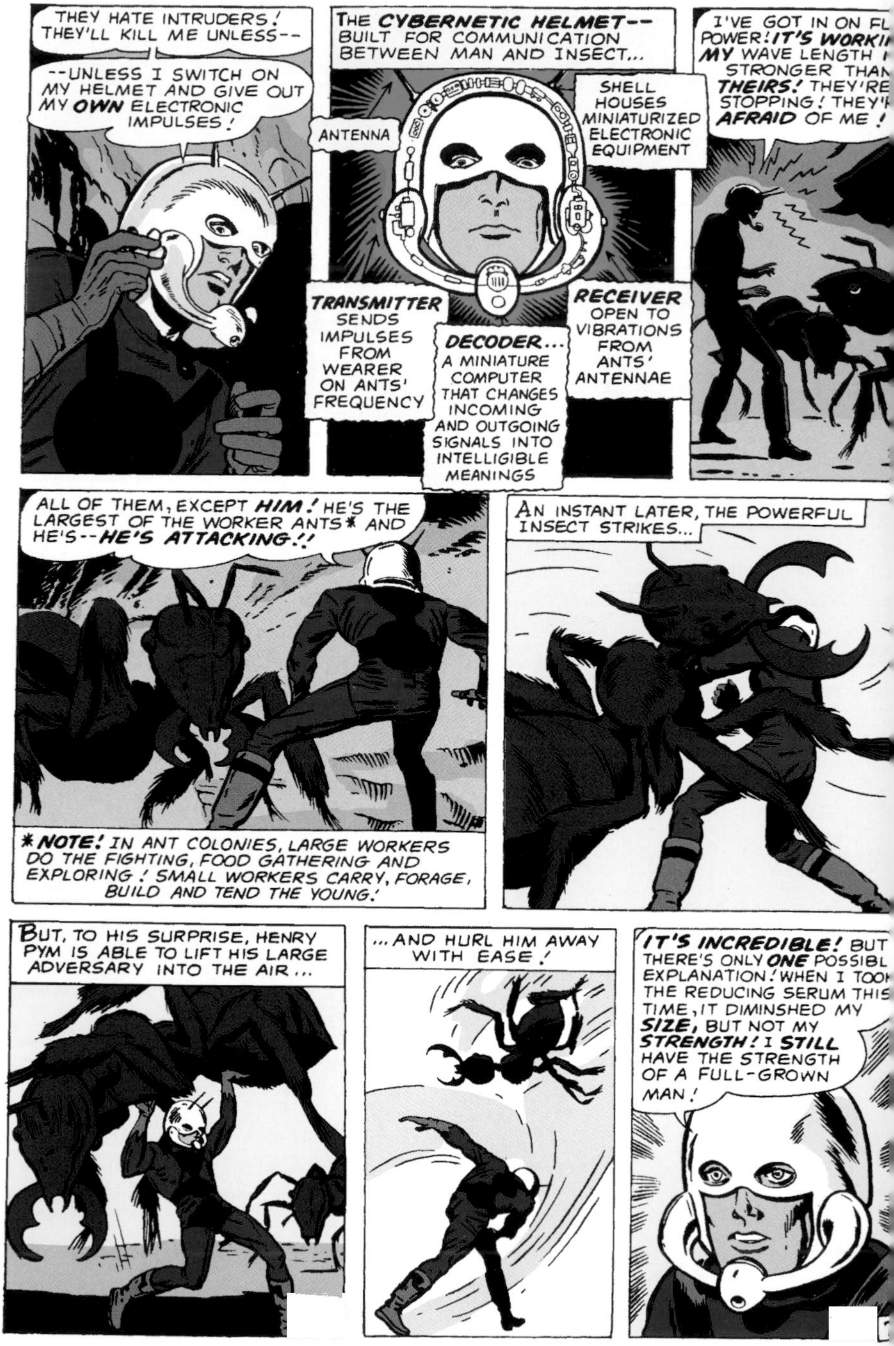

THEY HATE INTRUDERS! THEY'LL KILL ME UNLESS--
--UNLESS I SWITCH ON MY HELMET AND GIVE OUT MY OWN ELECTRONIC IMPULSES!
THE CYBERNETIC HELMET-- BUILT FOR COMMUNICATION BETWEEN MAN AND INSECT...
ANTENNA
SHELL HOUSES MINIATURIZED ELECTRONIC EQUIPMENT
TRANSMITTER SENDS IMPULSES FROM WEARER ON ANTS' FREQUENCY
DECODER... A MINIATURE COMPUTER THAT CHANGES INCOMING AND OUTGOING SIGNALS INTO INTELLIGIBLE MEANINGS
RECEIVER OPEN TO VIBRATIONS FROM ANTS' ANTENNAE
I'VE GOT IN ON FL POWER! IT'S WORKI MY WAVE LENGTH STRONGER THAN THEIRS! THEY'RE STOPPING! THEY' AFRAID OF ME!
ALL OF THEM, EXCEPT HIM! HE'S THE LARGEST OF THE WORKER ANTS* AND HE'S--HE'S ATTACKING!!
*NOTE! IN ANT COLONIES, LARGE WORKERS DO THE FIGHTING, FOOD GATHERING AND EXPLORING! SMALL WORKERS CARRY, FORAGE, BUILD AND TEND THE YOUNG!
AN INSTANT LATER, THE POWERFUL INSECT STRIKES...
BUT, TO HIS SURPRISE, HENRY PYM IS ABLE TO LIFT HIS LARGE ADVERSARY INTO THE AIR...
...AND HURL HIM AWAY WITH EASE!
IT'S INCREDIBLE! BUT THERE'S ONLY ONE POSSIBL EXPLANATION! WHEN I TOO THE REDUCING SERUM THIS TIME, IT DIMINISHED MY SIZE, BUT NOT MY STRENGTH! I STILL HAVE THE STRENGTH OF A FULL-GROWN MAN!

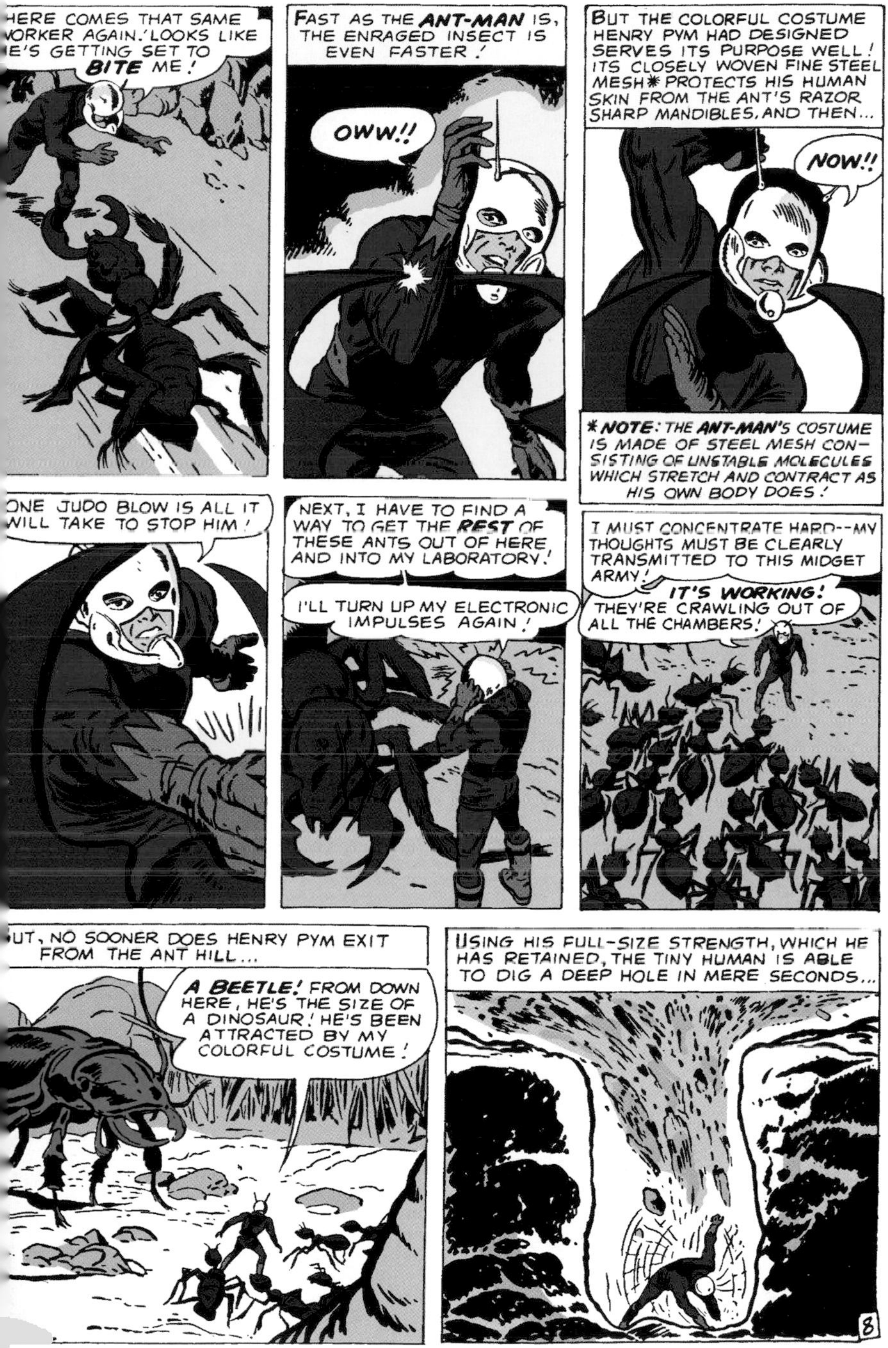
HERE COMES THAT SAME WORKER AGAIN! LOOKS LIKE HE'S GETTING SET TO BITE ME!
FAST AS THE ANT-MAN IS, THE ENRAGED INSECT IS EVEN FASTER!
OWW!!
BUT THE COLORFUL COSTUME HENRY PYM HAD DESIGNED SERVES ITS PURPOSE WELL! ITS CLOSELY WOVEN FINE STEEL MESH* PROTECTS HIS HUMAN SKIN FROM THE ANT'S RAZOR SHARP MANDIBLES, AND THEN...
NOW!!
*NOTE: THE ANT-MAN'S COSTUME IS MADE OF STEEL MESH CONSISTING OF UNSTABLE MOLECULES WHICH STRETCH AND CONTRACT AS HIS OWN BODY DOES!
ONE JUDO BLOW IS ALL IT WILL TAKE TO STOP HIM!
NEXT, I HAVE TO FIND A WAY TO GET THE REST OF THESE ANTS OUT OF HERE AND INTO MY LABORATORY!
I'LL TURN UP MY ELECTRONIC IMPULSES AGAIN!
I MUST CONCENTRATE HARD--MY THOUGHTS MUST BE CLEARLY TRANSMITTED TO THIS MIDGET ARMY!
IT'S WORKING! THEY'RE CRAWLING OUT OF ALL THE CHAMBERS!
BUT, NO SOONER DOES HENRY PYM EXIT FROM THE ANT HILL...
A BEETLE! FROM DOWN HERE, HE'S THE SIZE OF A DINOSAUR! HE'S BEEN ATTRACTED BY MY COLORFUL COSTUME!
USING HIS FULL-SIZE STRENGTH, WHICH HE HAS RETAINED, THE TINY HUMAN IS ABLE TO DIG A DEEP HOLE IN MERE SECONDS...
8

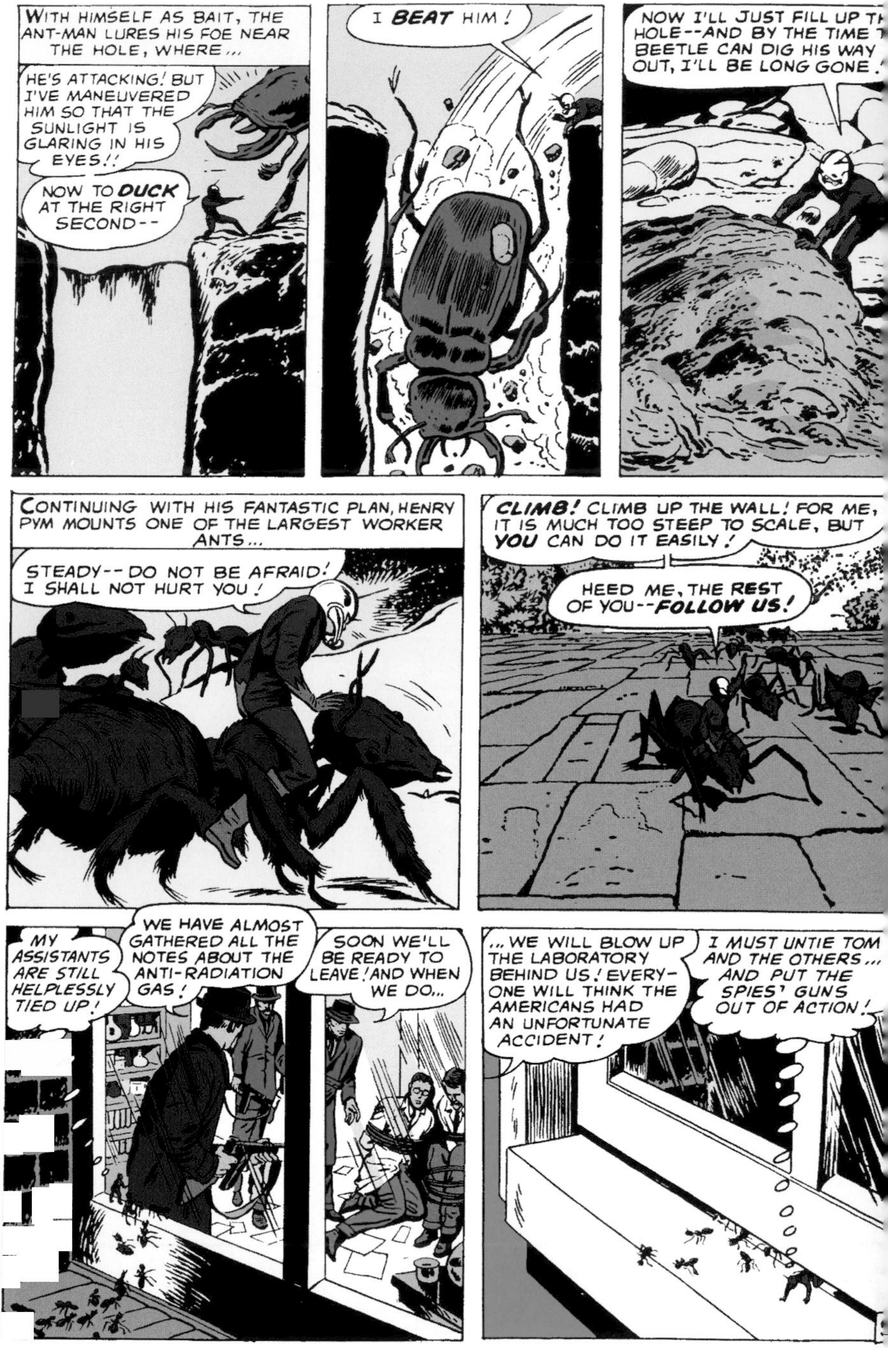
WITH HIMSELF AS BAIT, THE ANT-MAN LURES HIS FOE NEAR THE HOLE, WHERE...
HE'S ATTACKING! BUT I'VE MANEUVERED HIM SO THAT THE SUNLIGHT IS GLARING IN HIS EYES!!
NOW TO DUCK AT THE RIGHT SECOND--
I BEAT HIM!
NOW I'LL JUST FILL UP THE HOLE--AND BY THE TIME THE BEETLE CAN DIG HIS WAY OUT, I'LL BE LONG GONE.
CONTINUING WITH HIS FANTASTIC PLAN, HENRY PYM MOUNTS ONE OF THE LARGEST WORKER ANTS...
STEADY--DO NOT BE AFRAID! I SHALL NOT HURT YOU!
CLIMB! CLIMB UP THE WALL! FOR ME, IT IS MUCH TOO STEEP TO SCALE, BUT YOU CAN DO IT EASILY!
HEED ME, THE REST OF YOU--FOLLOW US!
MY ASSISTANTS ARE STILL HELPLESSLY TIED UP!
WE HAVE ALMOST GATHERED ALL THE NOTES ABOUT THE ANTI-RADIATION GAS!
SOON WE'LL BE READY TO LEAVE! AND WHEN WE DO...
...WE WILL BLOW UP THE LABORATORY BEHIND US! EVERYONE WILL THINK THE AMERICANS HAD AN UNFORTUNATE ACCIDENT!
I MUST UNTIE TOM AND THE OTHERS... AND PUT THE SPIES' GUNS OUT OF ACTION!

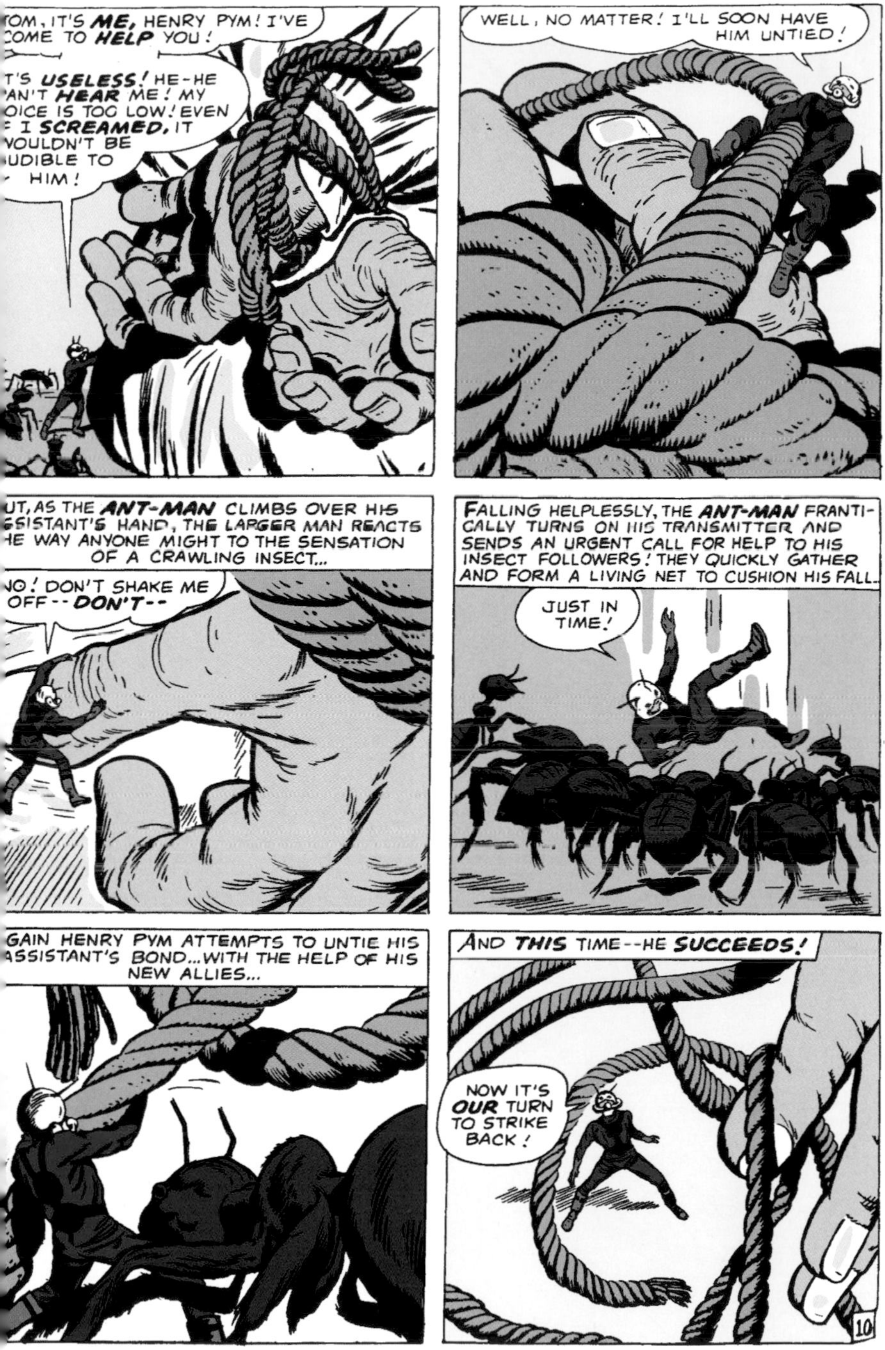
TOM, IT'S ME, HENRY PYM! I'VE COME TO HELP YOU!
T'S USELESS! HE-HE AN'T HEAR ME! MY OICE IS TOO LOW! EVEN I SCREAMED, IT VOULDN'T BE UDIBLE TO HIM!
WELL, NO MATTER! I'LL SOON HAVE HIM UNTIED!
UT, AS THE ANT-MAN CLIMBS OVER HIS SSISTANT'S HAND, THE LARGER MAN REACTS HE WAY ANYONE MIGHT TO THE SENSATION OF A CRAWLING INSECT...
NO! DON'T SHAKE ME OFF--DON'T--
FALLING HELPLESSLY, THE ANT-MAN FRANTICALLY TURNS ON HIS TRANSMITTER AND SENDS AN URGENT CALL FOR HELP TO HIS INSECT FOLLOWERS! THEY QUICKLY GATHER AND FORM A LIVING NET TO CUSHION HIS FALL.
JUST IN TIME!
GAIN HENRY PYM ATTEMPTS TO UNTIE HIS SSISTANT'S BOND...WITH THE HELP OF HIS NEW ALLIES...
AND THIS TIME--HE SUCCEEDS!
NOW IT'S OUR TURN TO STRIKE BACK!
10

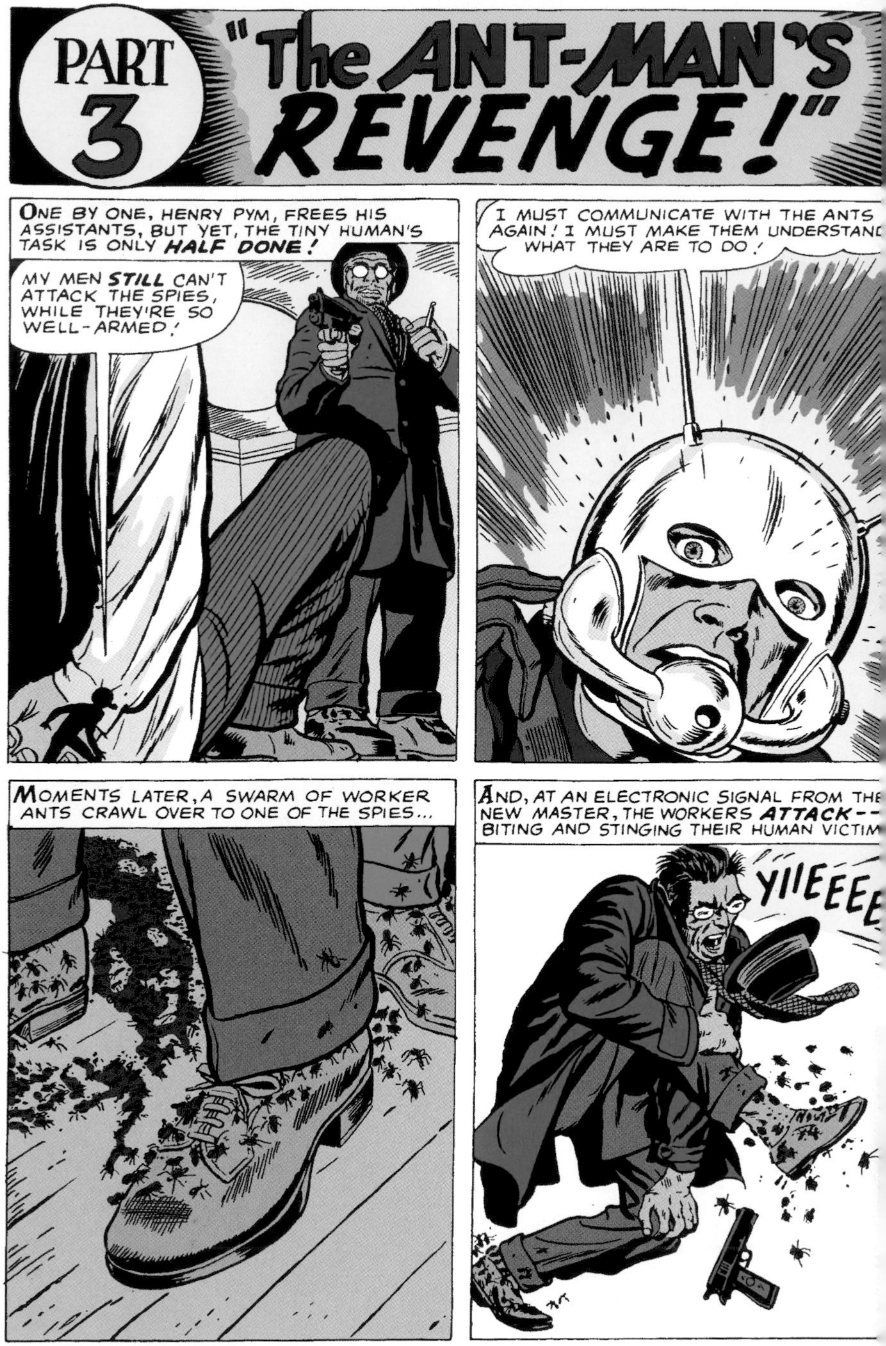
PART 3
"The ANT-MAN'S REVENGE!"
ONE BY ONE, HENRY PYM, FREES HIS ASSISTANTS, BUT YET, THE TINY HUMAN'S TASK IS ONLY HALF DONE!
MY MEN STILL CAN'T ATTACK THE SPIES, WHILE THEY'RE SO WELL-ARMED!
I MUST COMMUNICATE WITH THE ANTS AGAIN! I MUST MAKE THEM UNDERSTAN
WHAT THEY ARE TO DO!
MOMENTS LATER, A SWARM OF WORKER ANTS CRAWL OVER TO ONE OF THE SPIES...
AND, AT AN ELECTRONIC SIGNAL FROM THE NEW MASTER, THE WORKERS ATTACK-- BITING AND STINGING THEIR HUMAN VICTIM
YIIEEEE

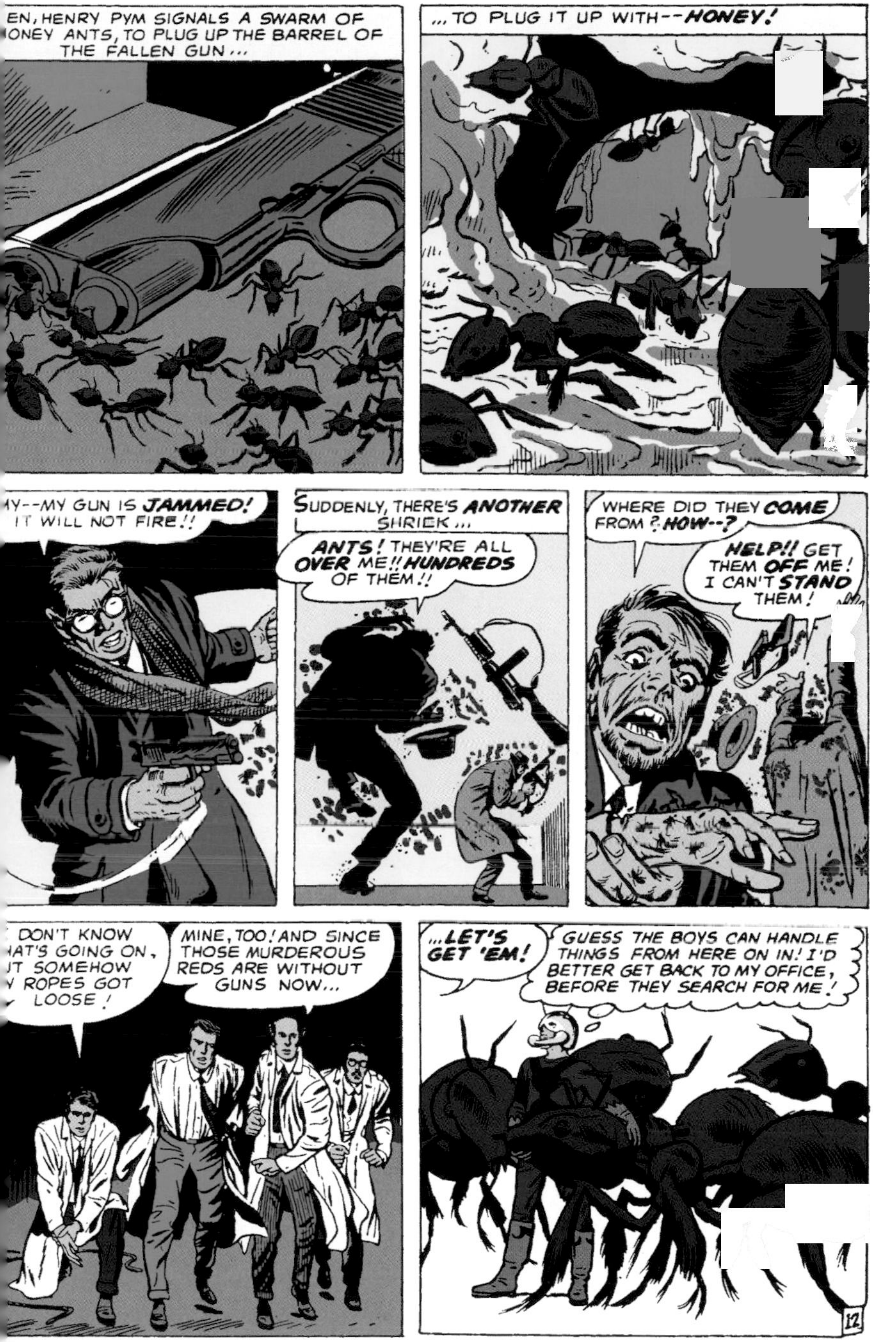
EN, HENRY PYM SIGNALS A SWARM OF ONEY ANTS, TO PLUG UP THE BARREL OF THE FALLEN GUN...
...TO PLUG IT UP WITH--HONEY!
Y--MY GUN IS JAMMED! IT WILL NOT FIRE!!
SUDDENLY, THERE'S ANOTHER SHRIEK...
ANTS! THEY'RE ALL OVER ME!! HUNDREDS OF THEM!!
WHERE DID THEY COME FROM? HOW--?
HELP!! GET THEM OFF ME! I CAN'T STAND THEM!
DON'T KNOW AT'S GOING ON, T SOMEHOW ROPES GOT LOOSE!
MINE, TOO! AND SINCE THOSE MURDEROUS REDS ARE WITHOUT GUNS NOW...
...LET'S GET 'EM!
GUESS THE BOYS CAN HANDLE THINGS FROM HERE ON IN! I'D BETTER GET BACK TO MY OFFICE, BEFORE THEY SEARCH FOR ME!
12

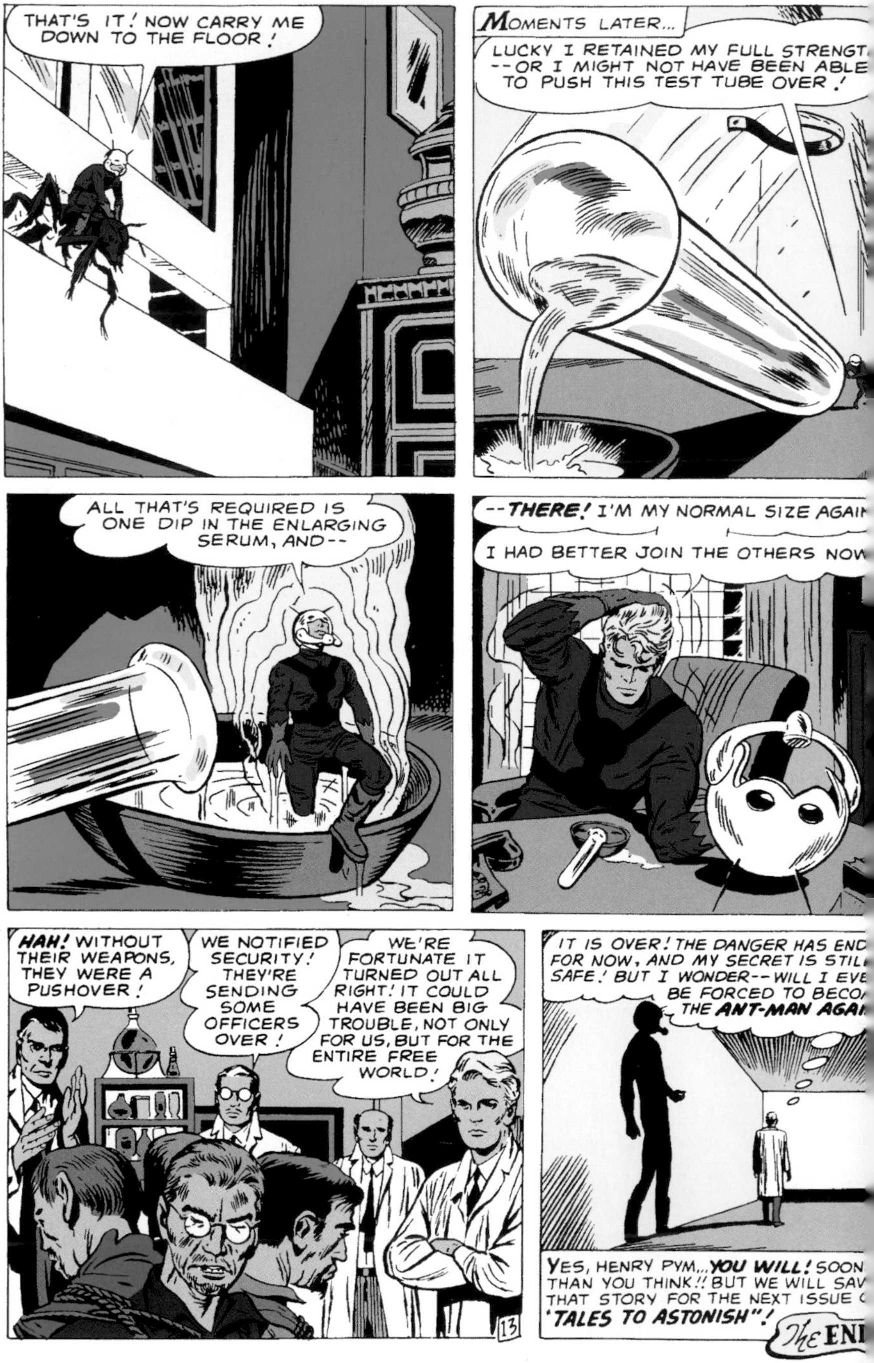
THAT'S IT! NOW CARRY ME DOWN TO THE FLOOR!
MOMENTS LATER...
LUCKY I RETAINED MY FULL STRENGT --OR I MIGHT NOT HAVE BEEN ABLE TO PUSH THIS TEST TUBE OVER!
ALL THAT'S REQUIRED IS ONE DIP IN THE ENLARGING SERUM, AND--
--THERE! I'M MY NORMAL SIZE AGAI
I HAD BETTER JOIN THE OTHERS NOW
HAH! WITHOUT THEIR WEAPONS, THEY WERE A PUSHOVER!
WE NOTIFIED SECURITY! THEY'RE SENDING SOME OFFICERS OVER!
WE'RE FORTUNATE IT TURNED OUT ALL RIGHT! IT COULD HAVE BEEN BIG TROUBLE, NOT ONLY FOR US, BUT FOR THE ENTIRE FREE WORLD!
13
IT IS OVER! THE DANGER HAS END FOR NOW, AND MY SECRET IS STIL SAFE! BUT I WONDER--WILL I EVE BE FORCED TO BECO THE ANT-MAN AGA
YES, HENRY PYM... YOU WILL! SOON THAN YOU THINK!! BUT WE WILL SAV THAT STORY FOR THE NEXT ISSUE O "TALES TO ASTONISH"!
THE EN

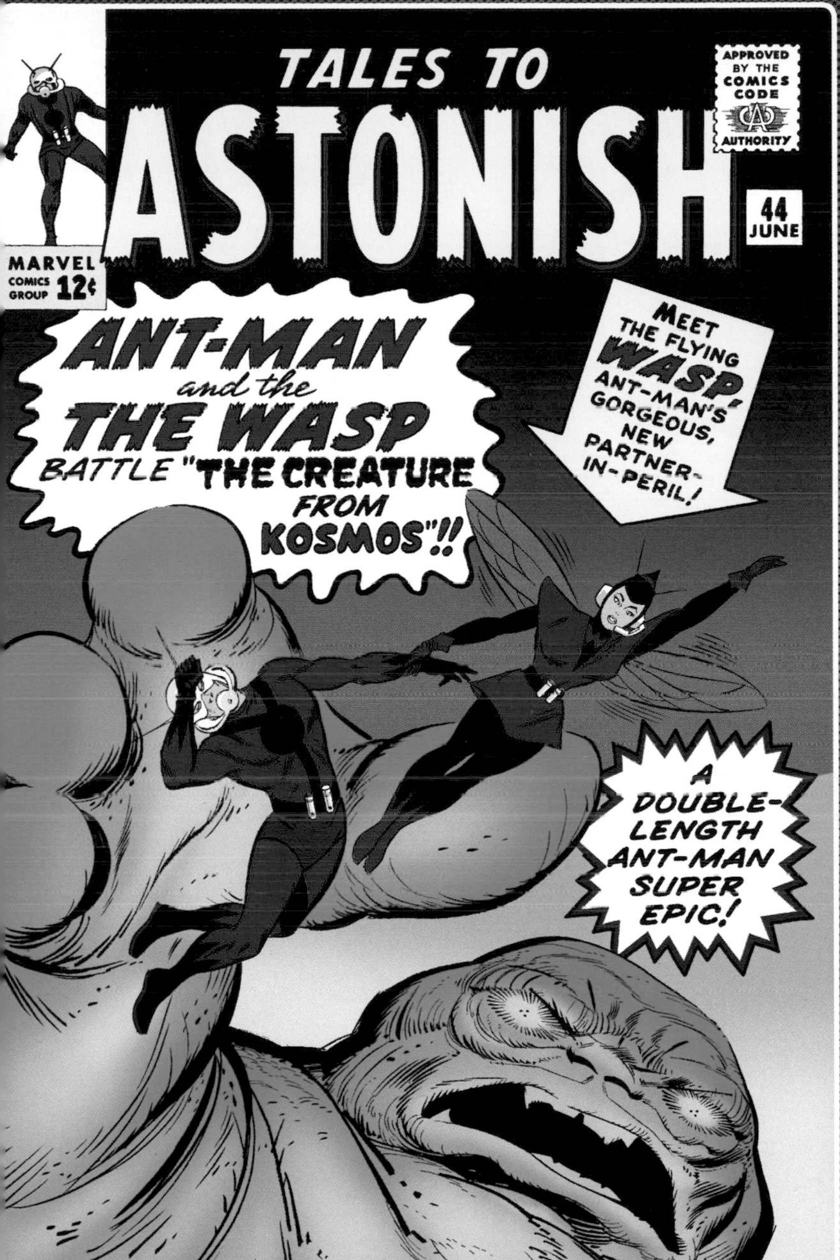
TALES TO ASTONISH
APPROVED BY THE COMICS CODE AUTHORITY
44 JUNE
MARVEL COMICS GROUP 12¢
ANT-MAN and the THE WASP BATTLE "THE CREATURE FROM KOSMOS"!!
MEET THE FLYING WASP, ANT-MAN'S GORGEOUS, NEW PARTNER-IN-PERIL!
A DOUBLE-LENGTH ANT-MAN SUPER EPIC!

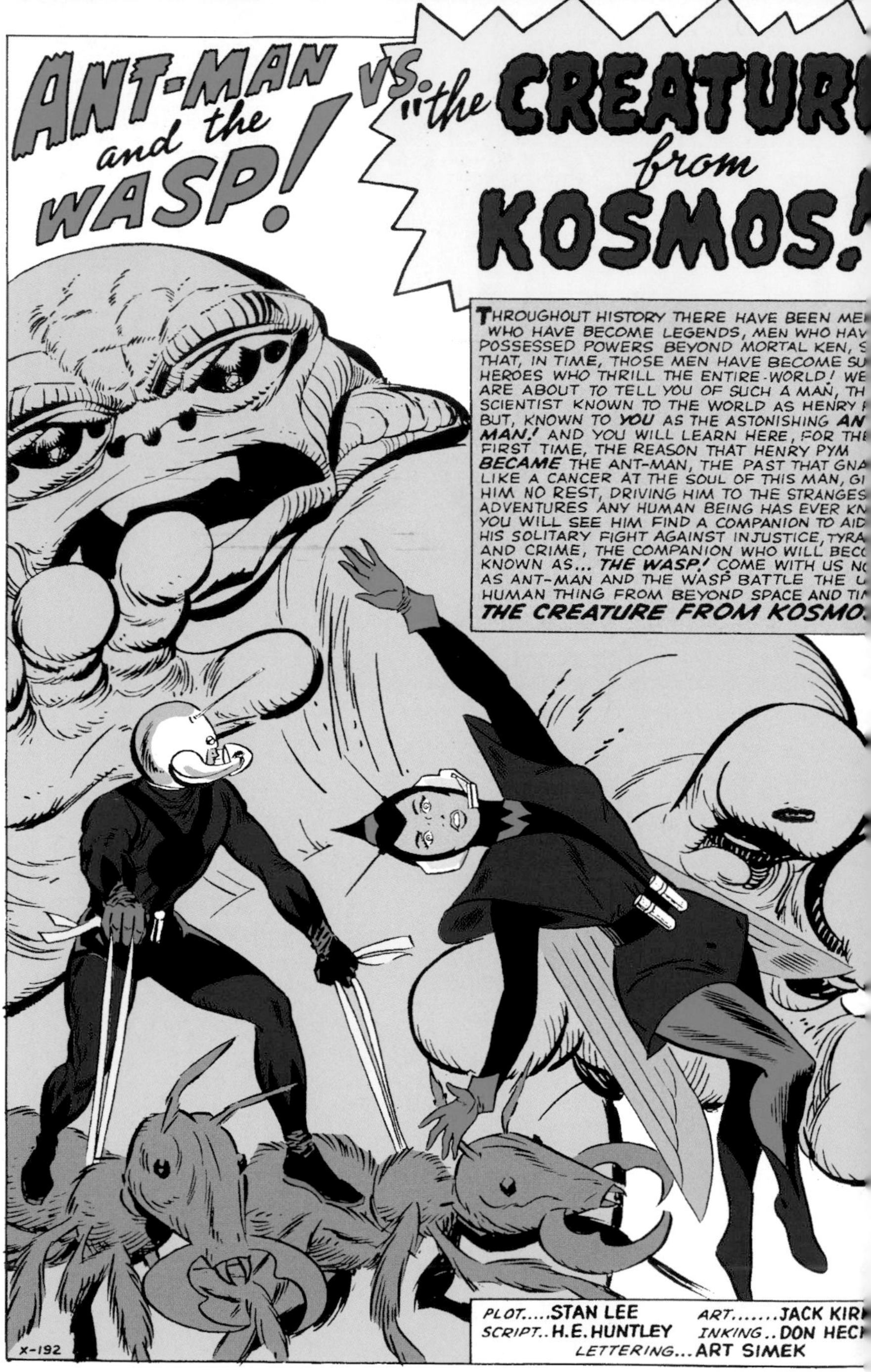
ANT-MAN and the WASP! VS. "the CREATUR from KOSMOS!
THROUGHOUT HISTORY THERE HAVE BEEN ME WHO HAVE BECOME LEGENDS, MEN WHO HAV POSSESSED POWERS BEYOND MORTAL KEN, S THAT, IN TIME, THOSE MEN HAVE BECOME SU HEROES WHO THRILL THE ENTIRE-WORLD! WE ARE ABOUT TO TELL YOU OF SUCH A MAN, TH SCIENTIST KNOWN TO THE WORLD AS HENRY BUT, KNOWN TO YOU AS THE ASTONISHING AN MAN! AND YOU WILL LEARN HERE, FOR TH FIRST TIME, THE REASON THAT HENRY PYM BECAME THE ANT-MAN, THE PAST THAT GNA LIKE A CANCER AT THE SOUL OF THIS MAN, GI HIM NO REST, DRIVING HIM TO THE STRANGES ADVENTURES ANY HUMAN BEING HAS EVER KN YOU WILL SEE HIM FIND A COMPANION TO AID HIS SOLITARY FIGHT AGAINST INJUSTICE, TYRA AND CRIME, THE COMPANION WHO WILL BEC KNOWN AS... THE WASP! COME WITH US N AS ANT-MAN AND THE WASP BATTLE THE U HUMAN THING FROM BEYOND SPACE AND TI THE CREATURE FROM KOSMO
PLOT.....STAN LEE
ART.......JACK KIR
SCRIPT..H.E. HUNTLEY
INKING..DON HEC
LETTERING...ART SIMEK
X-192

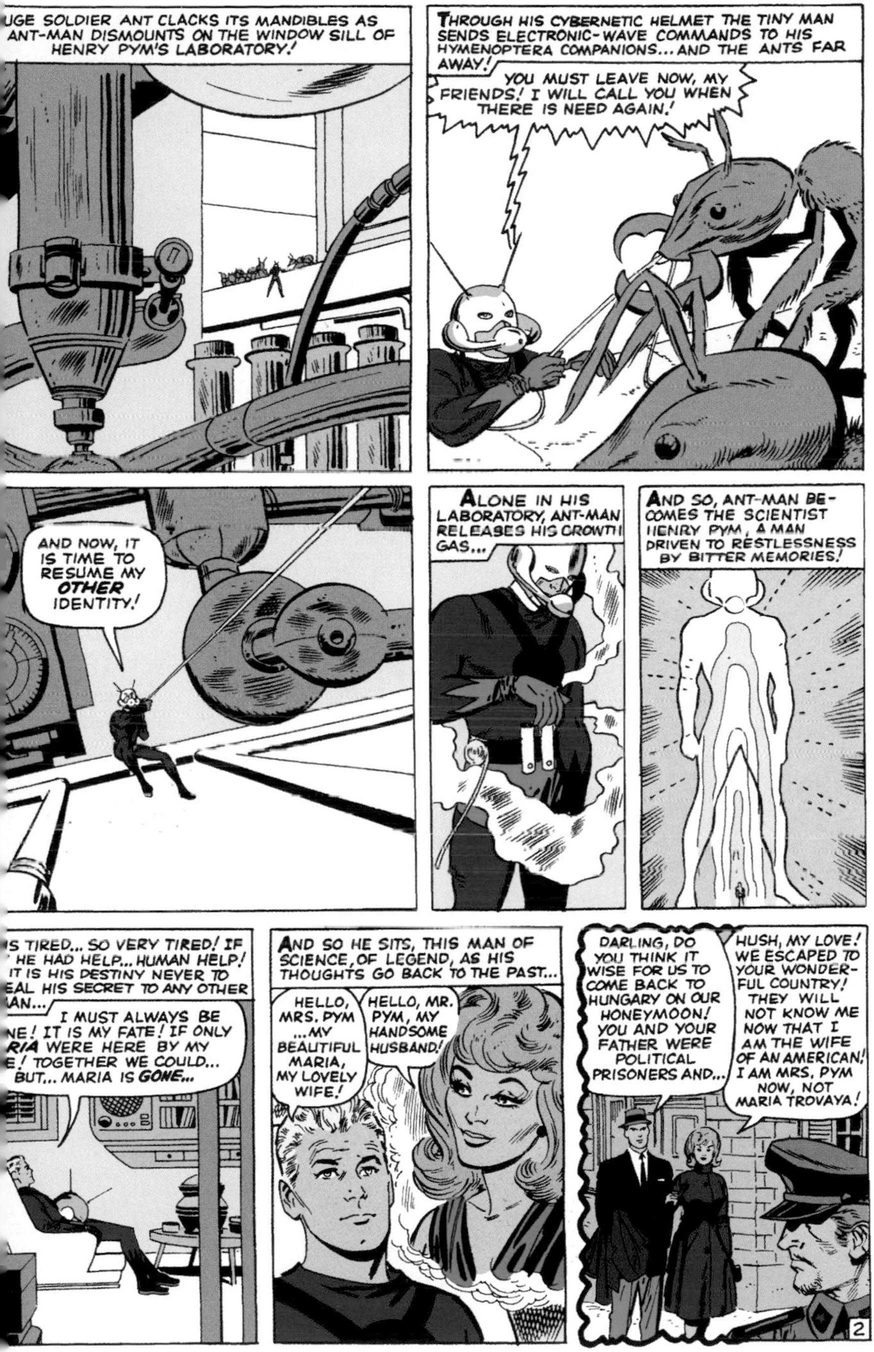
UGE SOLDIER ANT CLACKS ITS MANDIBLES AS ANT-MAN DISMOUNTS ON THE WINDOW SILL OF HENRY PYM'S LABORATORY!
THROUGH HIS CYBERNETIC HELMET THE TINY MAN SENDS ELECTRONIC-WAVE COMMANDS TO HIS HYMENOPTERA COMPANIONS... AND THE ANTS FAR AWAY!
YOU MUST LEAVE NOW, MY FRIENDS! I WILL CALL YOU WHEN THERE IS NEED AGAIN!
AND NOW, IT IS TIME TO RESUME MY OTHER IDENTITY!
ALONE IN HIS LABORATORY, ANT-MAN RELEASES HIS GROWTH GAS...
AND SO, ANT-MAN BECOMES THE SCIENTIST HENRY PYM, A MAN DRIVEN TO RESTLESSNESS BY BITTER MEMORIES!
S TIRED... SO VERY TIRED! IF HE HAD HELP... HUMAN HELP! IT IS HIS DESTINY NEVER TO EAL HIS SECRET TO ANY OTHER AN...
I MUST ALWAYS BE NE! IT IS MY FATE! IF ONLY RIA WERE HERE BY MY E! TOGETHER WE COULD... BUT... MARIA IS GONE...
AND SO HE SITS, THIS MAN OF SCIENCE, OF LEGEND, AS HIS THOUGHTS GO BACK TO THE PAST...
HELLO, MRS. PYM ...MY BEAUTIFUL MARIA, MY LOVELY WIFE!
HELLO, MR. PYM, MY HANDSOME HUSBAND!
DARLING, DO YOU THINK IT WISE FOR US TO COME BACK TO HUNGARY ON OUR HONEYMOON! YOU AND YOUR FATHER WERE POLITICAL PRISONERS AND...
HUSH, MY LOVE! WE ESCAPED TO YOUR WONDERFUL COUNTRY! THEY WILL NOT KNOW ME NOW THAT I AM THE WIFE OF AN AMERICAN! I AM MRS. PYM NOW, NOT MARIA TROVAYA!
2

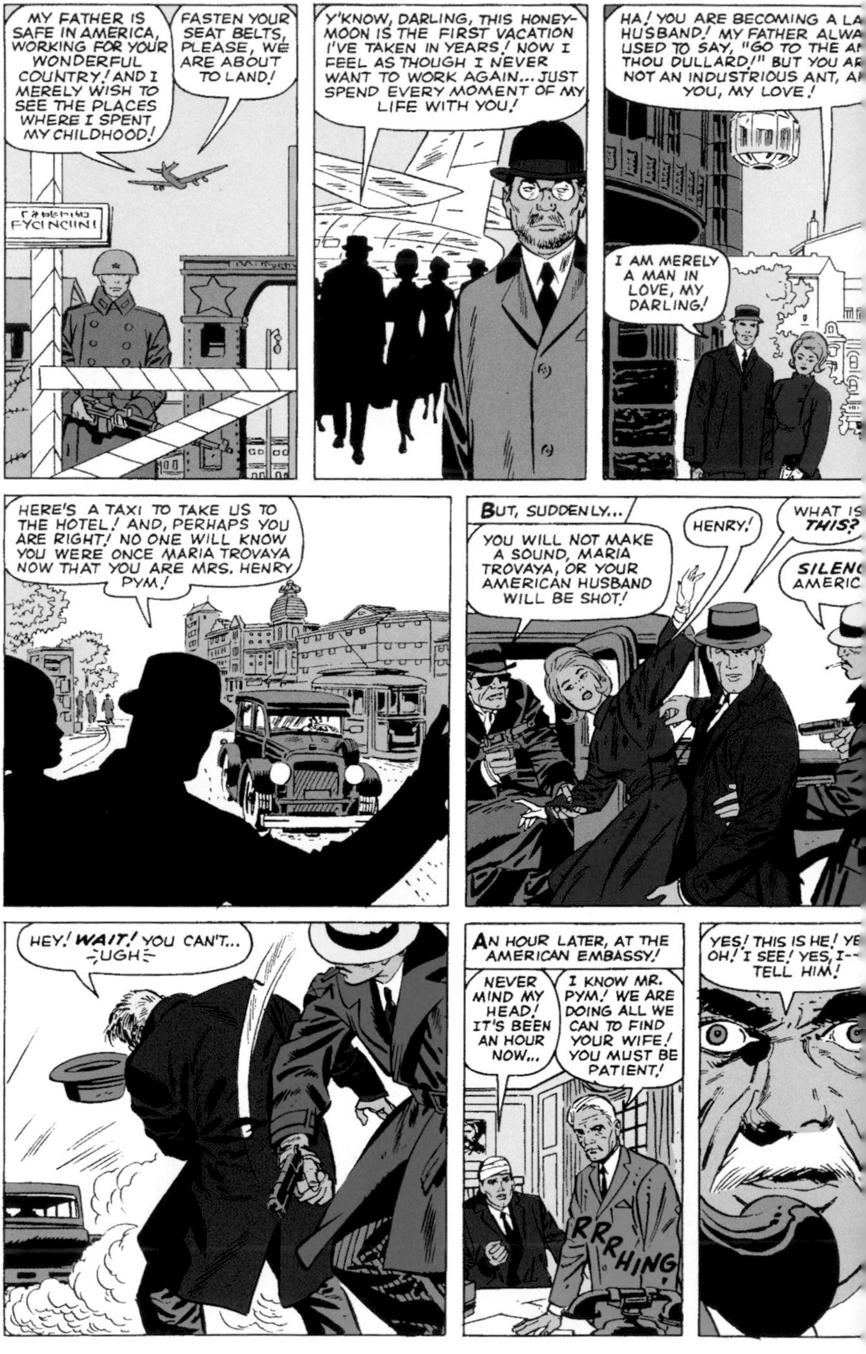
MY FATHER IS SAFE IN AMERICA, WORKING FOR YOUR WONDERFUL COUNTRY! AND I MERELY WISH TO SEE THE PLACES WHERE I SPENT MY CHILDHOOD!
FASTEN YOUR SEAT BELTS, PLEASE, WE ARE ABOUT TO LAND!
Y'KNOW, DARLING, THIS HONEY-MOON IS THE FIRST VACATION I'VE TAKEN IN YEARS! NOW I FEEL AS THOUGH I NEVER WANT TO WORK AGAIN... JUST SPEND EVERY MOMENT OF MY LIFE WITH YOU!
HA! YOU ARE BECOMING A LA
HUSBAND! MY FATHER ALWA
USED TO SAY, "GO TO THE A
THOU DULLARD!" BUT YOU A
NOT AN INDUSTRIOUS ANT, A
YOU, MY LOVE!
I AM MERELY A MAN IN LOVE, MY DARLING!
HERE'S A TAXI TO TAKE US TO THE HOTEL! AND, PERHAPS YOU ARE RIGHT! NO ONE WILL KNOW YOU WERE ONCE MARIA TROVAYA NOW THAT YOU ARE MRS. HENRY PYM!
BUT, SUDDENLY...
YOU WILL NOT MAKE A SOUND, MARIA TROVAYA, OR YOUR AMERICAN HUSBAND WILL BE SHOT!
HENRY!
WHAT IS THIS?
SILENC
AMERIC
HEY! WAIT! YOU CAN'T... UGH
AN HOUR LATER, AT THE AMERICAN EMBASSY!
NEVER MIND MY HEAD! IT'S BEEN AN HOUR NOW...
I KNOW MR. PYM! WE ARE DOING ALL WE CAN TO FIND YOUR WIFE! YOU MUST BE PATIENT!
RRRHING
YES! THIS IS HE! YE
OH! I SEE! YES, I--
TELL HIM!

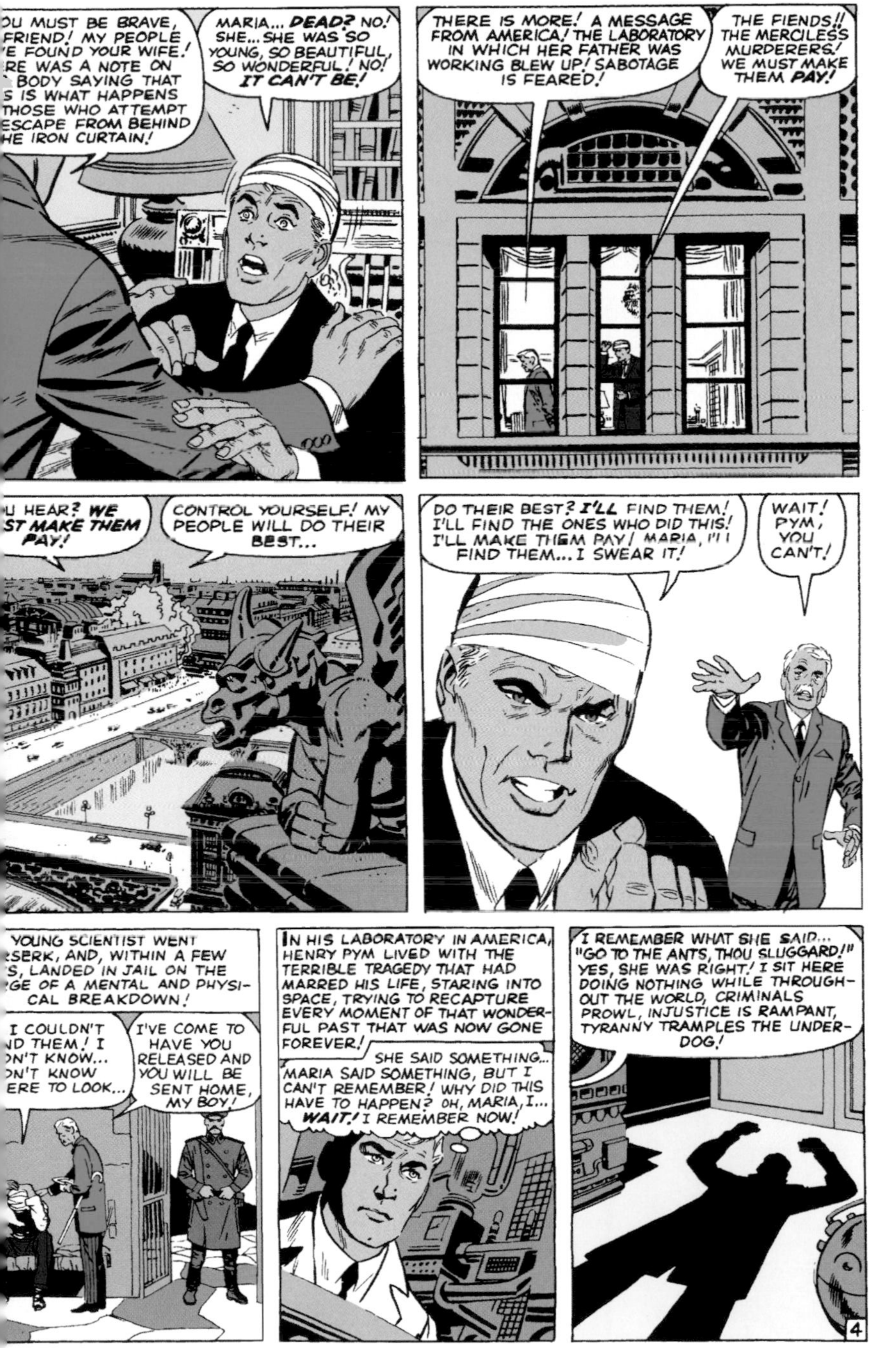

OU MUST BE BRAVE, FRIEND! MY PEOPLE 'E FOUND YOUR WIFE! RE WAS A NOTE ON BODY SAYING THAT S IS WHAT HAPPENS THOSE WHO ATTEMPT ESCAPE FROM BEHIND HE IRON CURTAIN!
MARIA... DEAD? NO! SHE... SHE WAS SO YOUNG, SO BEAUTIFUL, SO WONDERFUL! NO! IT CAN'T BE!
THERE IS MORE! A MESSAGE FROM AMERICA! THE LABORATORY IN WHICH HER FATHER WAS WORKING BLEW UP! SABOTAGE IS FEARED!
THE FIENDS!! THE MERCILESS MURDERERS! WE MUST MAKE THEM PAY!
U HEAR? WE ST MAKE THEM PAY!
CONTROL YOURSELF! MY PEOPLE WILL DO THEIR BEST...
DO THEIR BEST? I'LL FIND THEM! I'LL FIND THE ONES WHO DID THIS! I'LL MAKE THEM PAY! MARIA, I'LL FIND THEM... I SWEAR IT!
WAIT! PYM, YOU CAN'T!
YOUNG SCIENTIST WENT RSERK, AND, WITHIN A FEW 'S, LANDED IN JAIL ON THE RGE OF A MENTAL AND PHYSICAL BREAKDOWN!
I COULDN'T ND THEM! I ON'T KNOW... ON'T KNOW ERE TO LOOK...
I'VE COME TO HAVE YOU RELEASED AND YOU WILL BE SENT HOME, MY BOY!
IN HIS LABORATORY IN AMERICA, HENRY PYM LIVED WITH THE TERRIBLE TRAGEDY THAT HAD MARRED HIS LIFE, STARING INTO SPACE, TRYING TO RECAPTURE EVERY MOMENT OF THAT WONDERFUL PAST THAT WAS NOW GONE FOREVER!
SHE SAID SOMETHING... MARIA SAID SOMETHING, BUT I CAN'T REMEMBER! WHY DID THIS HAVE TO HAPPEN? OH, MARIA, I... WAIT! I REMEMBER NOW!
I REMEMBER WHAT SHE SAID... "GO TO THE ANTS, THOU SLUGGARD!" YES, SHE WAS RIGHT! I SIT HERE DOING NOTHING WHILE THROUGHOUT THE WORLD, CRIMINALS PROWL, INJUSTICE IS RAMPANT, TYRANNY TRAMPLES THE UNDERDOG!
4

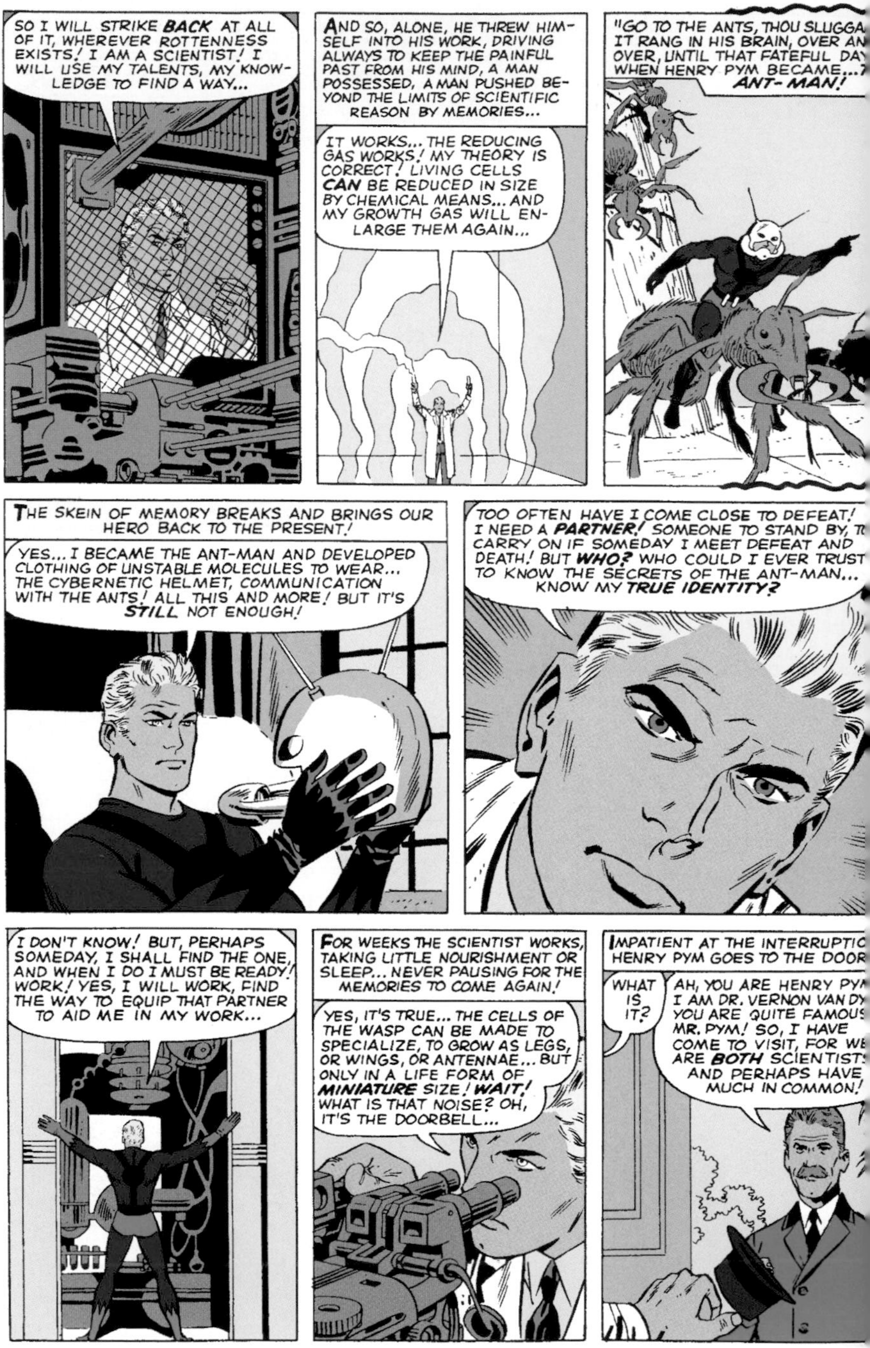

SO I WILL STRIKE BACK AT ALL OF IT, WHEREVER ROTTENNESS EXISTS! I AM A SCIENTIST! I WILL USE MY TALENTS, MY KNOWLEDGE TO FIND A WAY...
AND SO, ALONE, HE THREW HIMSELF INTO HIS WORK, DRIVING ALWAYS TO KEEP THE PAINFUL PAST FROM HIS MIND, A MAN POSSESSED, A MAN PUSHED BEYOND THE LIMITS OF SCIENTIFIC REASON BY MEMORIES...
IT WORKS... THE REDUCING GAS WORKS! MY THEORY IS CORRECT! LIVING CELLS CAN BE REDUCED IN SIZE BY CHEMICAL MEANS... AND MY GROWTH GAS WILL ENLARGE THEM AGAIN...
"GO TO THE ANTS, THOU SLUGGA IT RANG IN HIS BRAIN, OVER AN OVER, UNTIL THAT FATEFUL DAY WHEN HENRY PYM BECAME... ANT-MAN!
THE SKEIN OF MEMORY BREAKS AND BRINGS OUR HERO BACK TO THE PRESENT!
YES... I BECAME THE ANT-MAN AND DEVELOPED CLOTHING OF UNSTABLE MOLECULES TO WEAR... THE CYBERNETIC HELMET, COMMUNICATION WITH THE ANTS! ALL THIS AND MORE! BUT IT'S STILL NOT ENOUGH!
TOO OFTEN HAVE I COME CLOSE TO DEFEAT! I NEED A PARTNER! SOMEONE TO STAND BY, TO CARRY ON IF SOMEDAY I MEET DEFEAT AND DEATH! BUT WHO? WHO COULD I EVER TRUST TO KNOW THE SECRETS OF THE ANT-MAN... KNOW MY TRUE IDENTITY?
I DON'T KNOW! BUT, PERHAPS SOMEDAY, I SHALL FIND THE ONE, AND WHEN I DO I MUST BE READY! WORK! YES, I WILL WORK, FIND THE WAY TO EQUIP THAT PARTNER TO AID ME IN MY WORK...
FOR WEEKS THE SCIENTIST WORKS, TAKING LITTLE NOURISHMENT OR SLEEP... NEVER PAUSING FOR THE MEMORIES TO COME AGAIN!
YES, IT'S TRUE... THE CELLS OF THE WASP CAN BE MADE TO SPECIALIZE, TO GROW AS LEGS, OR WINGS, OR ANTENNAE... BUT ONLY IN A LIFE FORM OF MINIATURE SIZE! WAIT! WHAT IS THAT NOISE? OH, IT'S THE DOORBELL...
IMPATIENT AT THE INTERRUPTIO HENRY PYM GOES TO THE DOOR
WHAT IS IT?
AH, YOU ARE HENRY PYM I AM DR. VERNON VAN DY YOU ARE QUITE FAMOUS MR. PYM! SO, I HAVE COME TO VISIT, FOR WE ARE BOTH SCIENTISTS AND PERHAPS HAVE MUCH IN COMMON!

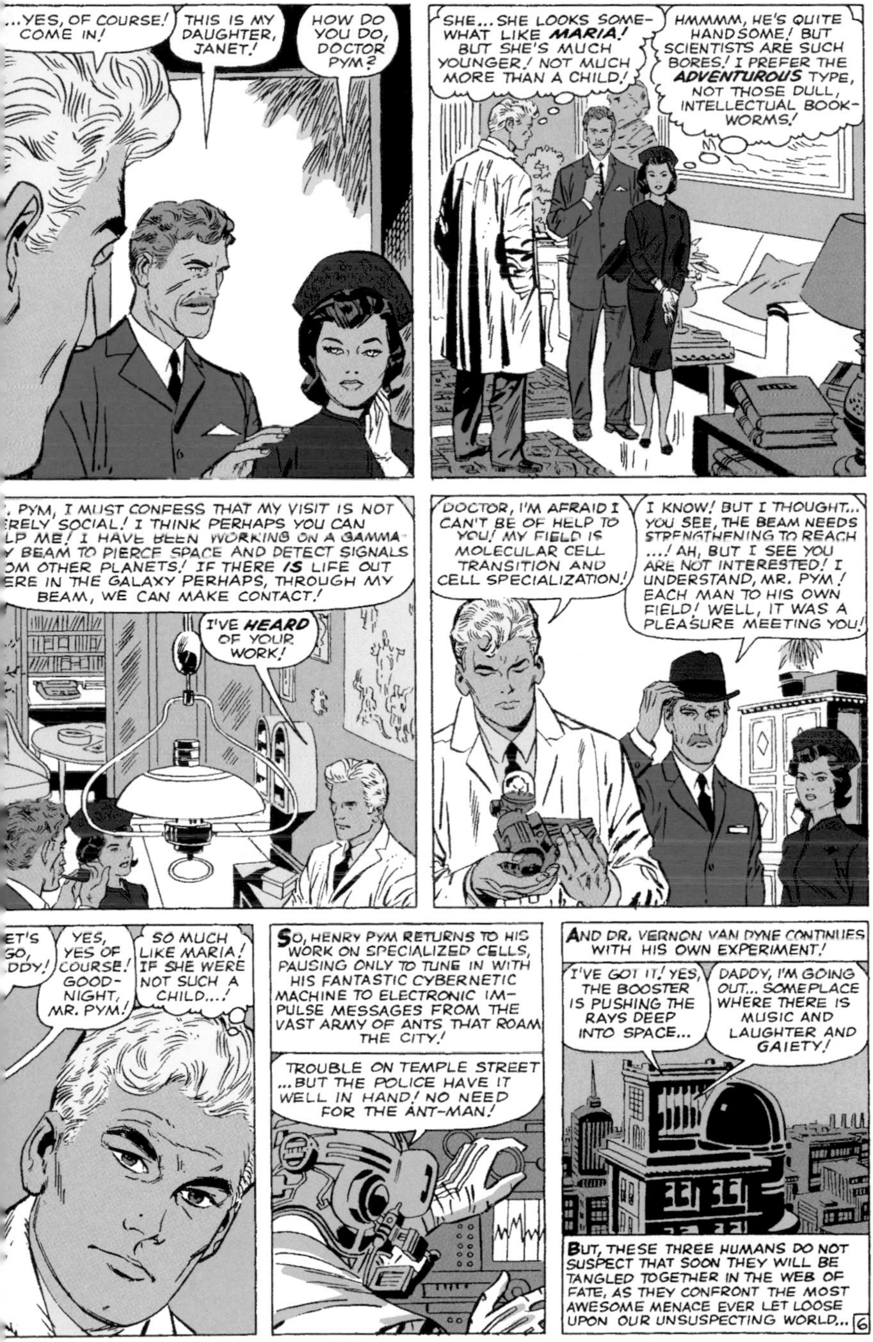
...YES, OF COURSE! COME IN!
THIS IS MY DAUGHTER, JANET!
HOW DO YOU DO, DOCTOR PYM?
SHE... SHE LOOKS SOMEWHAT LIKE MARIA! BUT SHE'S MUCH YOUNGER! NOT MUCH MORE THAN A CHILD!
HMMMM, HE'S QUITE HANDSOME! BUT SCIENTISTS ARE SUCH BORES! I PREFER THE ADVENTUROUS TYPE, NOT THOSE DULL, INTELLECTUAL BOOK-WORMS!
. PYM, I MUST CONFESS THAT MY VISIT IS NOT ERELY SOCIAL! I THINK PERHAPS YOU CAN LP ME! I HAVE BEEN WORKING ON A GAMMA Y BEAM TO PIERCE SPACE AND DETECT SIGNALS OM OTHER PLANETS! IF THERE IS LIFE OUT ERE IN THE GALAXY PERHAPS, THROUGH MY BEAM, WE CAN MAKE CONTACT!
I'VE HEARD OF YOUR WORK!
DOCTOR, I'M AFRAID I CAN'T BE OF HELP TO YOU! MY FIELD IS MOLECULAR CELL TRANSITION AND CELL SPECIALIZATION!
I KNOW! BUT I THOUGHT... YOU SEE, THE BEAM NEEDS STRENGTHENING TO REACH ...! AH, BUT I SEE YOU ARE NOT INTERESTED! I UNDERSTAND, MR. PYM! EACH MAN TO HIS OWN FIELD! WELL, IT WAS A PLEASURE MEETING YOU!
ET'S GO, DDY!
YES, YES OF COURSE! GOOD-NIGHT, MR. PYM!
SO MUCH LIKE MARIA! IF SHE WERE NOT SUCH A CHILD...!
SO, HENRY PYM RETURNS TO HIS WORK ON SPECIALIZED CELLS, PAUSING ONLY TO TUNE IN WITH HIS FANTASTIC CYBERNETIC MACHINE TO ELECTRONIC IMPULSE MESSAGES FROM THE VAST ARMY OF ANTS THAT ROAM THE CITY!
TROUBLE ON TEMPLE STREET ...BUT THE POLICE HAVE IT WELL IN HAND! NO NEED FOR THE ANT-MAN!
AND DR. VERNON VAN DYNE CONTINUES WITH HIS OWN EXPERIMENT!
I'VE GOT IT! YES, THE BOOSTER IS PUSHING THE RAYS DEEP INTO SPACE...
DADDY, I'M GOING OUT... SOMEPLACE WHERE THERE IS MUSIC AND LAUGHTER AND GAIETY!
BUT, THESE THREE HUMANS DO NOT SUSPECT THAT SOON THEY WILL BE TANGLED TOGETHER IN THE WEB OF FATE, AS THEY CONFRONT THE MOST AWESOME MENACE EVER LET LOOSE UPON OUR UNSUSPECTING WORLD...
6

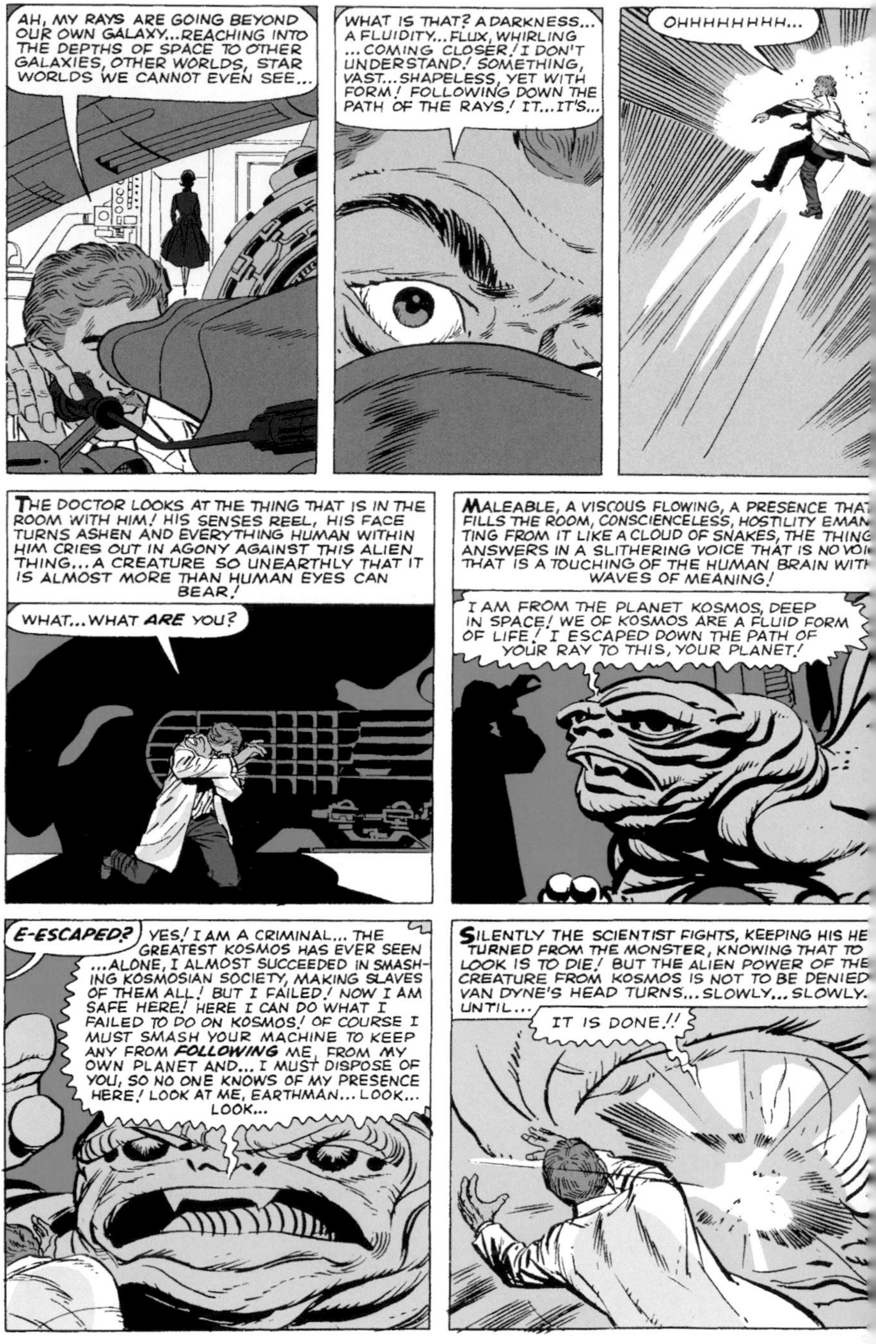
AH, MY RAYS ARE GOING BEYOND OUR OWN GALAXY... REACHING INTO THE DEPTHS OF SPACE TO OTHER GALAXIES, OTHER WORLDS, STAR WORLDS WE CANNOT EVEN SEE...
WHAT IS THAT? A DARKNESS... A FLUIDITY... FLUX, WHIRLING ... COMING CLOSER! I DON'T UNDERSTAND! SOMETHING, VAST... SHAPELESS, YET WITH FORM! FOLLOWING DOWN THE PATH OF THE RAYS! IT... IT'S...
OHHHHHHHH...
THE DOCTOR LOOKS AT THE THING THAT IS IN THE ROOM WITH HIM! HIS SENSES REEL, HIS FACE TURNS ASHEN AND EVERYTHING HUMAN WITHIN HIM CRIES OUT IN AGONY AGAINST THIS ALIEN THING... A CREATURE SO UNEARTHLY THAT IT IS ALMOST MORE THAN HUMAN EYES CAN BEAR!
WHAT... WHAT ARE YOU?
MALEABLE, A VISCOUS FLOWING, A PRESENCE THAT FILLS THE ROOM, CONSCIENCELESS, HOSTILITY EMANATING FROM IT LIKE A CLOUD OF SNAKES, THE THING ANSWERS IN A SLITHERING VOICE THAT IS NO VOI THAT IS A TOUCHING OF THE HUMAN BRAIN WITH WAVES OF MEANING!
I AM FROM THE PLANET KOSMOS, DEEP IN SPACE! WE OF KOSMOS ARE A FLUID FORM OF LIFE! I ESCAPED DOWN THE PATH OF YOUR RAY TO THIS, YOUR PLANET!
E-ESCAPED?
YES! I AM A CRIMINAL... THE GREATEST KOSMOS HAS EVER SEEN ...ALONE, I ALMOST SUCCEEDED IN SMASHING KOSMOSIAN SOCIETY, MAKING SLAVES OF THEM ALL! BUT I FAILED! NOW I AM SAFE HERE! HERE I CAN DO WHAT I FAILED TO DO ON KOSMOS! OF COURSE I MUST SMASH YOUR MACHINE TO KEEP ANY FROM FOLLOWING ME, FROM MY OWN PLANET AND... I MUST DISPOSE OF YOU, SO NO ONE KNOWS OF MY PRESENCE HERE! LOOK AT ME, EARTHMAN... LOOK... LOOK...
SILENTLY THE SCIENTIST FIGHTS, KEEPING HIS HE TURNED FROM THE MONSTER, KNOWING THAT TO LOOK IS TO DIE! BUT THE ALIEN POWER OF THE CREATURE FROM KOSMOS IS NOT TO BE DENIED VAN DYNE'S HEAD TURNS... SLOWLY... SLOWLY. UNTIL...
IT IS DONE!!

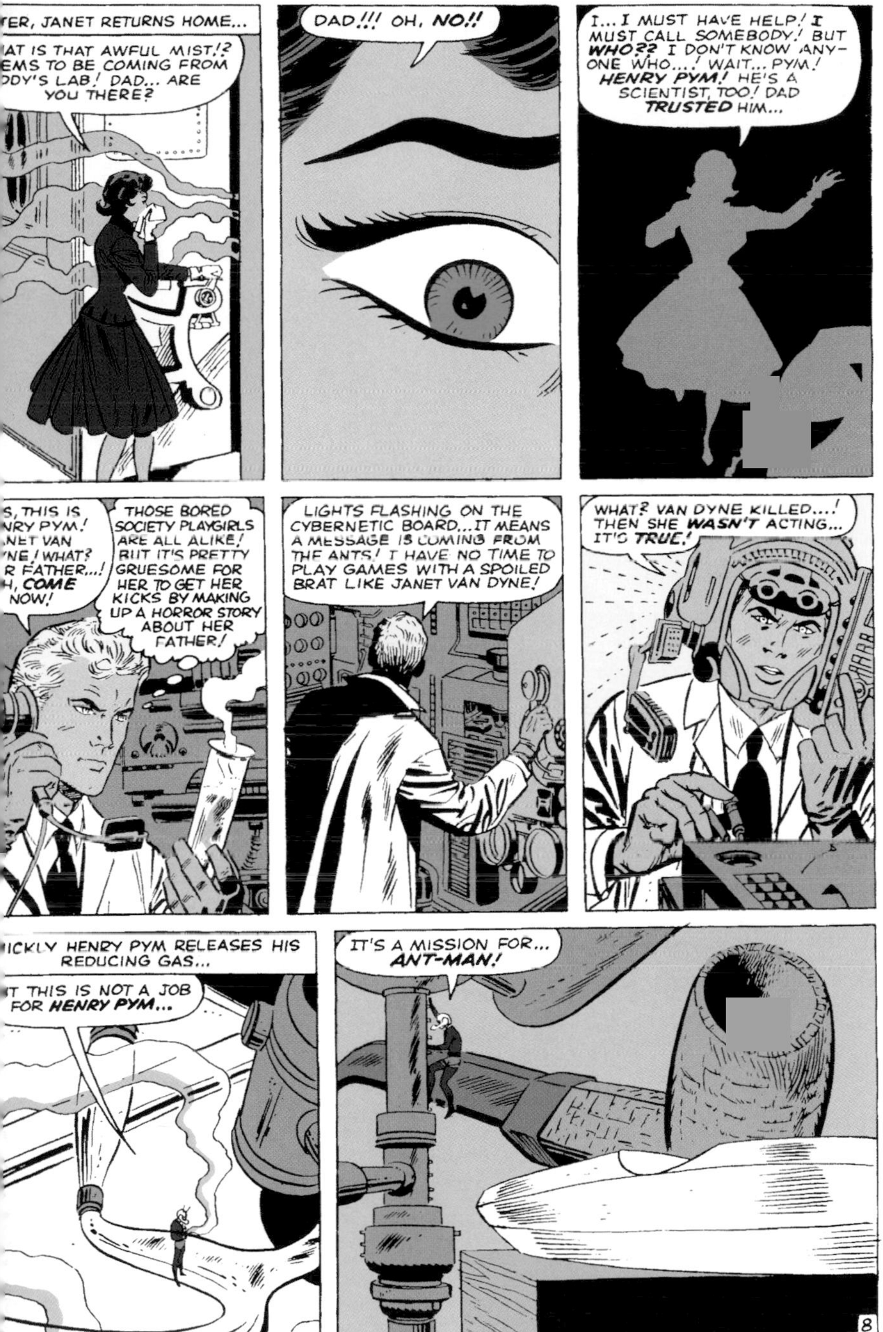
TER, JANET RETURNS HOME...
AT IS THAT AWFUL MIST!? EMS TO BE COMING FROM DDY'S LAB! DAD... ARE YOU THERE?
DAD!!! OH, NO!!
I... I MUST HAVE HELP! I MUST CALL SOMEBODY! BUT WHO?? I DON'T KNOW ANY-ONE WHO...! WAIT... PYM! HENRY PYM! HE'S A SCIENTIST, TOO! DAD TRUSTED HIM...
S, THIS IS NRY PYM! NET VAN NE! WHAT? R FATHER...! H, COME NOW!
THOSE BORED SOCIETY PLAYGIRLS ARE ALL ALIKE! BUT IT'S PRETTY GRUESOME FOR HER TO GET HER KICKS BY MAKING UP A HORROR STORY ABOUT HER FATHER!
LIGHTS FLASHING ON THE CYBERNETIC BOARD...IT MEANS A MESSAGE IS COMING FROM THE ANTS! I HAVE NO TIME TO PLAY GAMES WITH A SPOILED BRAT LIKE JANET VAN DYNE!
WHAT? VAN DYNE KILLED...! THEN SHE WASN'T ACTING... IT'S TRUE!
ICKLY HENRY PYM RELEASES HIS REDUCING GAS...
T THIS IS NOT A JOB FOR HENRY PYM...
IT'S A MISSION FOR... ANT-MAN!
8

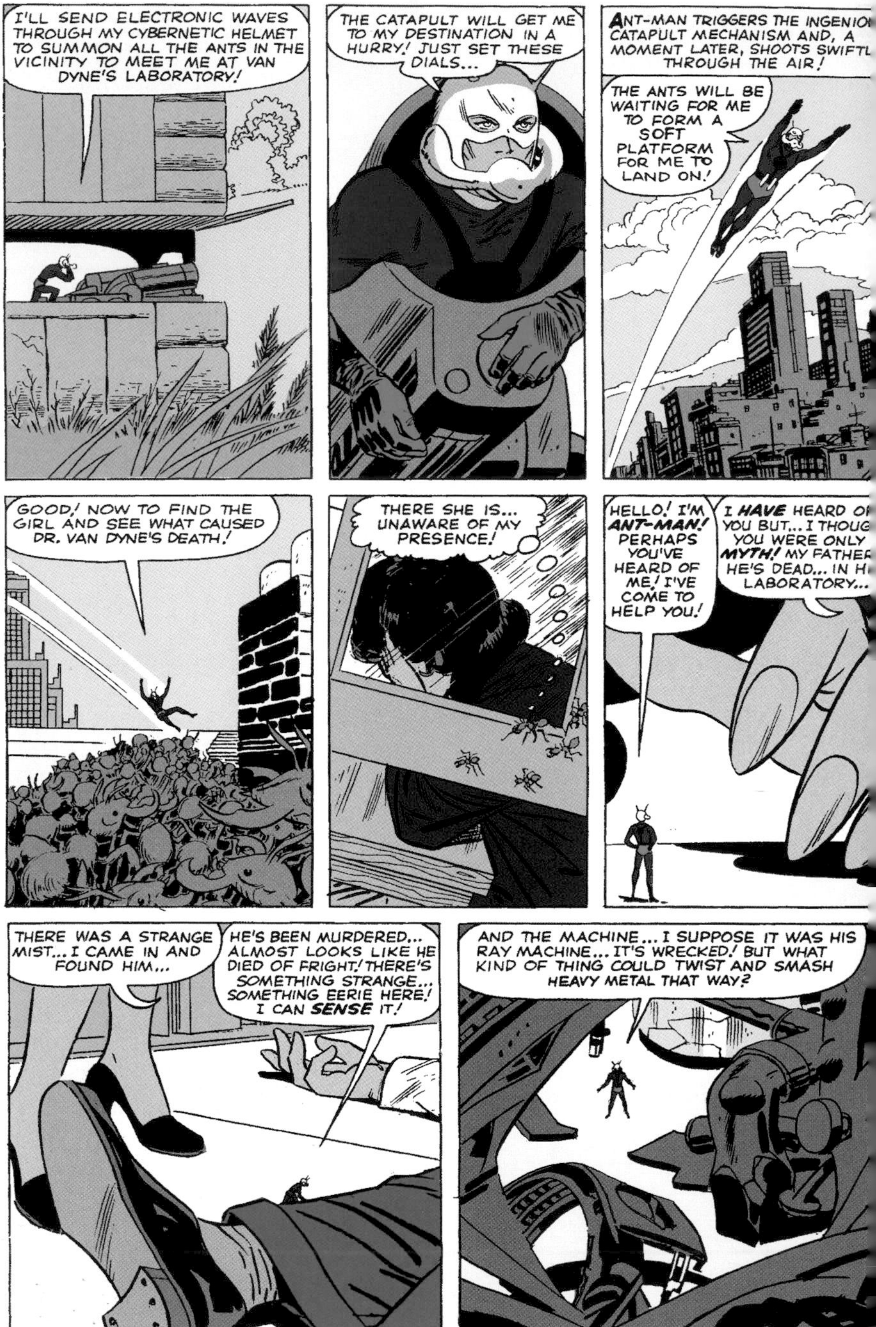
I'LL SEND ELECTRONIC WAVES THROUGH MY CYBERNETIC HELMET TO SUMMON ALL THE ANTS IN THE VICINITY TO MEET ME AT VAN DYNE'S LABORATORY!
THE CATAPULT WILL GET ME TO MY DESTINATION IN A HURRY! JUST SET THESE DIALS...
ANT-MAN TRIGGERS THE INGENIO CATAPULT MECHANISM AND, A MOMENT LATER, SHOOTS SWIFTL THROUGH THE AIR!
THE ANTS WILL BE WAITING FOR ME TO FORM A SOFT PLATFORM FOR ME TO LAND ON!
GOOD! NOW TO FIND THE GIRL AND SEE WHAT CAUSED DR. VAN DYNE'S DEATH!
THERE SHE IS... UNAWARE OF MY PRESENCE!
HELLO! I'M ANT-MAN! PERHAPS YOU'VE HEARD OF ME! I'VE COME TO HELP YOU!
I HAVE HEARD OF YOU BUT... I THOUG YOU WERE ONLY MYTH! MY FATHER HE'S DEAD... IN H LABORATORY...
THERE WAS A STRANGE MIST... I CAME IN AND FOUND HIM...
HE'S BEEN MURDERED... ALMOST LOOKS LIKE HE DIED OF FRIGHT! THERE'S SOMETHING STRANGE... SOMETHING EERIE HERE! I CAN SENSE IT!
AND THE MACHINE... I SUPPOSE IT WAS HIS RAY MACHINE... IT'S WRECKED! BUT WHAT KIND OF THING COULD TWIST AND SMASH HEAVY METAL THAT WAY?

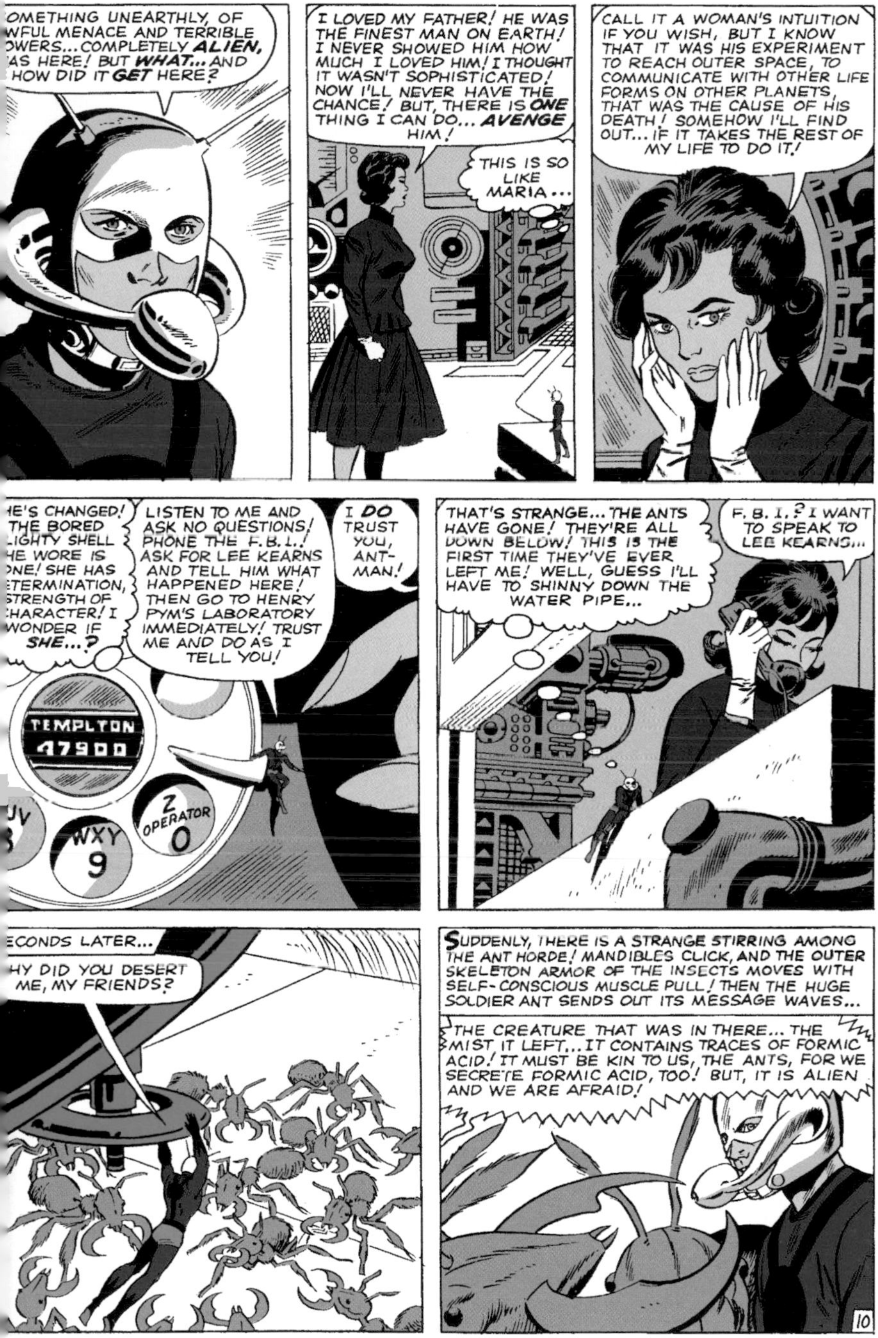
OMETHING UNEARTHLY, OF WFUL MENACE AND TERRIBLE OWERS... COMPLETELY ALIEN, AS HERE! BUT WHAT... AND HOW DID IT GET HERE?
I LOVED MY FATHER! HE WAS THE FINEST MAN ON EARTH! I NEVER SHOWED HIM HOW MUCH I LOVED HIM! I THOUGHT IT WASN'T SOPHISTICATED! NOW I'LL NEVER HAVE THE CHANCE! BUT, THERE IS ONE THING I CAN DO... AVENGE HIM!
THIS IS SO LIKE MARIA...
CALL IT A WOMAN'S INTUITION IF YOU WISH, BUT I KNOW THAT IT WAS HIS EXPERIMENT TO REACH OUTER SPACE, TO COMMUNICATE WITH OTHER LIFE FORMS ON OTHER PLANETS, THAT WAS THE CAUSE OF HIS DEATH! SOMEHOW I'LL FIND OUT... IF IT TAKES THE REST OF MY LIFE TO DO IT!
HE'S CHANGED! THE BORED LIGHTY SHELL HE WORE IS ONE! SHE HAS ETERMINATION, STRENGTH OF HARACTER! I WONDER IF SHE...?
LISTEN TO ME AND ASK NO QUESTIONS! PHONE THE F.B.I.! ASK FOR LEE KEARNS AND TELL HIM WHAT HAPPENED HERE! THEN GO TO HENRY PYM'S LABORATORY IMMEDIATELY! TRUST ME AND DO AS I TELL YOU!
I DO TRUST YOU, ANT-MAN!
TEMPLTON 47900
WXY 9
Z OPERATOR 0
THAT'S STRANGE... THE ANTS HAVE GONE! THEY'RE ALL DOWN BELOW! THIS IS THE FIRST TIME THEY'VE EVER LEFT ME! WELL, GUESS I'LL HAVE TO SHINNY DOWN THE WATER PIPE...
F.B.I.? I WANT TO SPEAK TO LEE KEARNS...
ECONDS LATER...
HY DID YOU DESERT ME, MY FRIENDS?
SUDDENLY, THERE IS A STRANGE STIRRING AMONG THE ANT HORDE! MANDIBLES CLICK, AND THE OUTER SKELETON ARMOR OF THE INSECTS MOVES WITH SELF-CONSCIOUS MUSCLE PULL! THEN THE HUGE SOLDIER ANT SENDS OUT ITS MESSAGE WAVES...
THE CREATURE THAT WAS IN THERE... THE MIST IT LEFT... IT CONTAINS TRACES OF FORMIC ACID! IT MUST BE KIN TO US, THE ANTS, FOR WE SECRETE FORMIC ACID, TOO! BUT, IT IS ALIEN AND WE ARE AFRAID!
10

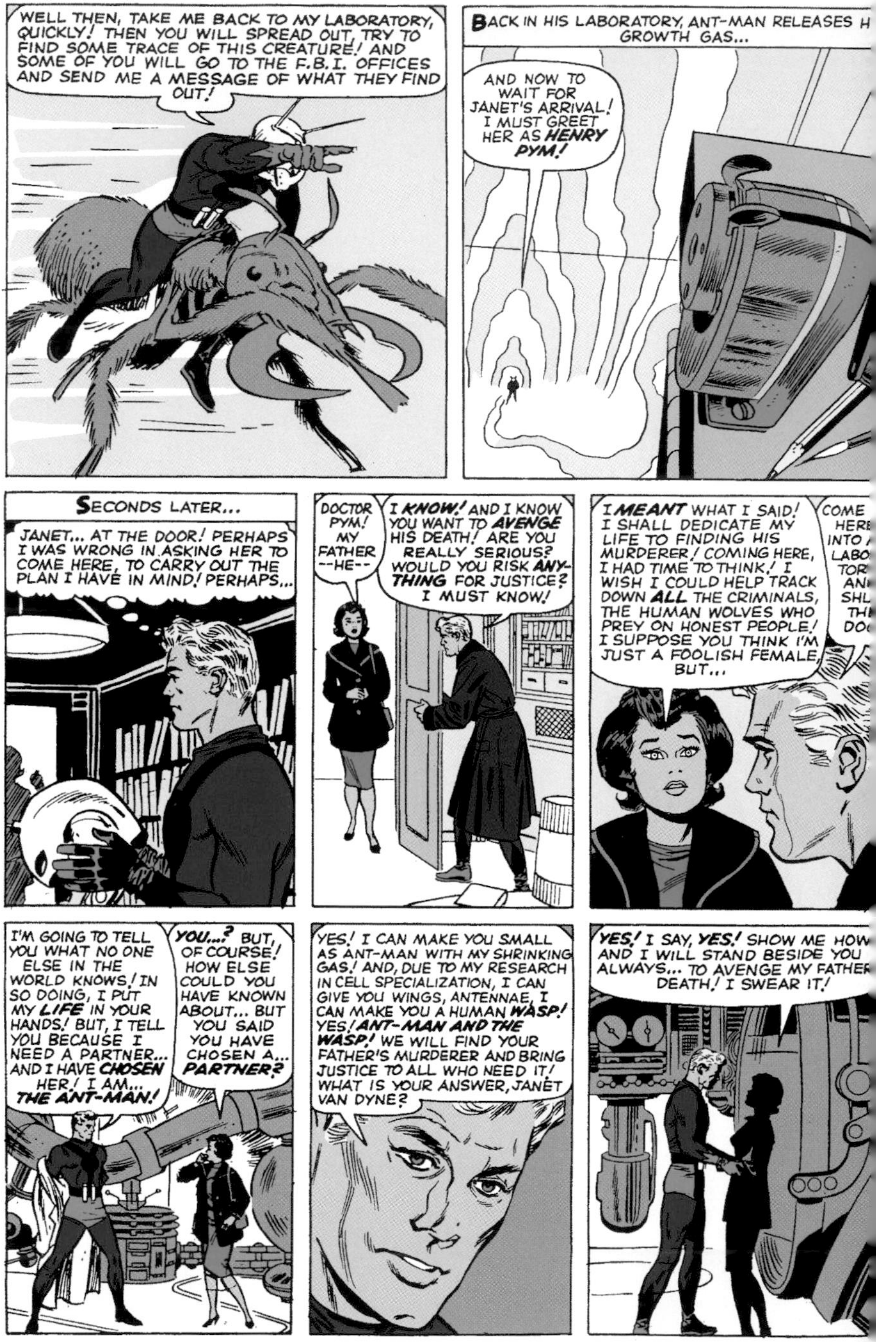
WELL THEN, TAKE ME BACK TO MY LABORATORY, QUICKLY! THEN YOU WILL SPREAD OUT, TRY TO FIND SOME TRACE OF THIS CREATURE! AND SOME OF YOU WILL GO TO THE F.B.I. OFFICES AND SEND ME A MESSAGE OF WHAT THEY FIND OUT!
BACK IN HIS LABORATORY, ANT-MAN RELEASES H
GROWTH GAS...
AND NOW TO WAIT FOR JANET'S ARRIVAL! I MUST GREET HER AS HENRY PYM!
SECONDS LATER...
JANET... AT THE DOOR! PERHAPS I WAS WRONG IN ASKING HER TO COME HERE, TO CARRY OUT THE PLAN I HAVE IN MIND! PERHAPS...
DOCTOR PYM! MY FATHER --HE--
I KNOW! AND I KNOW YOU WANT TO AVENGE HIS DEATH! ARE YOU REALLY SERIOUS? WOULD YOU RISK ANYTHING FOR JUSTICE? I MUST KNOW!
I MEANT WHAT I SAID! I SHALL DEDICATE MY LIFE TO FINDING HIS MURDERER! COMING HERE, I HAD TIME TO THINK! I WISH I COULD HELP TRACK DOWN ALL THE CRIMINALS, THE HUMAN WOLVES WHO PREY ON HONEST PEOPLE! I SUPPOSE YOU THINK I'M JUST A FOOLISH FEMALE, BUT...
I'M GOING TO TELL YOU WHAT NO ONE ELSE IN THE WORLD KNOWS! IN SO DOING, I PUT MY LIFE IN YOUR HANDS! BUT, I TELL YOU BECAUSE I NEED A PARTNER... AND I HAVE CHOSEN HER! I AM... THE ANT-MAN!
YOU...? BUT, OF COURSE! HOW ELSE COULD YOU HAVE KNOWN ABOUT... BUT YOU SAID YOU HAVE CHOSEN A... PARTNER?
YES! I CAN MAKE YOU SMALL AS ANT-MAN WITH MY SHRINKING GAS! AND, DUE TO MY RESEARCH IN CELL SPECIALIZATION, I CAN GIVE YOU WINGS, ANTENNAE, I CAN MAKE YOU A HUMAN WASP! YES! ANT-MAN AND THE WASP! WE WILL FIND YOUR FATHER'S MURDERER AND BRING JUSTICE TO ALL WHO NEED IT! WHAT IS YOUR ANSWER, JANET VAN DYNE?
YES! I SAY, YES! SHOW ME HOW AND I WILL STAND BESIDE YOU ALWAYS... TO AVENGE MY FATHER DEATH! I SWEAR IT!

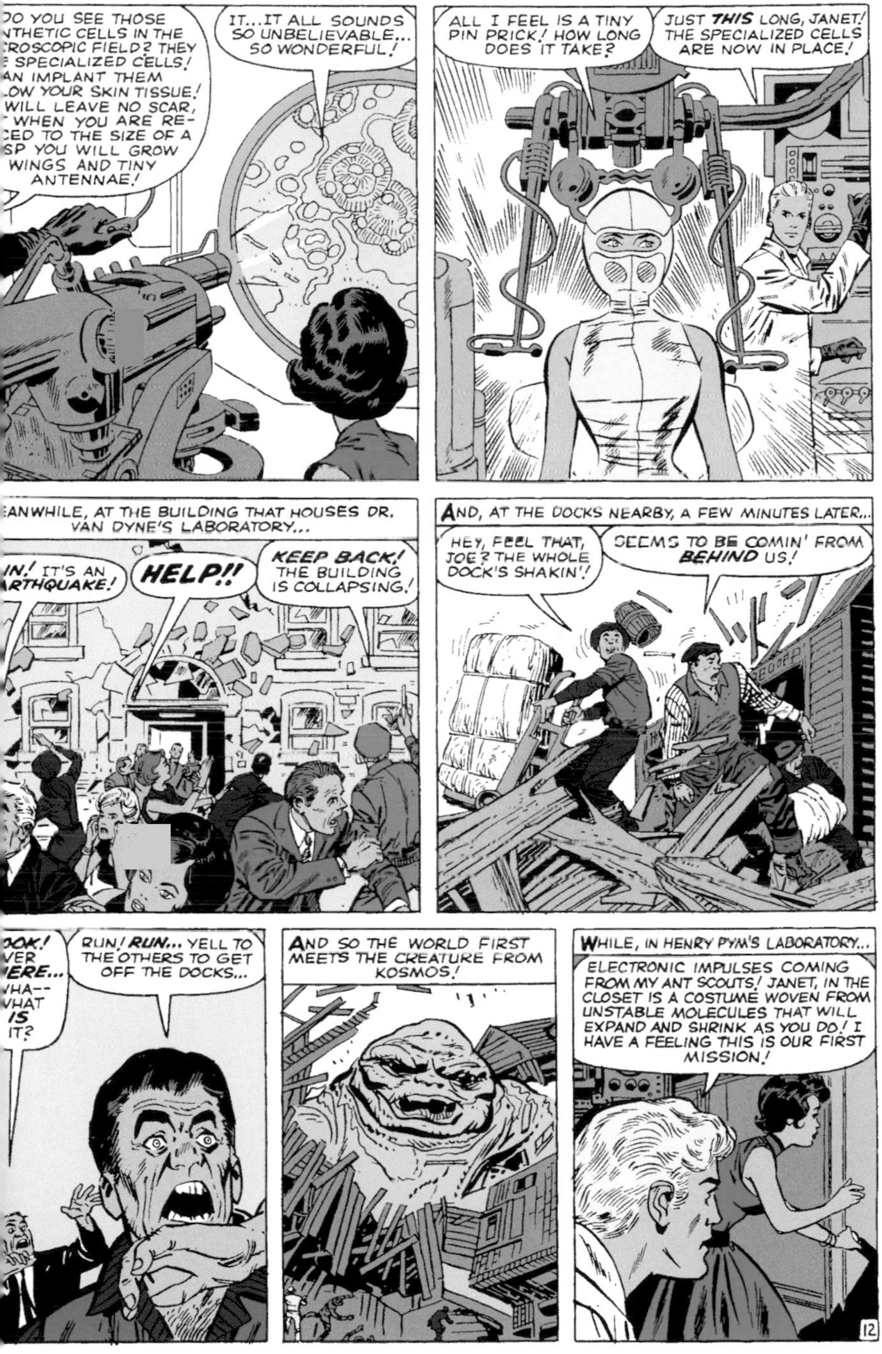

DO YOU SEE THOSE
NTHETIC CELLS IN THE
CROSCOPIC FIELD? THEY
E SPECIALIZED CELLS!
AN IMPLANT THEM
LOW YOUR SKIN TISSUE!
WILL LEAVE NO SCAR;
T WHEN YOU ARE RE-
CED TO THE SIZE OF A
SP YOU WILL GROW
WINGS AND TINY
ANTENNAE!
IT...IT ALL SOUNDS SO UNBELIEVABLE... SO WONDERFUL!
ALL I FEEL IS A TINY PIN PRICK! HOW LONG DOES IT TAKE?
JUST THIS LONG, JANET! THE SPECIALIZED CELLS ARE NOW IN PLACE!
EANWHILE, AT THE BUILDING THAT HOUSES DR. VAN DYNE'S LABORATORY...
N! IT'S AN
RTHQUAKE!
HELP!!
KEEP BACK! THE BUILDING IS COLLAPSING!
AND, AT THE DOCKS NEARBY, A FEW MINUTES LATER...
HEY, FEEL THAT, JOE? THE WHOLE DOCK'S SHAKIN'!
SEEMS TO BE COMIN' FROM BEHIND US!
OOK!
VER
ERE...
WHA--
WHAT
IS
IT?
RUN! RUN... YELL TO THE OTHERS TO GET OFF THE DOCKS...
AND SO THE WORLD FIRST MEETS THE CREATURE FROM KOSMOS!
WHILE, IN HENRY PYM'S LABORATORY...
ELECTRONIC IMPULSES COMING FROM MY ANT SCOUTS! JANET, IN THE CLOSET IS A COSTUME WOVEN FROM UNSTABLE MOLECULES THAT WILL EXPAND AND SHRINK AS YOU DO! I HAVE A FEELING THIS IS OUR FIRST MISSION!
12

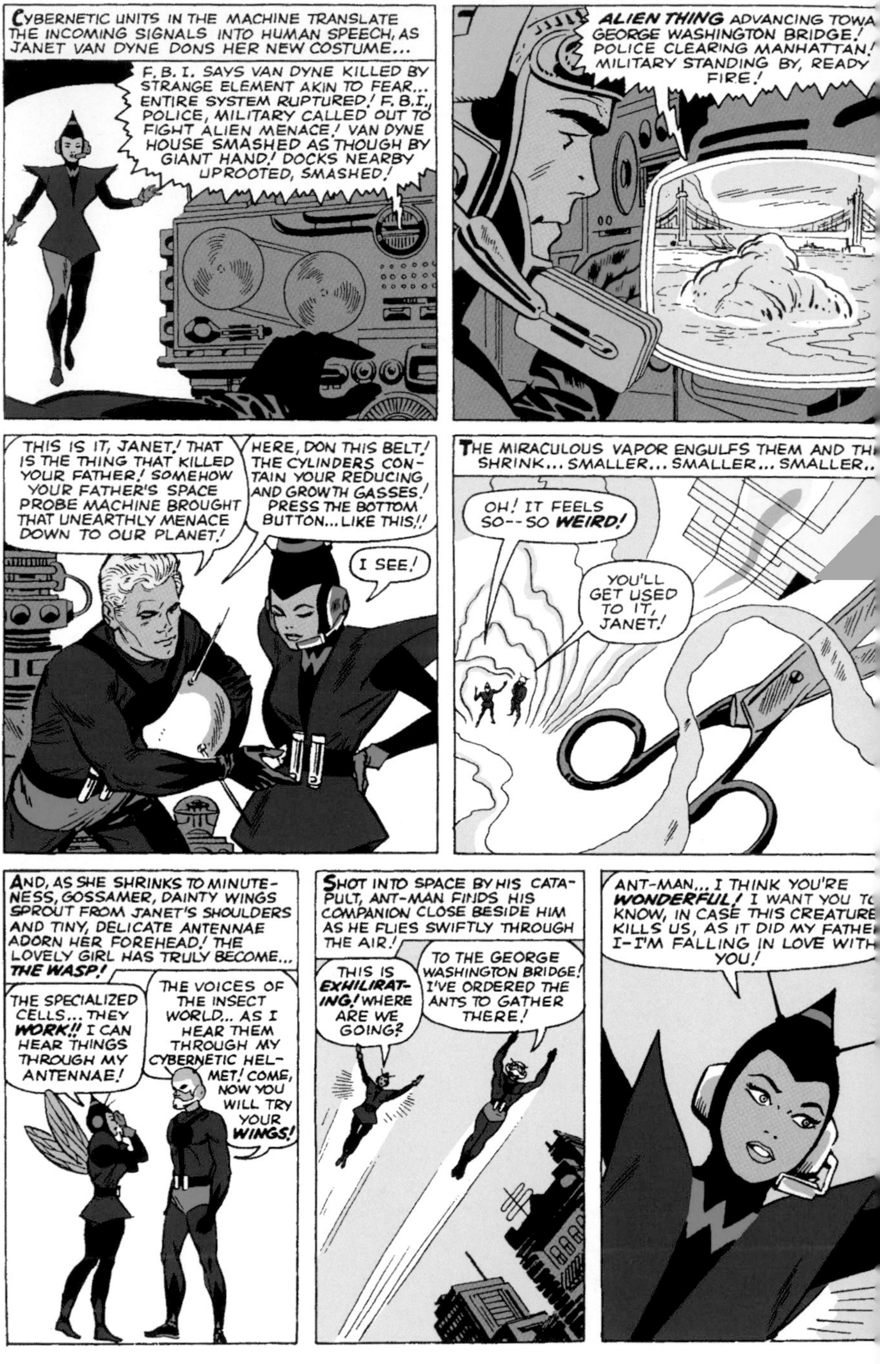
CYBERNETIC UNITS IN THE MACHINE TRANSLATE THE INCOMING SIGNALS INTO HUMAN SPEECH, AS JANET VAN DYNE DONS HER NEW COSTUME...
F.B.I. SAYS VAN DYNE KILLED BY STRANGE ELEMENT AKIN TO FEAR... ENTIRE SYSTEM RUPTURED! F.B.I., POLICE, MILITARY CALLED OUT TO FIGHT ALIEN MENACE! VAN DYNE HOUSE SMASHED AS THOUGH BY GIANT HAND! DOCKS NEARBY UPROOTED, SMASHED!
ALIEN THING ADVANCING TOWA GEORGE WASHINGTON BRIDGE! POLICE CLEARING MANHATTAN! MILITARY STANDING BY, READY FIRE!
THIS IS IT, JANET! THAT IS THE THING THAT KILLED YOUR FATHER! SOMEHOW YOUR FATHER'S SPACE PROBE MACHINE BROUGHT THAT UNEARTHLY MENACE DOWN TO OUR PLANET!
HERE, DON THIS BELT! THE CYLINDERS CONTAIN YOUR REDUCING AND GROWTH GASSES! PRESS THE BOTTOM BUTTON...LIKE THIS!!
I SEE!
THE MIRACULOUS VAPOR ENGULFS THEM AND TH SHRINK... SMALLER... SMALLER... SMALLER...
OH! IT FEELS SO--SO WEIRD!
YOU'LL GET USED TO IT, JANET!
AND, AS SHE SHRINKS TO MINUTENESS, GOSSAMER, DAINTY WINGS SPROUT FROM JANET'S SHOULDERS AND TINY, DELICATE ANTENNAE ADORN HER FOREHEAD! THE LOVELY GIRL HAS TRULY BECOME... THE WASP!
THE SPECIALIZED CELLS... THEY WORK!! I CAN HEAR THINGS THROUGH MY ANTENNAE!
THE VOICES OF THE INSECT WORLD... AS I HEAR THEM THROUGH MY CYBERNETIC HELMET! COME, NOW YOU WILL TRY YOUR WINGS!
SHOT INTO SPACE BY HIS CATAPULT, ANT-MAN FINDS HIS COMPANION CLOSE BESIDE HIM AS HE FLIES SWIFTLY THROUGH THE AIR!
THIS IS EXHILIRATING! WHERE ARE WE GOING?
TO THE GEORGE WASHINGTON BRIDGE! I'VE ORDERED THE ANTS TO GATHER THERE!
ANT-MAN... I THINK YOU'RE WONDERFUL! I WANT YOU TO KNOW, IN CASE THIS CREATURE KILLS US, AS IT DID MY FATHE I-I'M FALLING IN LOVE WITH YOU!

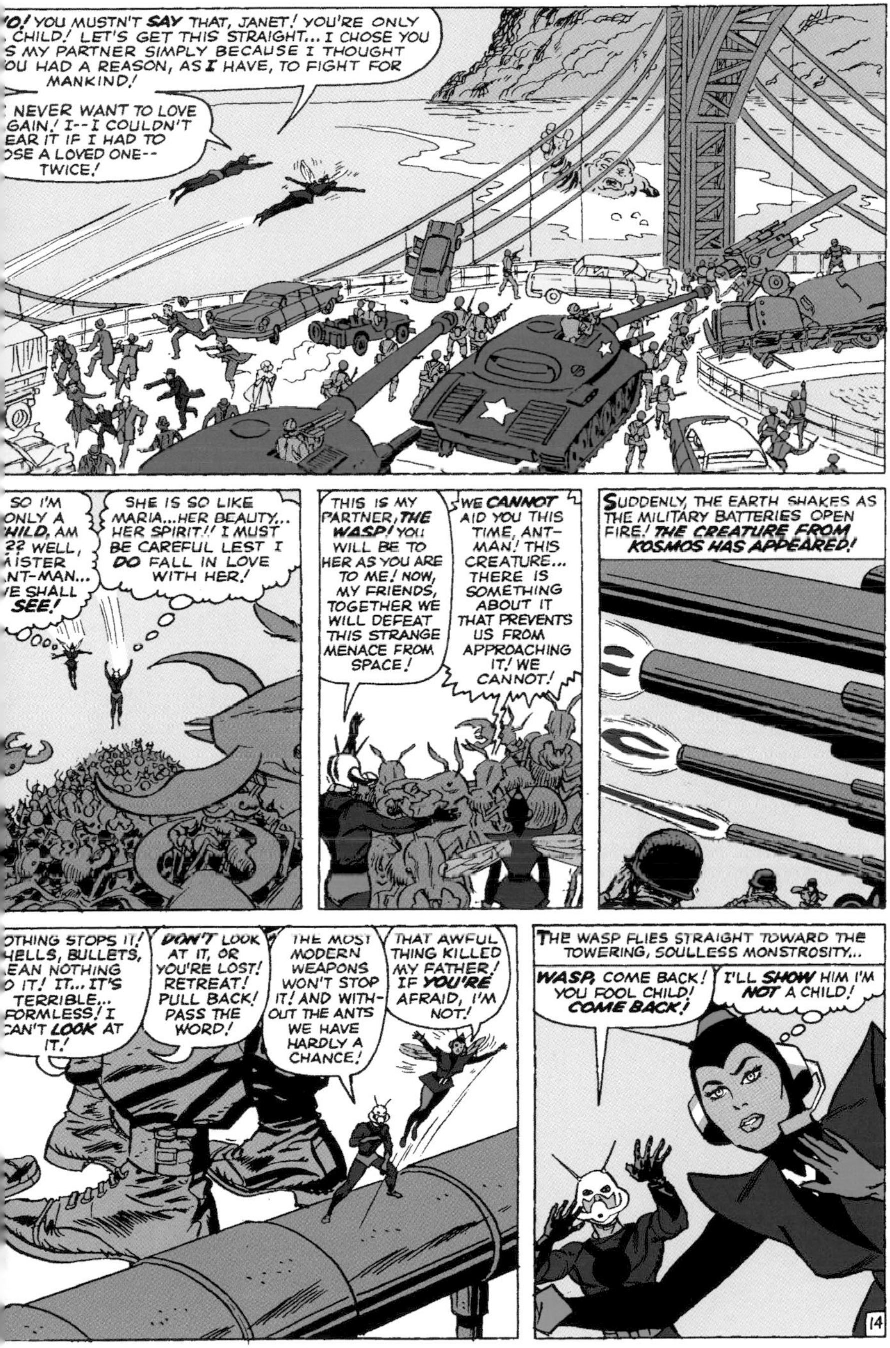

'O! YOU MUSTN'T SAY THAT, JANET! YOU'RE ONLY CHILD! LET'S GET THIS STRAIGHT... I CHOSE YOU S MY PARTNER SIMPLY BECAUSE I THOUGHT OU HAD A REASON, AS I HAVE, TO FIGHT FOR MANKIND!
NEVER WANT TO LOVE GAIN! I--I COULDN'T EAR IT IF I HAD TO OSE A LOVED ONE-- TWICE!
SO I'M ONLY A HILD, AM ? WELL, MISTER NT-MAN... E SHALL SEE!
SHE IS SO LIKE MARIA...HER BEAUTY... HER SPIRIT!! I MUST BE CAREFUL LEST I DO FALL IN LOVE WITH HER!
THIS IS MY PARTNER, THE WASP! YOU WILL BE TO HER AS YOU ARE TO ME! NOW, MY FRIENDS, TOGETHER WE WILL DEFEAT THIS STRANGE MENACE FROM SPACE!
WE CANNOT AID YOU THIS TIME, ANT-MAN! THIS CREATURE... THERE IS SOMETHING ABOUT IT THAT PREVENTS US FROM APPROACHING IT! WE CANNOT!
SUDDENLY, THE EARTH SHAKES AS THE MILITARY BATTERIES OPEN FIRE! THE CREATURE FROM KOSMOS HAS APPEARED!
OTHING STOPS IT! HELLS, BULLETS, EAN NOTHING O IT! IT... IT'S TERRIBLE... FORMLESS! I CAN'T LOOK AT IT!
DON'T LOOK AT IT, OR YOU'RE LOST! RETREAT! PULL BACK! PASS THE WORD!
THE MOST MODERN WEAPONS WON'T STOP IT! AND WITH-OUT THE ANTS WE HAVE HARDLY A CHANCE!
THAT AWFUL THING KILLED MY FATHER! IF YOU'RE AFRAID, I'M NOT!
THE WASP FLIES STRAIGHT TOWARD THE TOWERING, SOULLESS MONSTROSITY...
WASP, COME BACK! YOU FOOL CHILD! COME BACK!
I'LL SHOW HIM I'M NOT A CHILD!
14

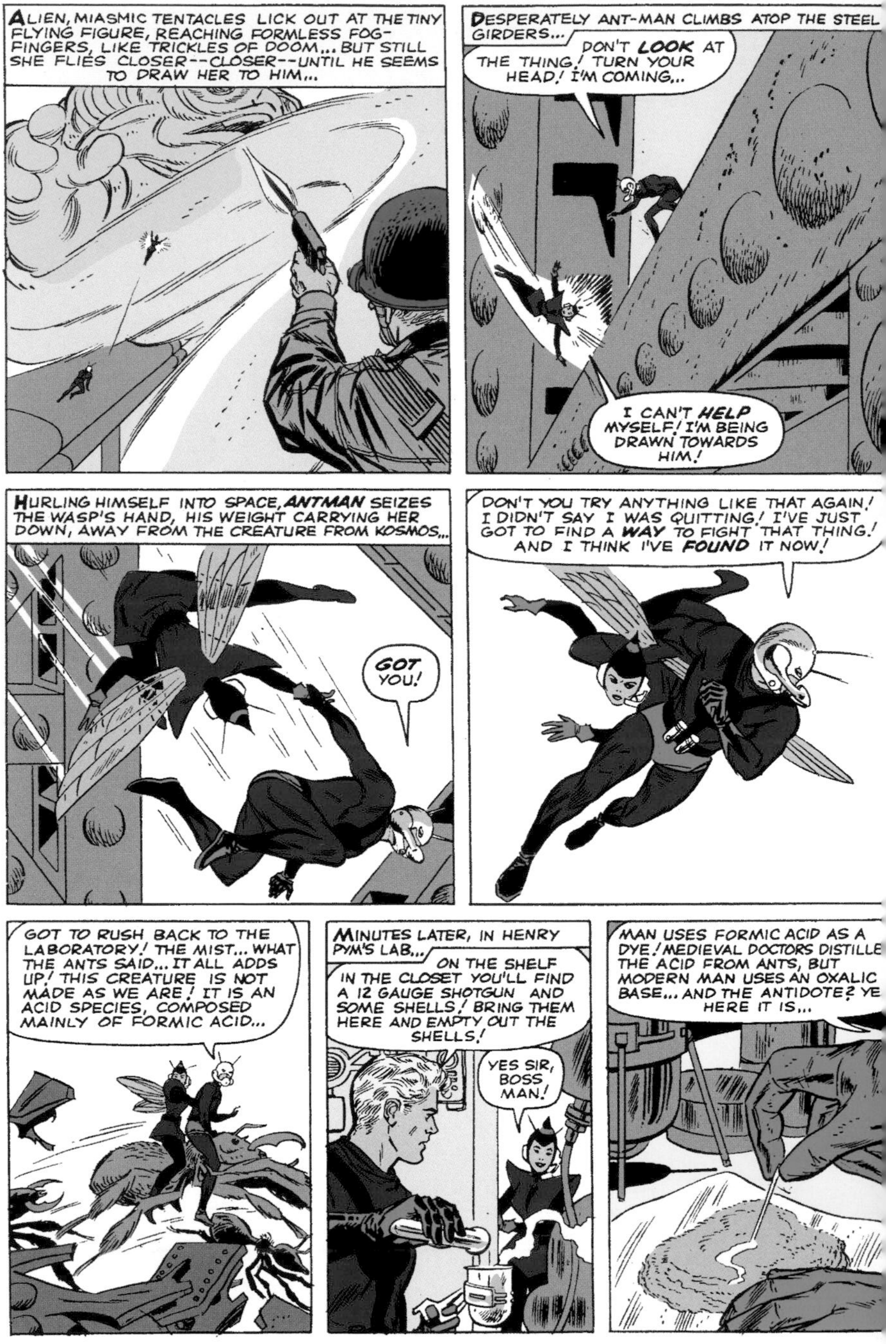
ALIEN, MIASMIC TENTACLES LICK OUT AT THE TINY FLYING FIGURE, REACHING FORMLESS FOG-FINGERS, LIKE TRICKLES OF DOOM... BUT STILL SHE FLIES CLOSER--CLOSER--UNTIL HE SEEMS TO DRAW HER TO HIM...
DESPERATELY ANT-MAN CLIMBS ATOP THE STEEL GIRDERS...
DON'T LOOK AT THE THING! TURN YOUR HEAD! I'M COMING...
I CAN'T HELP MYSELF! I'M BEING DRAWN TOWARDS HIM!
HURLING HIMSELF INTO SPACE, ANTMAN SEIZES THE WASP'S HAND, HIS WEIGHT CARRYING HER DOWN, AWAY FROM THE CREATURE FROM KOSMOS...
GOT YOU!
DON'T YOU TRY ANYTHING LIKE THAT AGAIN! I DIDN'T SAY I WAS QUITTING! I'VE JUST GOT TO FIND A WAY TO FIGHT THAT THING! AND I THINK I'VE FOUND IT NOW!
GOT TO RUSH BACK TO THE LABORATORY! THE MIST... WHAT THE ANTS SAID... IT ALL ADDS UP! THIS CREATURE IS NOT MADE AS WE ARE! IT IS AN ACID SPECIES, COMPOSED MAINLY OF FORMIC ACID...
MINUTES LATER, IN HENRY PYM'S LAB...
ON THE SHELF IN THE CLOSET YOU'LL FIND A 12 GAUGE SHOTGUN AND SOME SHELLS! BRING THEM HERE AND EMPTY OUT THE SHELLS!
YES SIR, BOSS MAN!
MAN USES FORMIC ACID AS A DYE! MEDIEVAL DOCTORS DISTILLE THE ACID FROM ANTS, BUT MODERN MAN USES AN OXALIC BASE... AND THE ANTIDOTE? YE HERE IT IS...

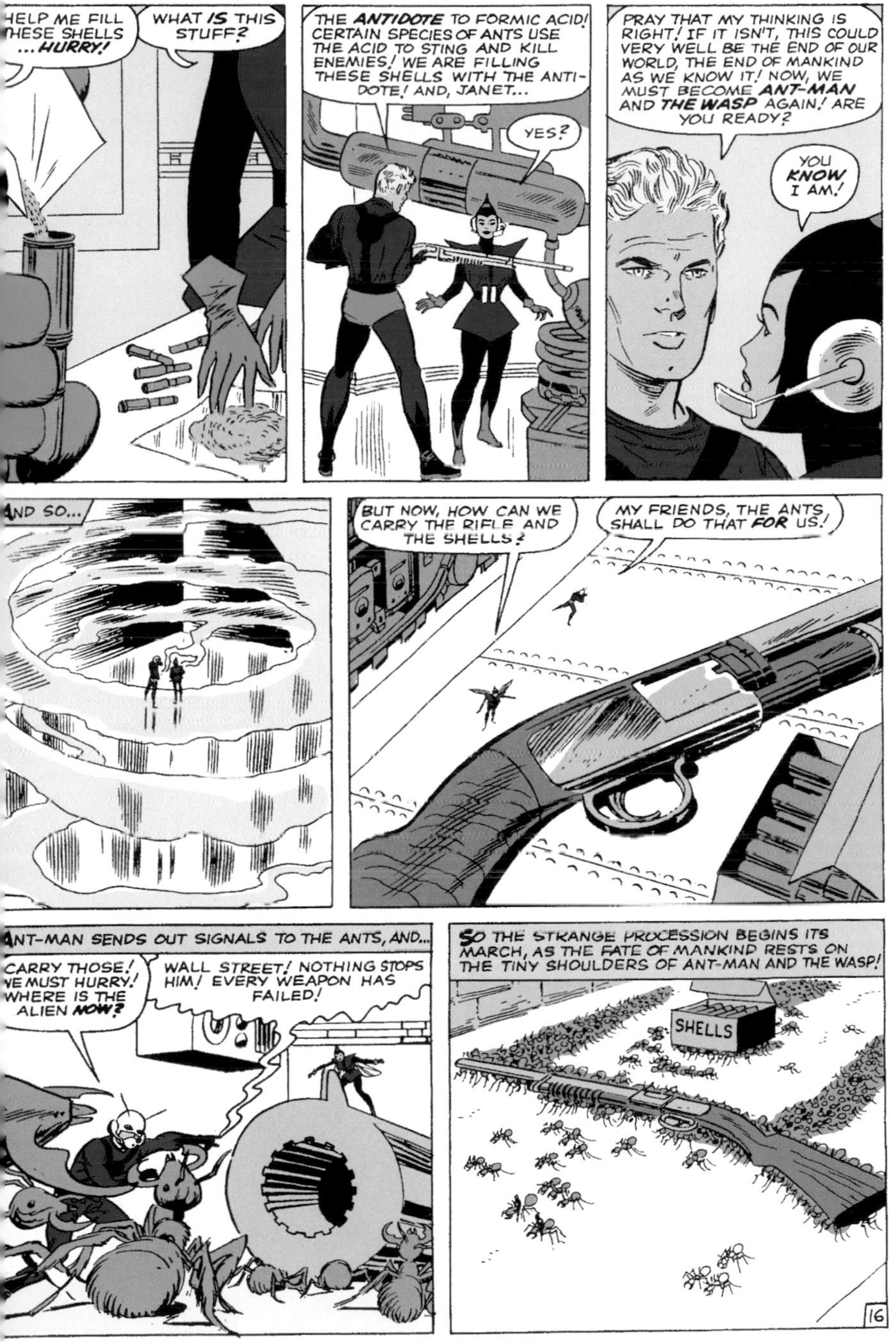

HELP ME FILL THESE SHELLS ...HURRY!
WHAT IS THIS STUFF?
THE ANTIDOTE TO FORMIC ACID! CERTAIN SPECIES OF ANTS USE THE ACID TO STING AND KILL ENEMIES! WE ARE FILLING THESE SHELLS WITH THE ANTIDOTE! AND, JANET...
YES?
PRAY THAT MY THINKING IS RIGHT! IF IT ISN'T, THIS COULD VERY WELL BE THE END OF OUR WORLD, THE END OF MANKIND AS WE KNOW IT! NOW, WE MUST BECOME ANT-MAN AND THE WASP AGAIN! ARE YOU READY?
YOU KNOW I AM!
AND SO...
BUT NOW, HOW CAN WE CARRY THE RIFLE AND THE SHELLS?
MY FRIENDS, THE ANTS, SHALL DO THAT FOR US!
ANT-MAN SENDS OUT SIGNALS TO THE ANTS, AND...
CARRY THOSE! WE MUST HURRY! WHERE IS THE ALIEN NOW?
WALL STREET! NOTHING STOPS HIM! EVERY WEAPON HAS FAILED!
SO THE STRANGE PROCESSION BEGINS ITS MARCH, AS THE FATE OF MANKIND RESTS ON THE TINY SHOULDERS OF ANT-MAN AND THE WASP!
SHELLS
16

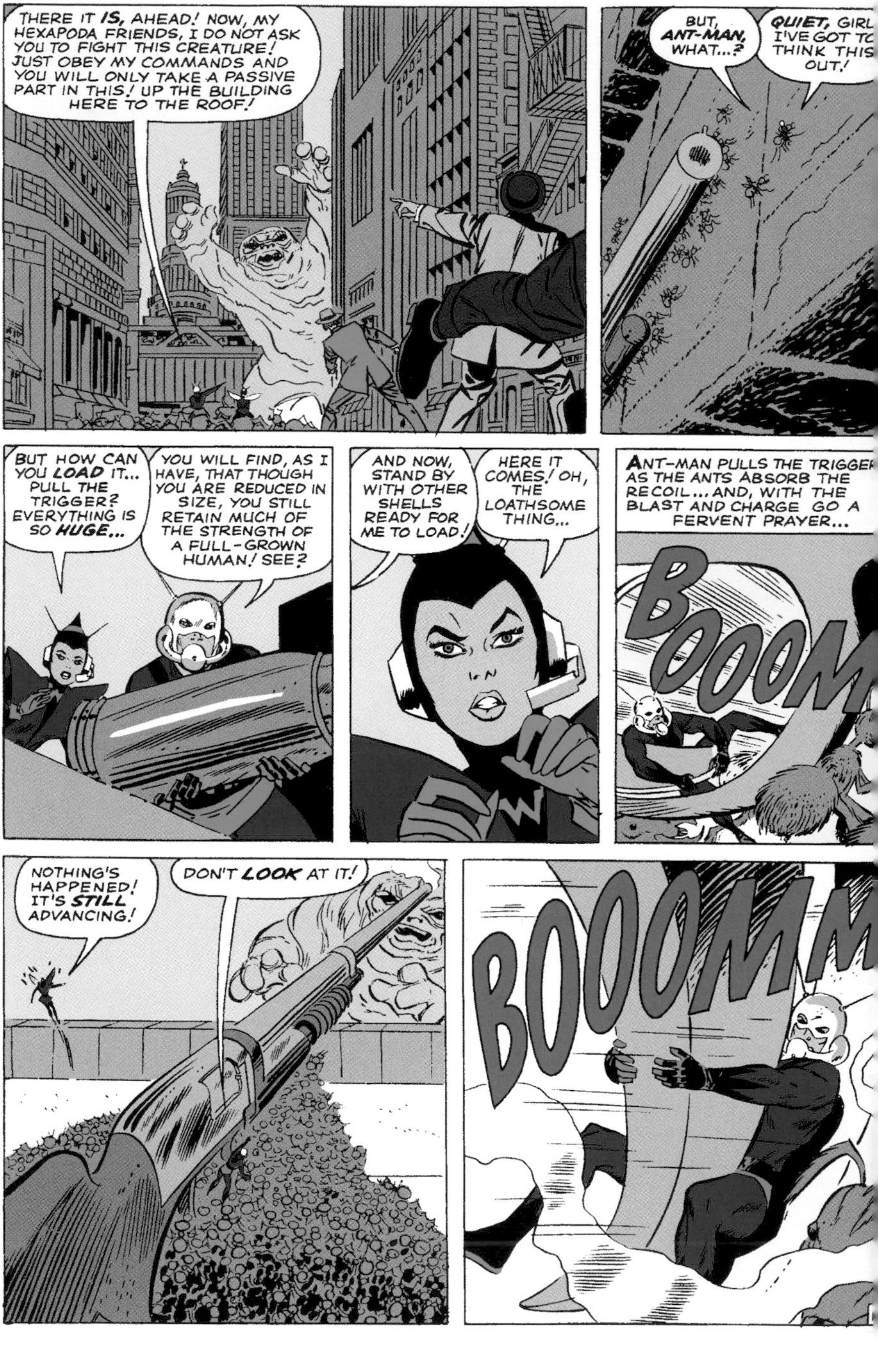
THERE IT IS, AHEAD! NOW, MY HEXAPODA FRIENDS, I DO NOT ASK YOU TO FIGHT THIS CREATURE! JUST OBEY MY COMMANDS AND YOU WILL ONLY TAKE A PASSIVE PART IN THIS! UP THE BUILDING HERE TO THE ROOF!
BUT, ANT-MAN, WHAT...?
QUIET, GIRL! I'VE GOT TO THINK THIS OUT!
BUT HOW CAN YOU LOAD IT... PULL THE TRIGGER? EVERYTHING IS SO HUGE...
YOU WILL FIND, AS I HAVE, THAT THOUGH YOU ARE REDUCED IN SIZE, YOU STILL RETAIN MUCH OF THE STRENGTH OF A FULL-GROWN HUMAN! SEE?
AND NOW, STAND BY WITH OTHER SHELLS READY FOR ME TO LOAD!
HERE IT COMES! OH, THE LOATHSOME THING...
ANT-MAN PULLS THE TRIGGER AS THE ANTS ABSORB THE RECOIL... AND, WITH THE BLAST AND CHARGE GO A FERVENT PRAYER...
BOOOM
NOTHING'S HAPPENED! IT'S STILL ADVANCING!
DON'T LOOK AT IT!
BOOOMM

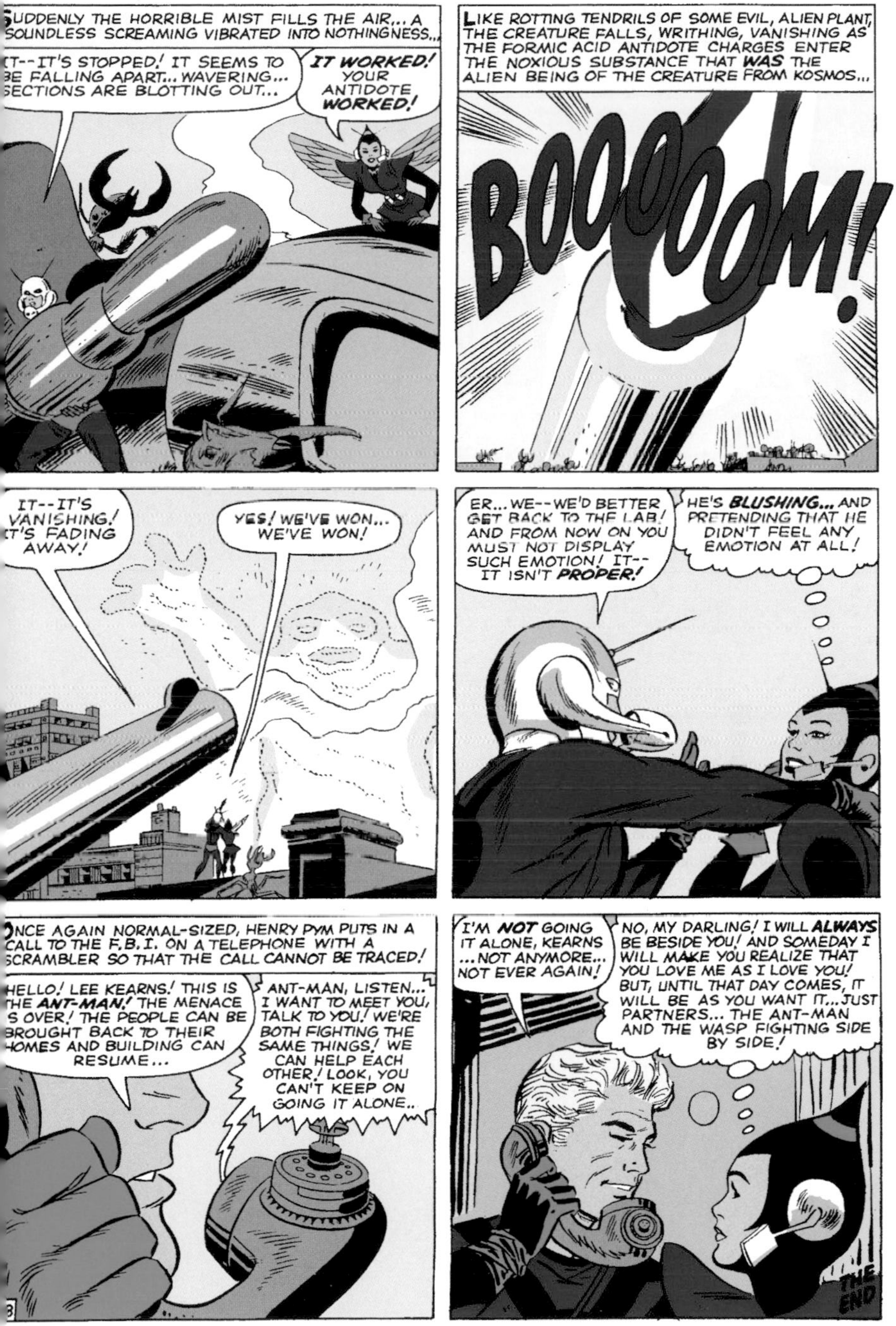

SUDDENLY THE HORRIBLE MIST FILLS THE AIR... A SOUNDLESS SCREAMING VIBRATED INTO NOTHINGNESS...
IT--IT'S STOPPED! IT SEEMS TO BE FALLING APART... WAVERING... SECTIONS ARE BLOTTING OUT...
IT WORKED! YOUR ANTIDOTE WORKED!
LIKE ROTTING TENDRILS OF SOME EVIL, ALIEN PLANT, THE CREATURE FALLS, WRITHING, VANISHING AS THE FORMIC ACID ANTIDOTE CHARGES ENTER THE NOXIOUS SUBSTANCE THAT WAS THE ALIEN BEING OF THE CREATURE FROM KOSMOS...
BOOOOOM!
IT--IT'S VANISHING! IT'S FADING AWAY!
YES! WE'VE WON... WE'VE WON!
ER... WE--WE'D BETTER GET BACK TO THE LAB! AND FROM NOW ON YOU MUST NOT DISPLAY SUCH EMOTION! IT--IT ISN'T PROPER!
HE'S BLUSHING... AND PRETENDING THAT HE DIDN'T FEEL ANY EMOTION AT ALL!
ONCE AGAIN NORMAL-SIZED, HENRY PYM PUTS IN A CALL TO THE F.B.I. ON A TELEPHONE WITH A SCRAMBLER SO THAT THE CALL CANNOT BE TRACED!
HELLO! LEE KEARNS! THIS IS THE ANT-MAN! THE MENACE IS OVER! THE PEOPLE CAN BE BROUGHT BACK TO THEIR HOMES AND BUILDING CAN RESUME...
ANT-MAN, LISTEN... I WANT TO MEET YOU, TALK TO YOU! WE'RE BOTH FIGHTING THE SAME THINGS! WE CAN HELP EACH OTHER! LOOK, YOU CAN'T KEEP ON GOING IT ALONE..
I'M NOT GOING IT ALONE, KEARNS ...NOT ANYMORE... NOT EVER AGAIN!
NO, MY DARLING! I WILL ALWAYS BE BESIDE YOU! AND SOMEDAY I WILL MAKE YOU REALIZE THAT YOU LOVE ME AS I LOVE YOU! BUT, UNTIL THAT DAY COMES, IT WILL BE AS YOU WANT IT... JUST PARTNERS... THE ANT-MAN AND THE WASP FIGHTING SIDE BY SIDE!
THE END

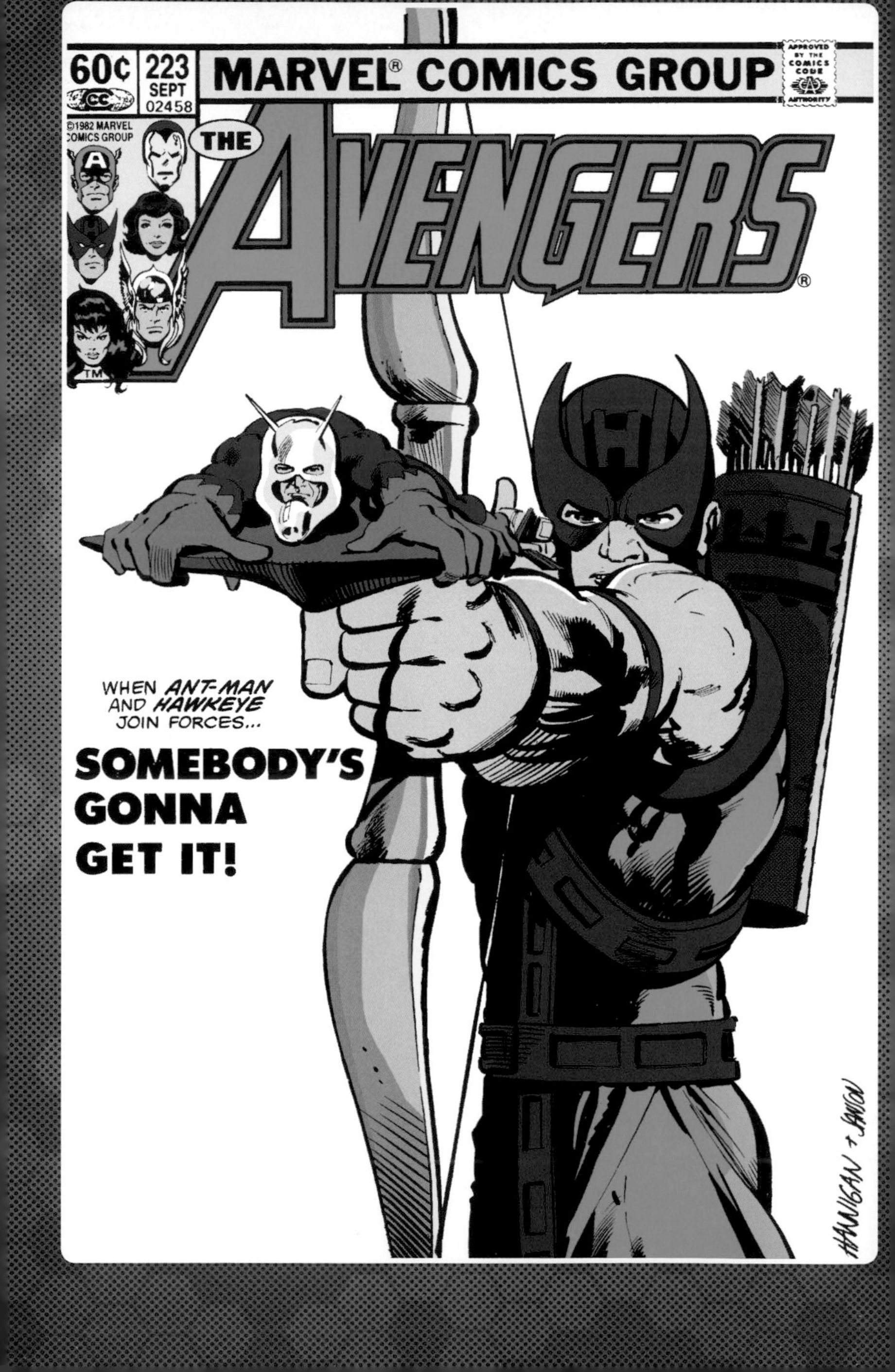
60¢
223
SEPT
02458
MARVEL® COMICS GROUP
APPROVED BY THE COMICS CODE AUTHORITY
©1982 MARVEL COMICS GROUP
THE AVENGERS®
WHEN ANT-MAN AND HAWKEYE JOIN FORCES...
SOMEBODY'S GONNA GET IT!

And there came a day when *Earth's mightiest heroes* found themselves *united* against a common threat. On that day, the *Avengers* were born—to fight the foes no *single* super hero could withstand!

Stan Lee PRESENTS: THE MIGHTY AVENGERS!®

DAVID MICHELINIE WRITER · GREG LAROCQUE PENCILER · BRETT BREEDING & CREW INKERS · CHRISTIE SCHEELE COLORIST · RICK PARKER LETTERER · MARK GRUENWALD EDITOR · JIM SHOOTER EDITOR-IN-CHIEF

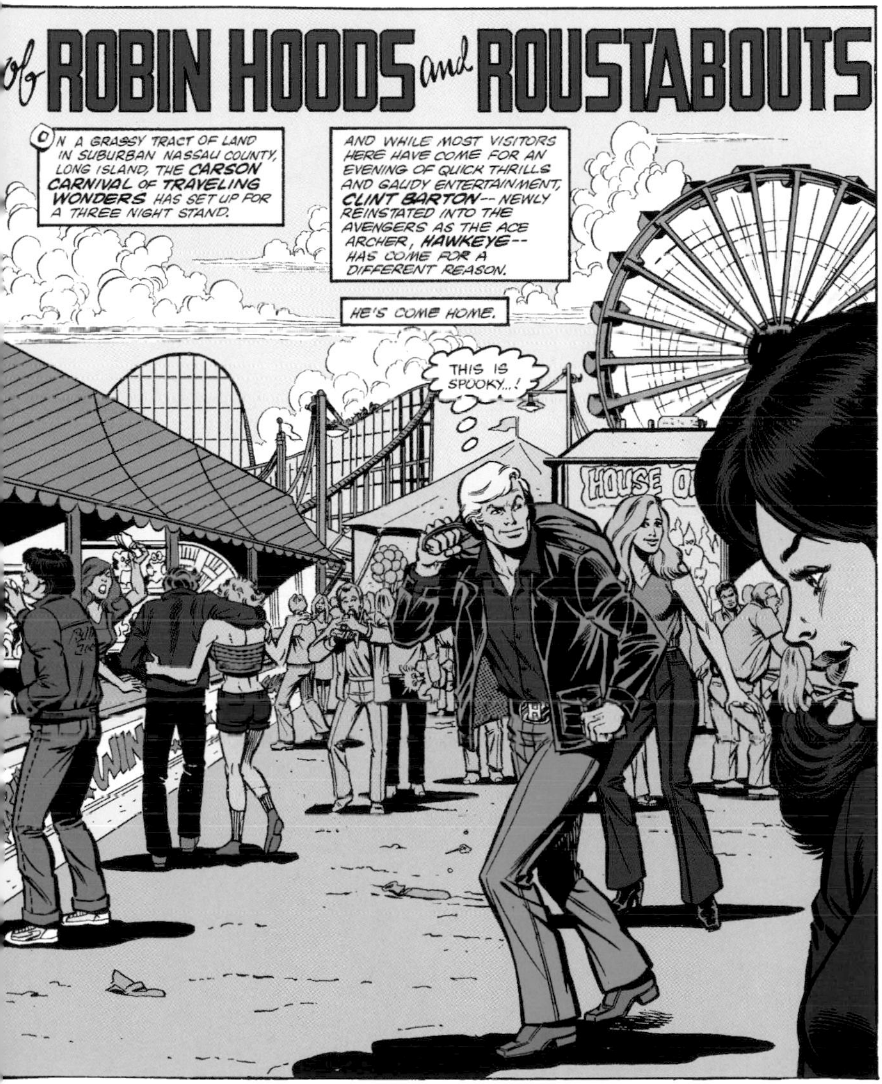

of ROBIN HOODS and ROUSTABOUTS
ON A GRASSY TRACT OF LAND IN SUBURBAN NASSAU COUNTY, LONG ISLAND, THE CARSON CARNIVAL OF TRAVELING WONDERS HAS SET UP FOR A THREE NIGHT STAND.
AND WHILE MOST VISITORS HERE HAVE COME FOR AN EVENING OF QUICK THRILLS AND GAUDY ENTERTAINMENT, CLINT BARTON-- NEWLY REINSTATED INTO THE AVENGERS AS THE ACE ARCHER, HAWKEYE-- HAS COME FOR A DIFFERENT REASON.
HE'S COME HOME.
THIS IS SPOOKY...!
HOUSE O

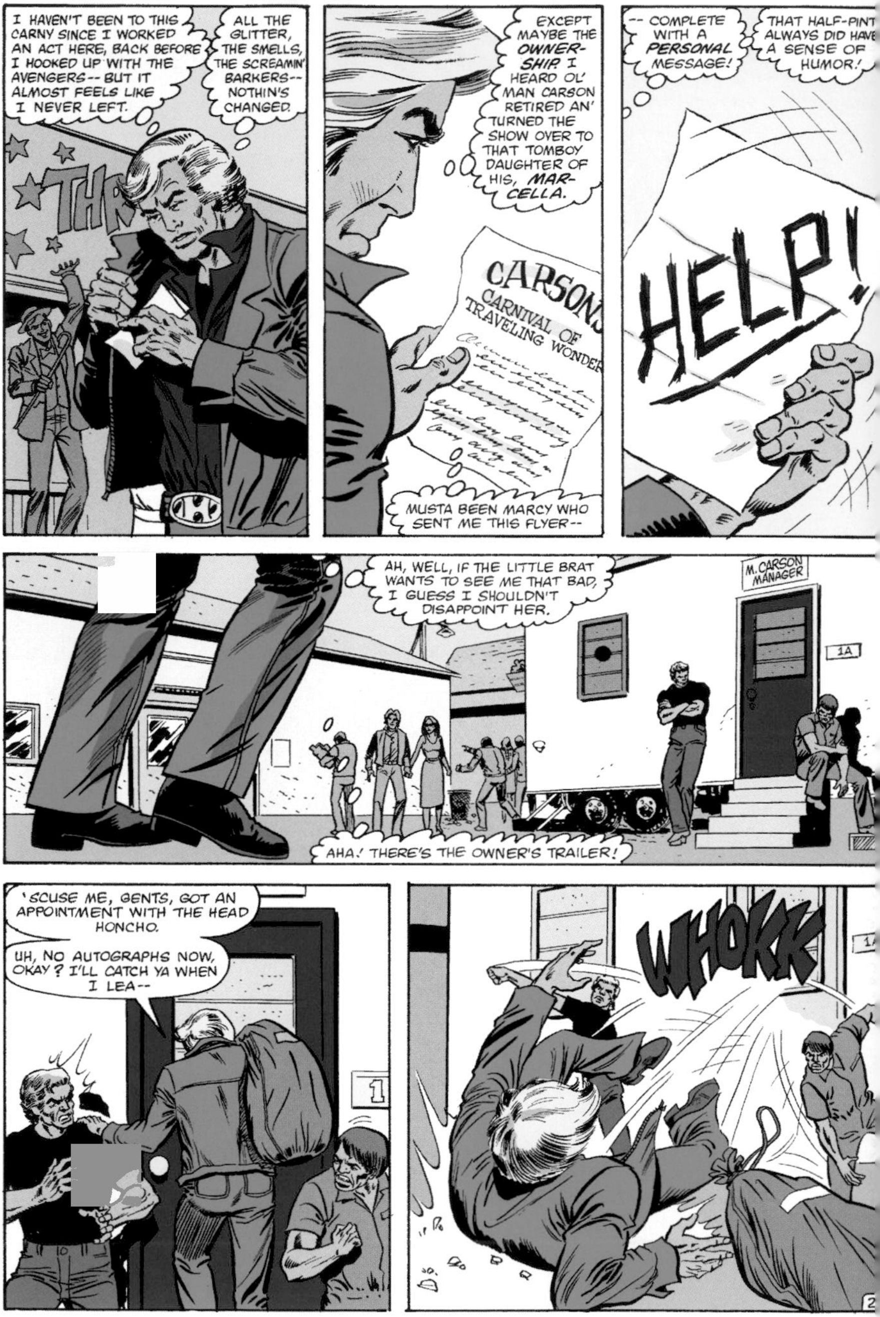
I HAVEN'T BEEN TO THIS CARNY SINCE I WORKED AN ACT HERE, BACK BEFORE I HOOKED UP WITH THE AVENGERS-- BUT IT ALMOST FEELS LIKE I NEVER LEFT.
ALL THE GLITTER, THE SMELLS, THE SCREAMIN' BARKERS-- NOTHIN'S CHANGED.
EXCEPT MAYBE THE OWNERSHIP. I HEARD OL' MAN CARSON RETIRED AN' TURNED THE SHOW OVER TO THAT TOMBOY DAUGHTER OF HIS, MARCELLA.
CARSON'S CARNIVAL OF TRAVELING WONDERS
MUSTA BEEN MARCY WHO SENT ME THIS FLYER--
-- COMPLETE WITH A PERSONAL MESSAGE!
THAT HALF-PINT ALWAYS DID HAVE A SENSE OF HUMOR!
HELP!
AH, WELL, IF THE LITTLE BRAT WANTS TO SEE ME THAT BAD, I GUESS I SHOULDN'T DISAPPOINT HER.
M. CARSON MANAGER
1A
AHA! THERE'S THE OWNER'S TRAILER!
'SCUSE ME, GENTS, GOT AN APPOINTMENT WITH THE HEAD HONCHO.
UH, NO AUTOGRAPHS NOW, OKAY? I'LL CATCH YA WHEN I LEA--
1
WHOKK

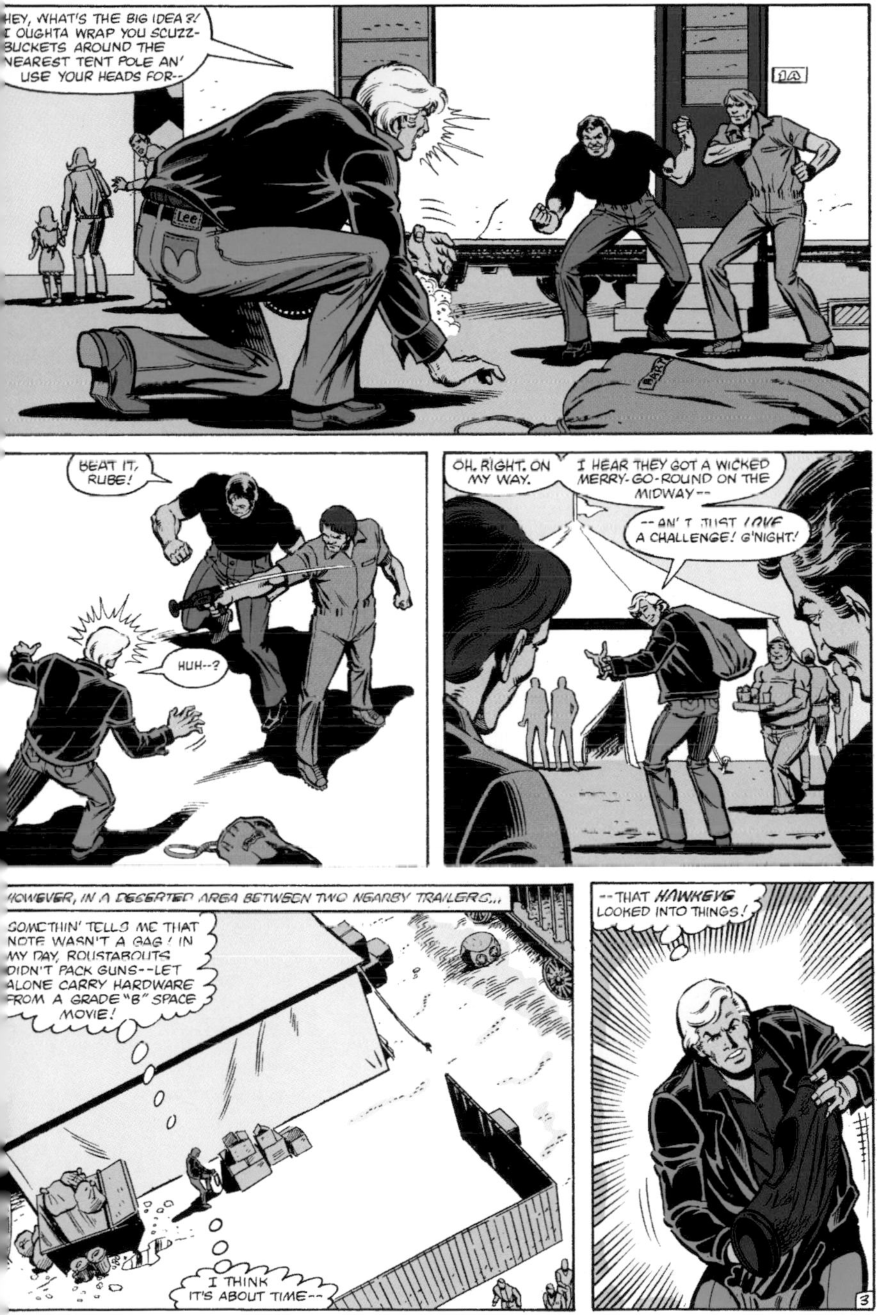
HEY, WHAT'S THE BIG IDEA?! I OUGHTA WRAP YOU SCUZZ-BUCKETS AROUND THE NEAREST TENT POLE AN' USE YOUR HEADS FOR--
1A
BEAT IT, RUBE!
HUH--?
OH, RIGHT. ON MY WAY.
I HEAR THEY GOT A WICKED MERRY-GO-ROUND ON THE MIDWAY--
--AN' I JUST LOVE A CHALLENGE! G'NIGHT!
HOWEVER, IN A DESERTED AREA BETWEEN TWO NEARBY TRAILERS...
SOMETHIN' TELLS ME THAT NOTE WASN'T A GAG! IN MY DAY, ROUSTABOUTS DIDN'T PACK GUNS--LET ALONE CARRY HARDWARE FROM A GRADE "B" SPACE MOVIE!
I THINK IT'S ABOUT TIME--
--THAT HAWKEYE LOOKED INTO THINGS!
3

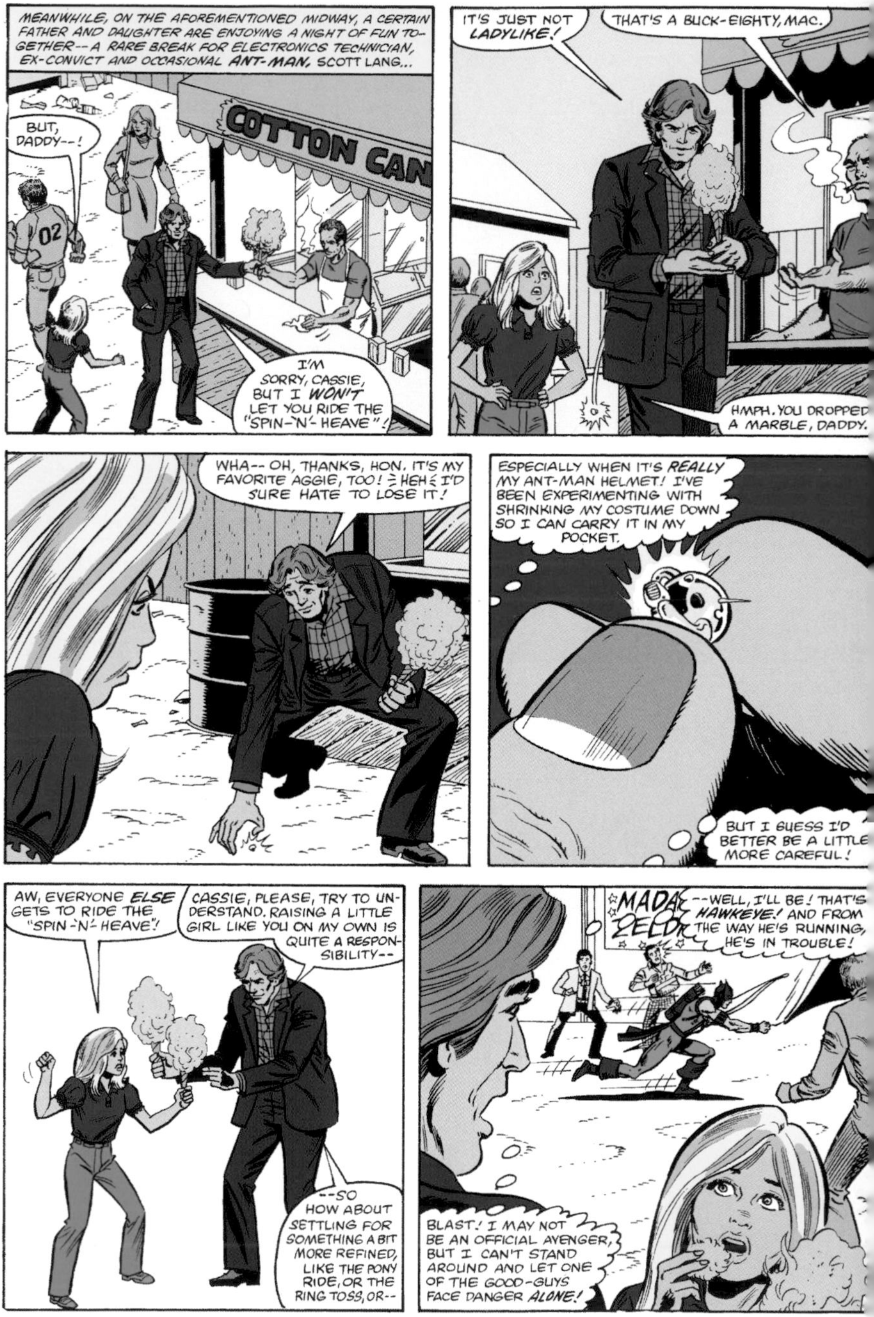
MEANWHILE, ON THE AFOREMENTIONED MIDWAY, A CERTAIN FATHER AND DAUGHTER ARE ENJOYING A NIGHT OF FUN TOGETHER-- A RARE BREAK FOR ELECTRONICS TECHNICIAN, EX-CONVICT AND OCCASIONAL ANT-MAN, SCOTT LANG...
COTTON CAN
BUT, DADDY--!
02
I'M SORRY, CASSIE, BUT I WON'T LET YOU RIDE THE "SPIN-'N'-HEAVE"!
IT'S JUST NOT LADYLIKE!
THAT'S A BUCK-EIGHTY, MAC.
HMPH. YOU DROPPED A MARBLE, DADDY.
WHA-- OH, THANKS, HON. IT'S MY FAVORITE AGGIE, TOO! HEH I'D SURE HATE TO LOSE IT!
ESPECIALLY WHEN IT'S REALLY MY ANT-MAN HELMET! I'VE BEEN EXPERIMENTING WITH SHRINKING MY COSTUME DOWN SO I CAN CARRY IT IN MY POCKET.
BUT I GUESS I'D BETTER BE A LITTLE MORE CAREFUL!
AW, EVERYONE ELSE GETS TO RIDE THE "SPIN-'N'-HEAVE"!
CASSIE, PLEASE, TRY TO UNDERSTAND. RAISING A LITTLE GIRL LIKE YOU ON MY OWN IS QUITE A RESPONSIBILITY--
--SO HOW ABOUT SETTLING FOR SOMETHING A BIT MORE REFINED, LIKE THE PONY RIDE, OR THE RING TOSS, OR--
--WELL, I'LL BE! THAT'S HAWKEYE! AND FROM THE WAY HE'S RUNNING, HE'S IN TROUBLE!
BLAST! I MAY NOT BE AN OFFICIAL AVENGER, BUT I CAN'T STAND AROUND AND LET ONE OF THE GOOD-GUYS FACE DANGER ALONE!

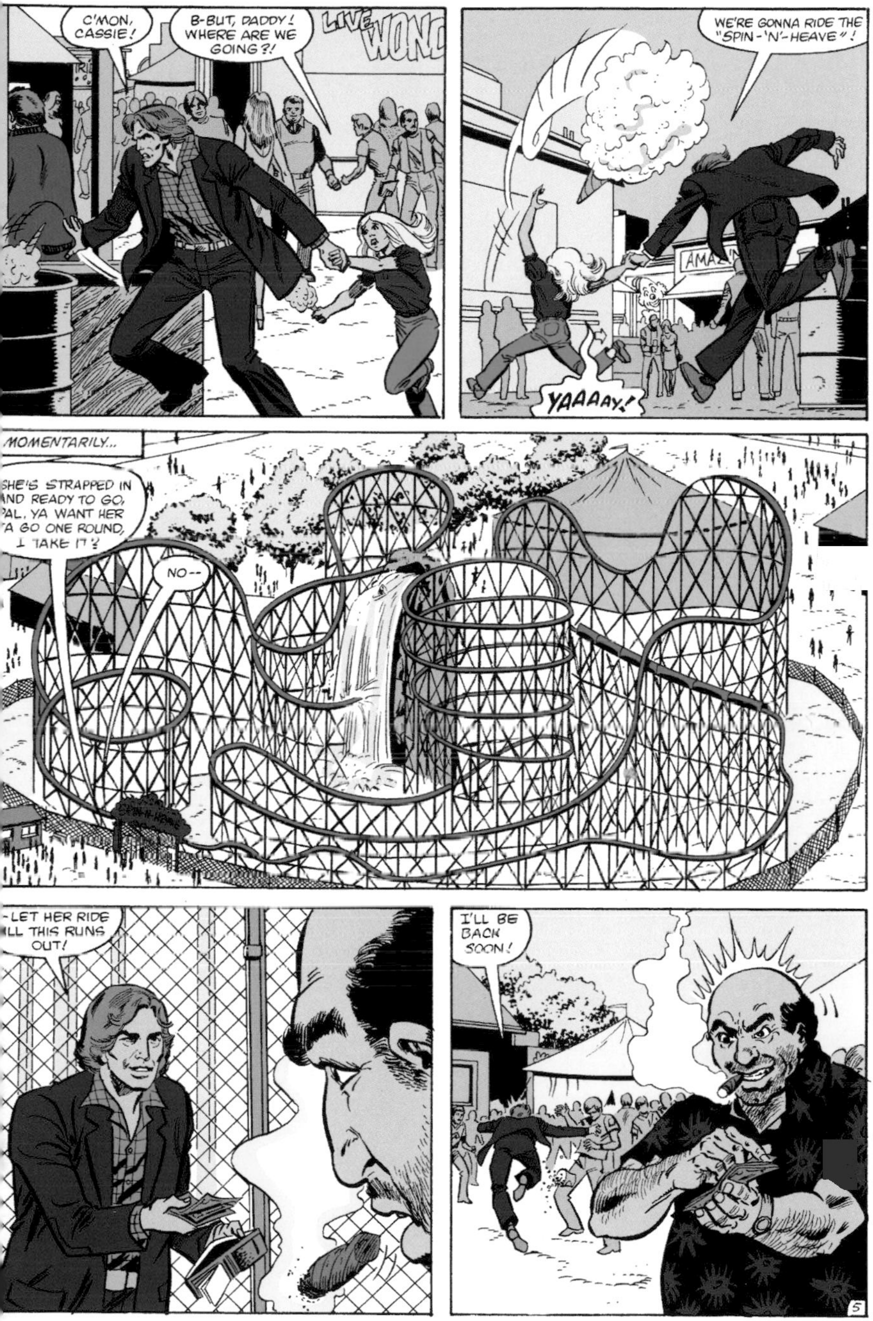
C'MON, CASSIE!
B-BUT, DADDY! WHERE ARE WE GOING?!
LIVE WONC
WE'RE GONNA RIDE THE "SPIN-'N'-HEAVE"!
YAAAAY!
MOMENTARILY...
SHE'S STRAPPED IN AND READY TO GO, PAL. YA WANT HER TA GO ONE ROUND, I TAKE IT?
NO--
-LET HER RIDE TILL THIS RUNS OUT!
I'LL BE BACK SOON!
5

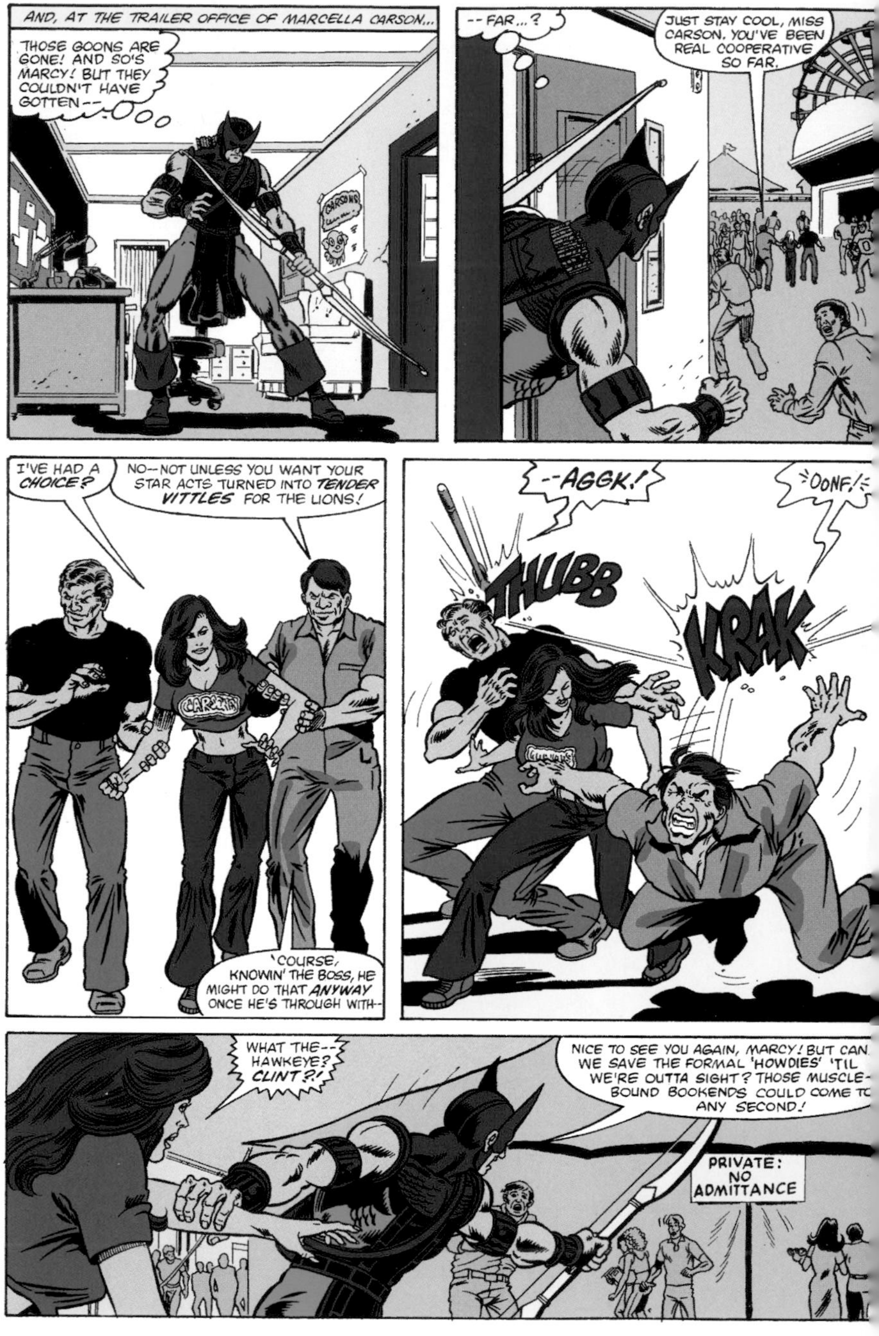
AND, AT THE TRAILER OFFICE OF MARCELLA CARSON...
THOSE GOONS ARE GONE! AND SO'S MARCY! BUT THEY COULDN'T HAVE GOTTEN--
--FAR...?
JUST STAY COOL, MISS CARSON. YOU'VE BEEN REAL COOPERATIVE SO FAR.
I'VE HAD A CHOICE?
NO--NOT UNLESS YOU WANT YOUR STAR ACTS TURNED INTO TENDER VITTLES FOR THE LIONS!
'COURSE, KNOWIN' THE BOSS, HE MIGHT DO THAT ANYWAY ONCE HE'S THROUGH WITH-
--AGGK!
OONF!
THUBB
KRAK
WHAT THE-- HAWKEYE? CLINT?!
NICE TO SEE YOU AGAIN, MARCY! BUT CAN WE SAVE THE FORMAL 'HOWDIES' 'TIL WE'RE OUTTA SIGHT? THOSE MUSCLE-BOUND BOOKENDS COULD COME TO ANY SECOND!
PRIVATE: NO ADMITTANCE

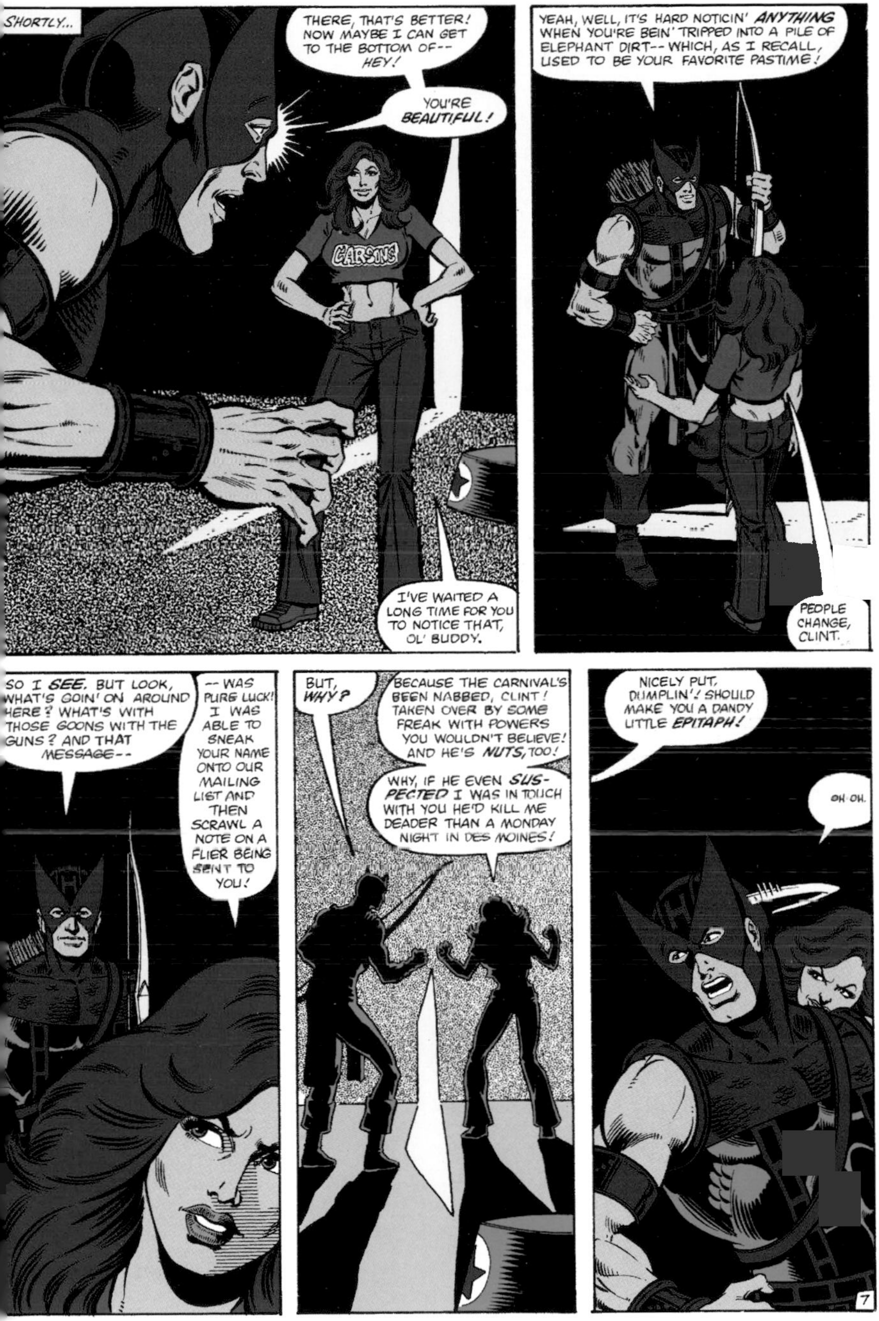
SHORTLY...
THERE, THAT'S BETTER! NOW MAYBE I CAN GET TO THE BOTTOM OF-- HEY!
YOU'RE BEAUTIFUL!
I'VE WAITED A LONG TIME FOR YOU TO NOTICE THAT, OL' BUDDY.
YEAH, WELL, IT'S HARD NOTICIN' ANYTHING WHEN YOU'RE BEIN' TRIPPED INTO A PILE OF ELEPHANT DIRT-- WHICH, AS I RECALL, USED TO BE YOUR FAVORITE PASTIME!
PEOPLE CHANGE, CLINT.
SO I SEE. BUT LOOK, WHAT'S GOIN' ON AROUND HERE? WHAT'S WITH THOSE GOONS WITH THE GUNS? AND THAT MESSAGE--
--WAS PURE LUCK! I WAS ABLE TO SNEAK YOUR NAME ONTO OUR MAILING LIST AND THEN SCRAWL A NOTE ON A FLIER BEING SENT TO YOU!
BUT, WHY?
BECAUSE THE CARNIVAL'S BEEN NABBED, CLINT! TAKEN OVER BY SOME FREAK WITH POWERS YOU WOULDN'T BELIEVE! AND HE'S NUTS, TOO!
WHY, IF HE EVEN SUSPECTED I WAS IN TOUCH WITH YOU HE'D KILL ME DEADER THAN A MONDAY NIGHT IN DES MOINES!
NICELY PUT, DUMPLIN'! SHOULD MAKE YOU A DANDY LITTLE EPITAPH!
OH-OH.
7

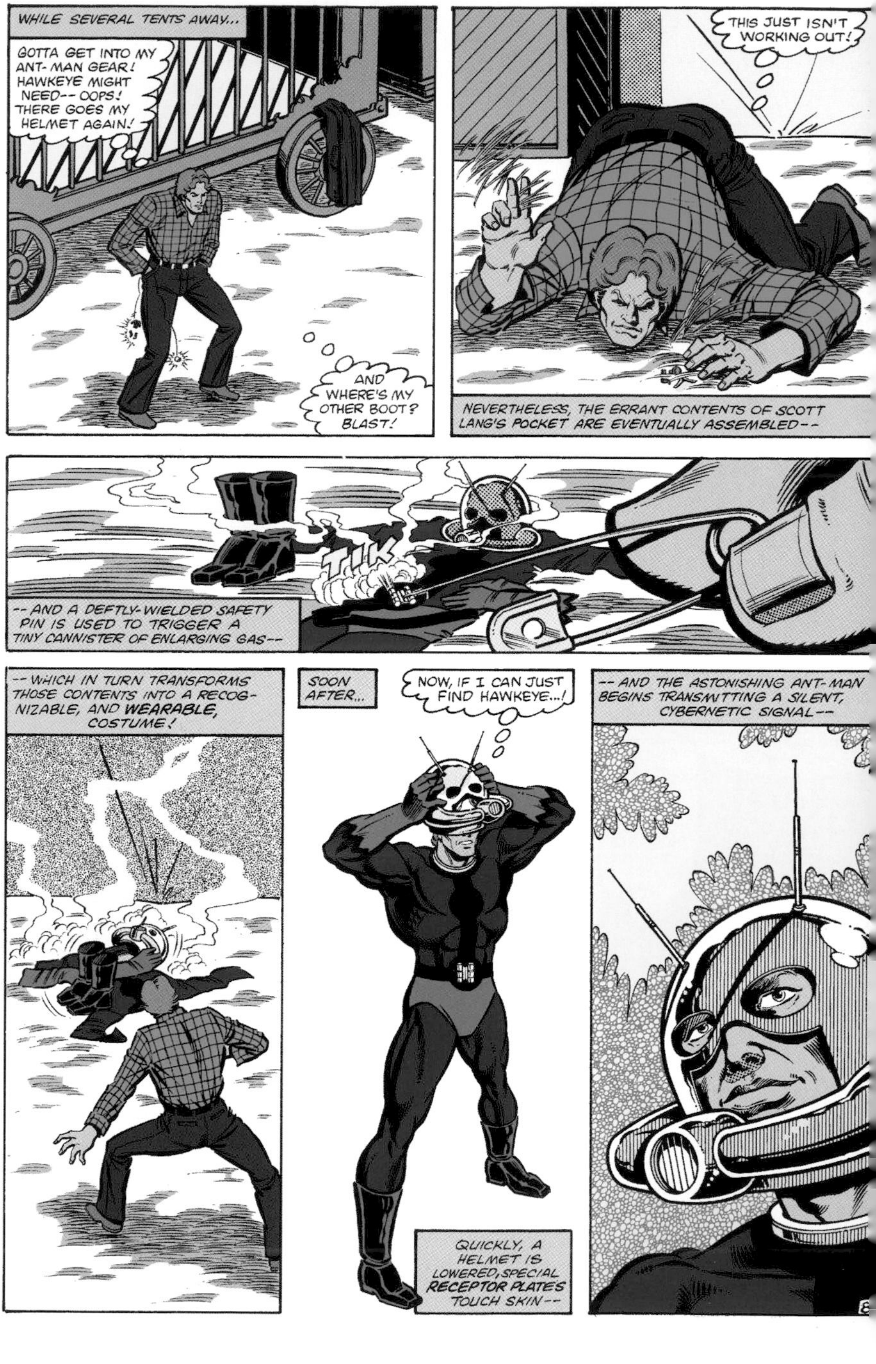
WHILE SEVERAL TENTS AWAY...
GOTTA GET INTO MY ANT-MAN GEAR! HAWKEYE MIGHT NEED-- OOPS! THERE GOES MY HELMET AGAIN!
AND WHERE'S MY OTHER BOOT? BLAST!
THIS JUST ISN'T WORKING OUT!
NEVERTHELESS, THE ERRANT CONTENTS OF SCOTT LANG'S POCKET ARE EVENTUALLY ASSEMBLED--
TIK
--AND A DEFTLY-WIELDED SAFETY PIN IS USED TO TRIGGER A TINY CANNISTER OF ENLARGING GAS--
--WHICH IN TURN TRANSFORMS THOSE CONTENTS INTO A RECOGNIZABLE, AND WEARABLE, COSTUME!
SOON AFTER...
NOW, IF I CAN JUST FIND HAWKEYE...!
QUICKLY, A HELMET IS LOWERED, SPECIAL RECEPTOR PLATES TOUCH SKIN--
--AND THE ASTONISHING ANT-MAN BEGINS TRANSMITTING A SILENT, CYBERNETIC SIGNAL--
8

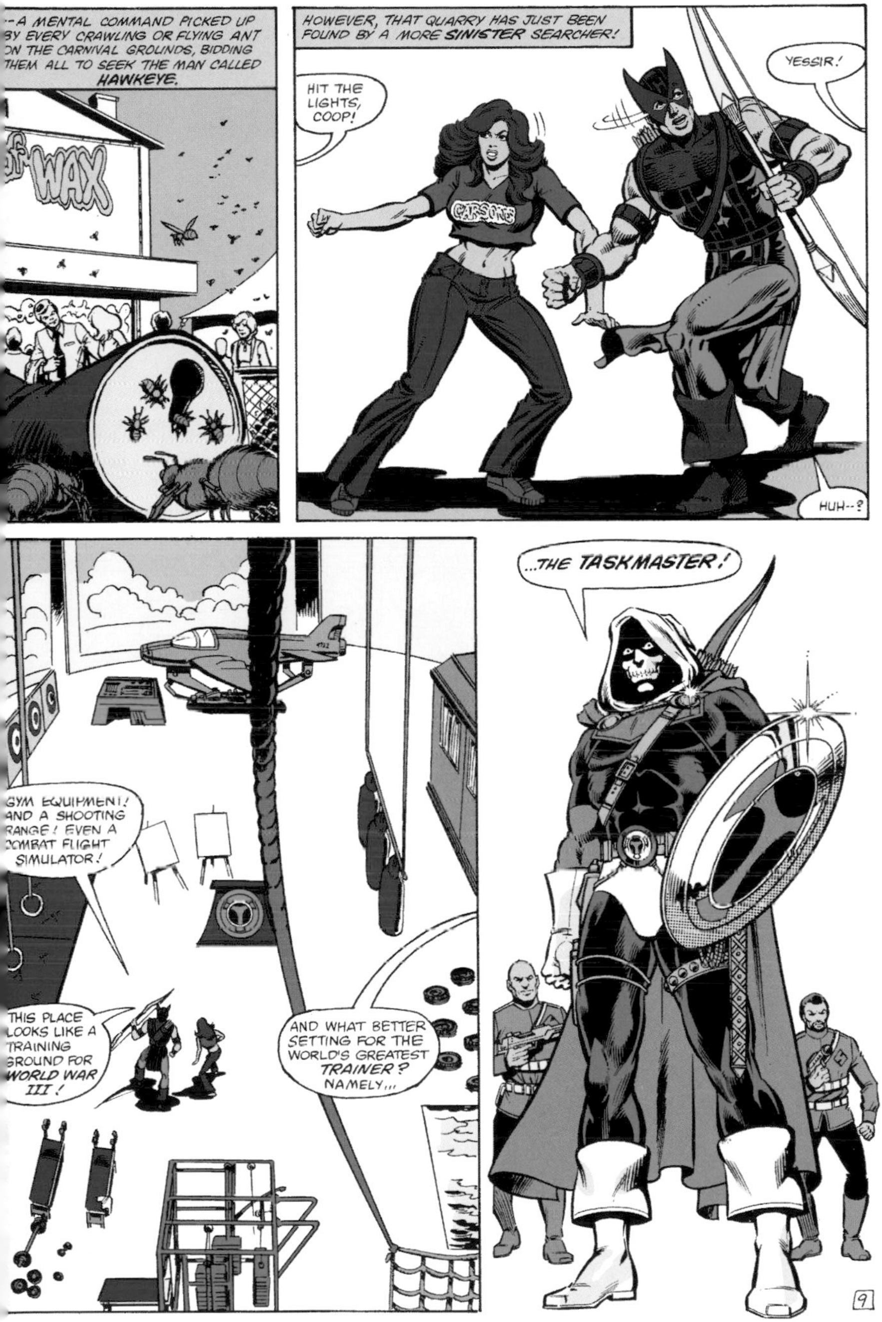
--A MENTAL COMMAND PICKED UP BY EVERY CRAWLING OR FLYING ANT ON THE CARNIVAL GROUNDS, BIDDING THEM ALL TO SEEK THE MAN CALLED HAWKEYE.
WAX
HOWEVER, THAT QUARRY HAS JUST BEEN FOUND BY A MORE SINISTER SEARCHER!
HIT THE LIGHTS, COOP!
YESSIR!
HUH--?
GYM EQUIPMENT! AND A SHOOTING RANGE! EVEN A COMBAT FLIGHT SIMULATOR!
THIS PLACE LOOKS LIKE A TRAINING GROUND FOR WORLD WAR III!
AND WHAT BETTER SETTING FOR THE WORLD'S GREATEST TRAINER? NAMELY...
...THE TASKMASTER!
9

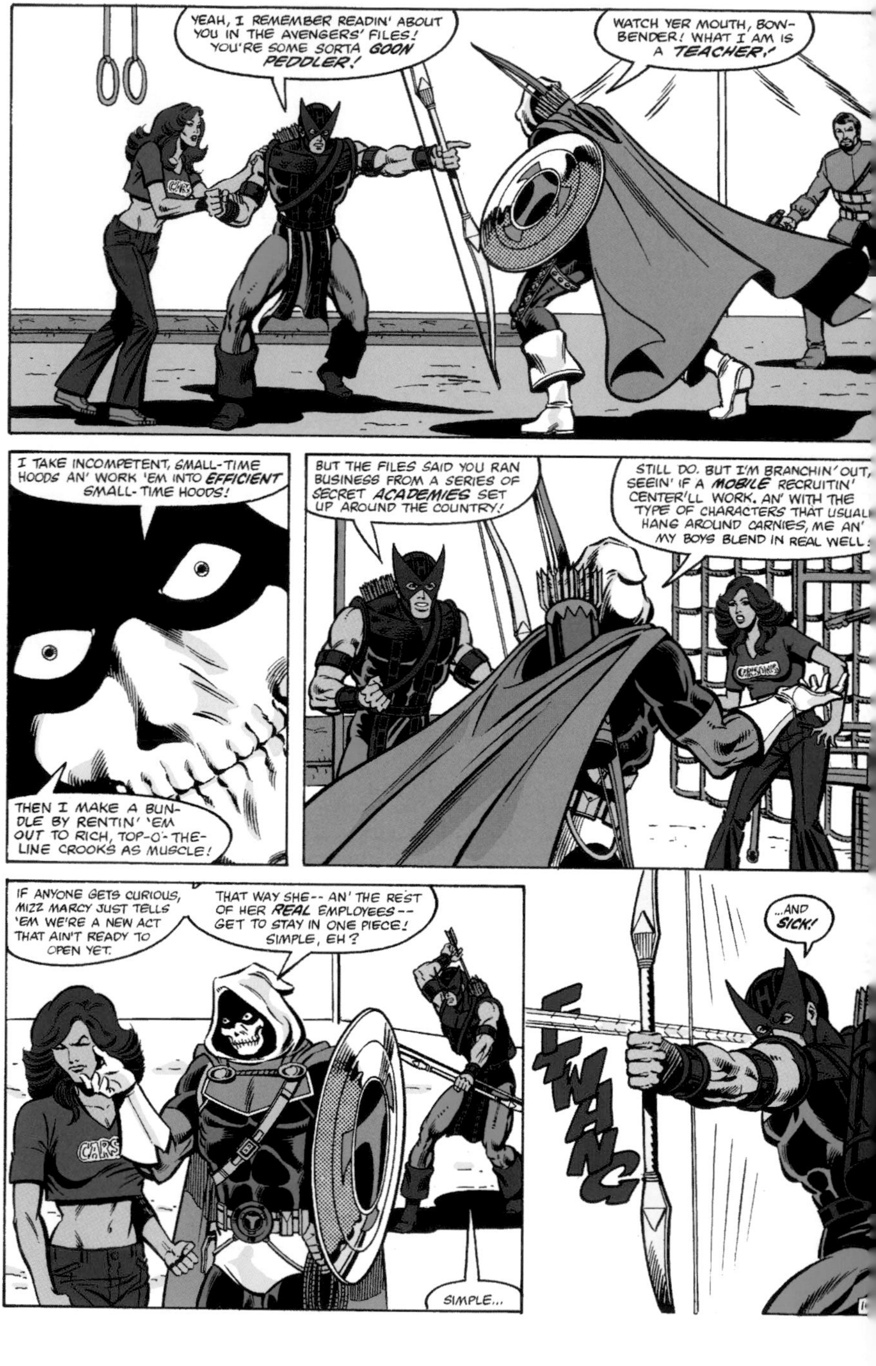
YEAH, I REMEMBER READIN' ABOUT YOU IN THE AVENGERS' FILES! YOU'RE SOME SORTA GOON PEDDLER!
WATCH YER MOUTH, BOW-BENDER! WHAT I AM IS A TEACHER!
I TAKE INCOMPETENT, SMALL-TIME HOODS AN' WORK 'EM INTO EFFICIENT SMALL-TIME HOODS!
THEN I MAKE A BUNDLE BY RENTIN' 'EM OUT TO RICH, TOP-O'-THE-LINE CROOKS AS MUSCLE!
BUT THE FILES SAID YOU RAN BUSINESS FROM A SERIES OF SECRET ACADEMIES SET UP AROUND THE COUNTRY!
STILL DO. BUT I'M BRANCHIN' OUT, SEEIN' IF A MOBILE RECRUITIN' CENTER'LL WORK. AN' WITH THE TYPE OF CHARACTERS THAT USUALL HANG AROUND CARNIES, ME AN' MY BOYS BLEND IN REAL WELL!
IF ANYONE GETS CURIOUS, MIZZ MARCY JUST TELLS 'EM WE'RE A NEW ACT THAT AIN'T READY TO OPEN YET.
THAT WAY SHE-- AN' THE REST OF HER REAL EMPLOYEES -- GET TO STAY IN ONE PIECE! SIMPLE, EH?
SIMPLE...
...AND SICK!
FWANG

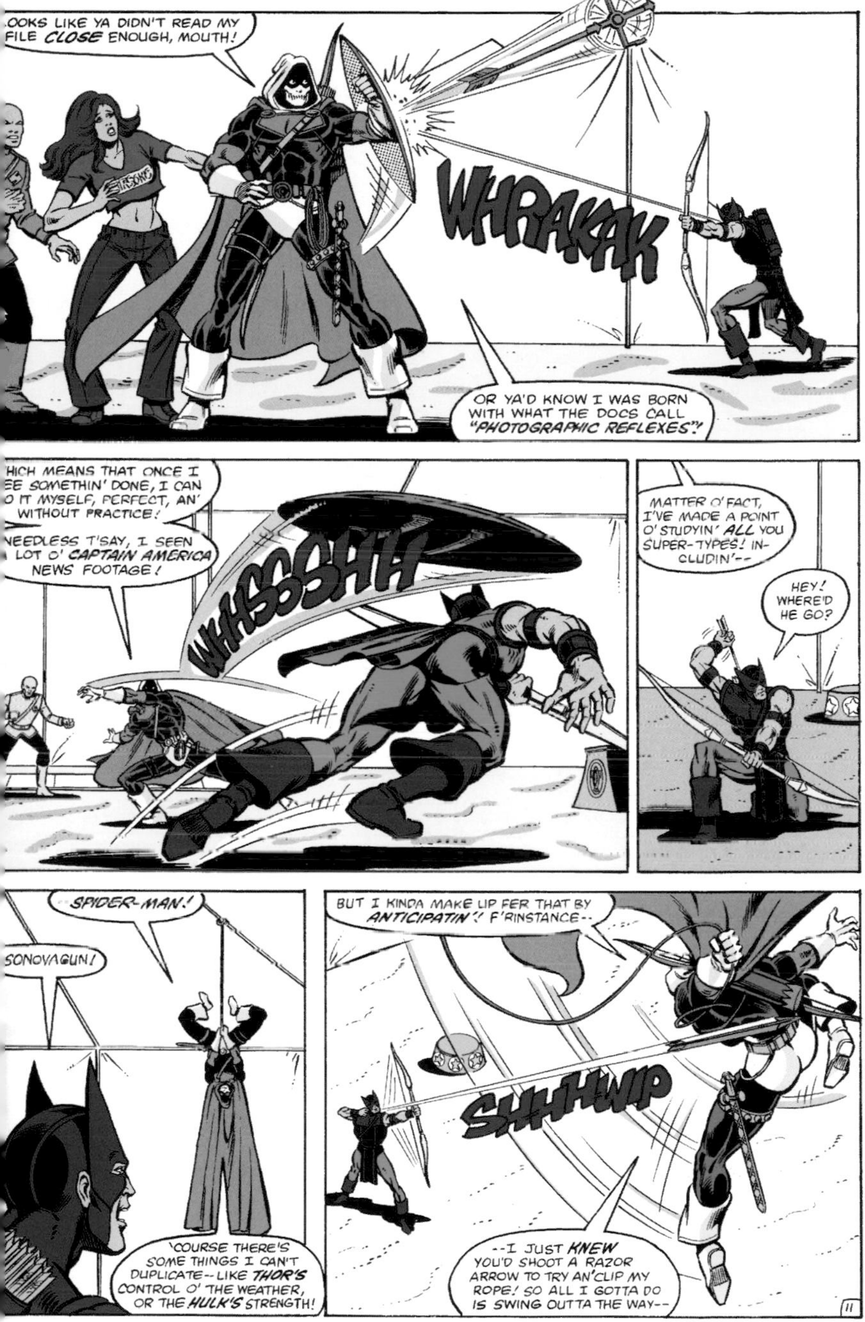

LOOKS LIKE YA DIDN'T READ MY FILE CLOSE ENOUGH, MOUTH!
WHRAKAK
OR YA'D KNOW I WAS BORN WITH WHAT THE DOCS CALL "PHOTOGRAPHIC REFLEXES"!
WHICH MEANS THAT ONCE I SEE SOMETHIN' DONE, I CAN DO IT MYSELF, PERFECT, AN' WITHOUT PRACTICE!
NEEDLESS T'SAY, I SEEN A LOT O' CAPTAIN AMERICA NEWS FOOTAGE!
WHSSSHH
MATTER O' FACT, I'VE MADE A POINT O' STUDYIN' ALL YOU SUPER-TYPES! IN-CLUDIN'--
HEY! WHERE'D HE GO?
--SPIDER-MAN!
SONOVAGUN!
'COURSE THERE'S SOME THINGS I CAN'T DUPLICATE--LIKE THOR'S CONTROL O' THE WEATHER, OR THE HULK'S STRENGTH!
BUT I KINDA MAKE UP FER THAT BY ANTICIPATIN'! F'RINSTANCE--
SHHHWIP
--I JUST KNEW YOU'D SHOOT A RAZOR ARROW TO TRY AN' CLIP MY ROPE! SO ALL I GOTTA DO IS SWING OUTTA THE WAY--
11

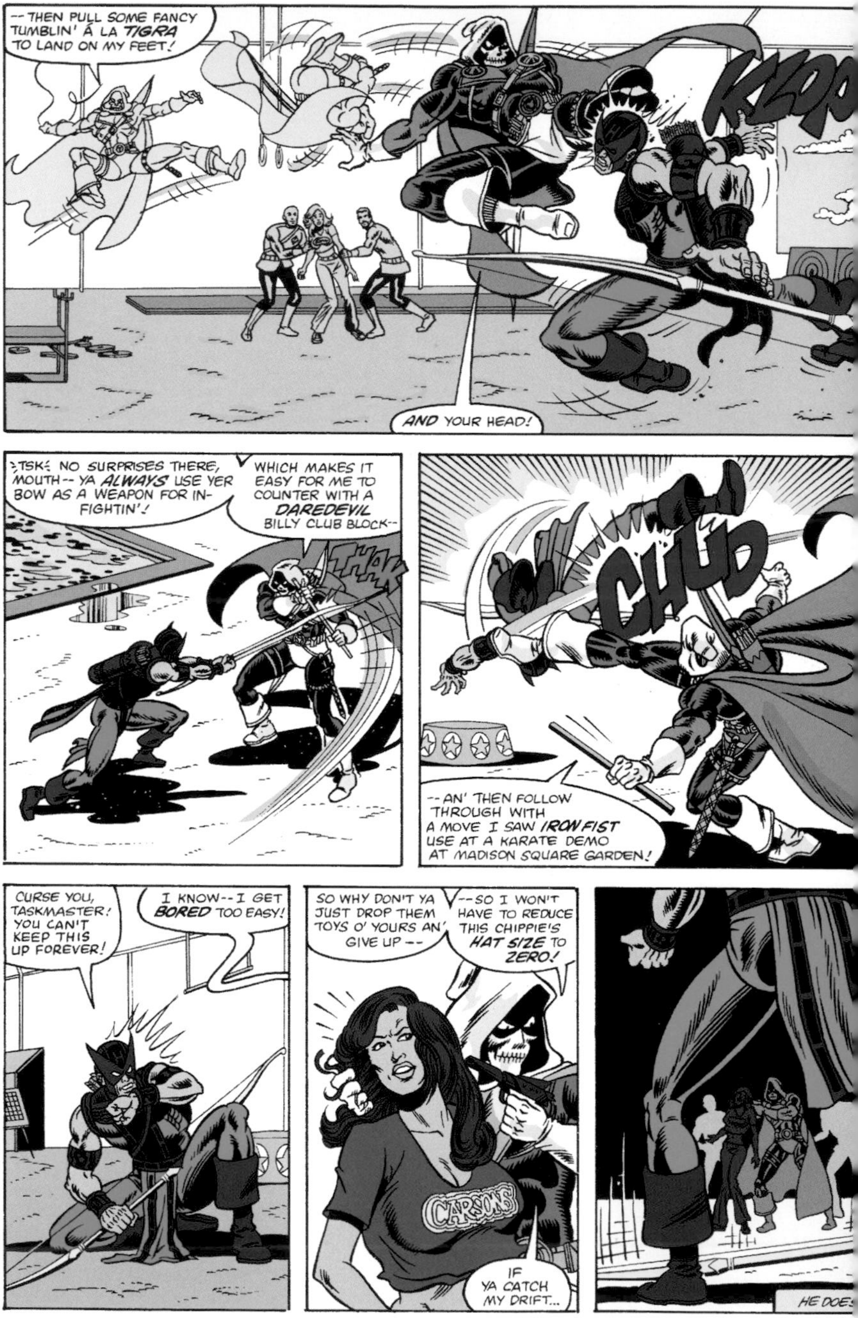
-- THEN PULL SOME FANCY TUMBLIN' Á LA TIGRA TO LAND ON MY FEET!
KLOP
AND YOUR HEAD!
TSK! NO SURPRISES THERE, MOUTH -- YA ALWAYS USE YER BOW AS A WEAPON FOR IN-FIGHTIN'!
WHICH MAKES IT EASY FOR ME TO COUNTER WITH A DAREDEVIL BILLY CLUB BLOCK--
THAK
CHUD
-- AN' THEN FOLLOW THROUGH WITH A MOVE I SAW IRON FIST USE AT A KARATE DEMO AT MADISON SQUARE GARDEN!
CURSE YOU, TASKMASTER! YOU CAN'T KEEP THIS UP FOREVER!
I KNOW -- I GET BORED TOO EASY!
SO WHY DON'T YA JUST DROP THEM TOYS O' YOURS AN' GIVE UP --
-- SO I WON'T HAVE TO REDUCE THIS CHIPPIE'S HAT SIZE TO ZERO!
CARSONS
IF YA CATCH MY DRIFT...
HE DOES

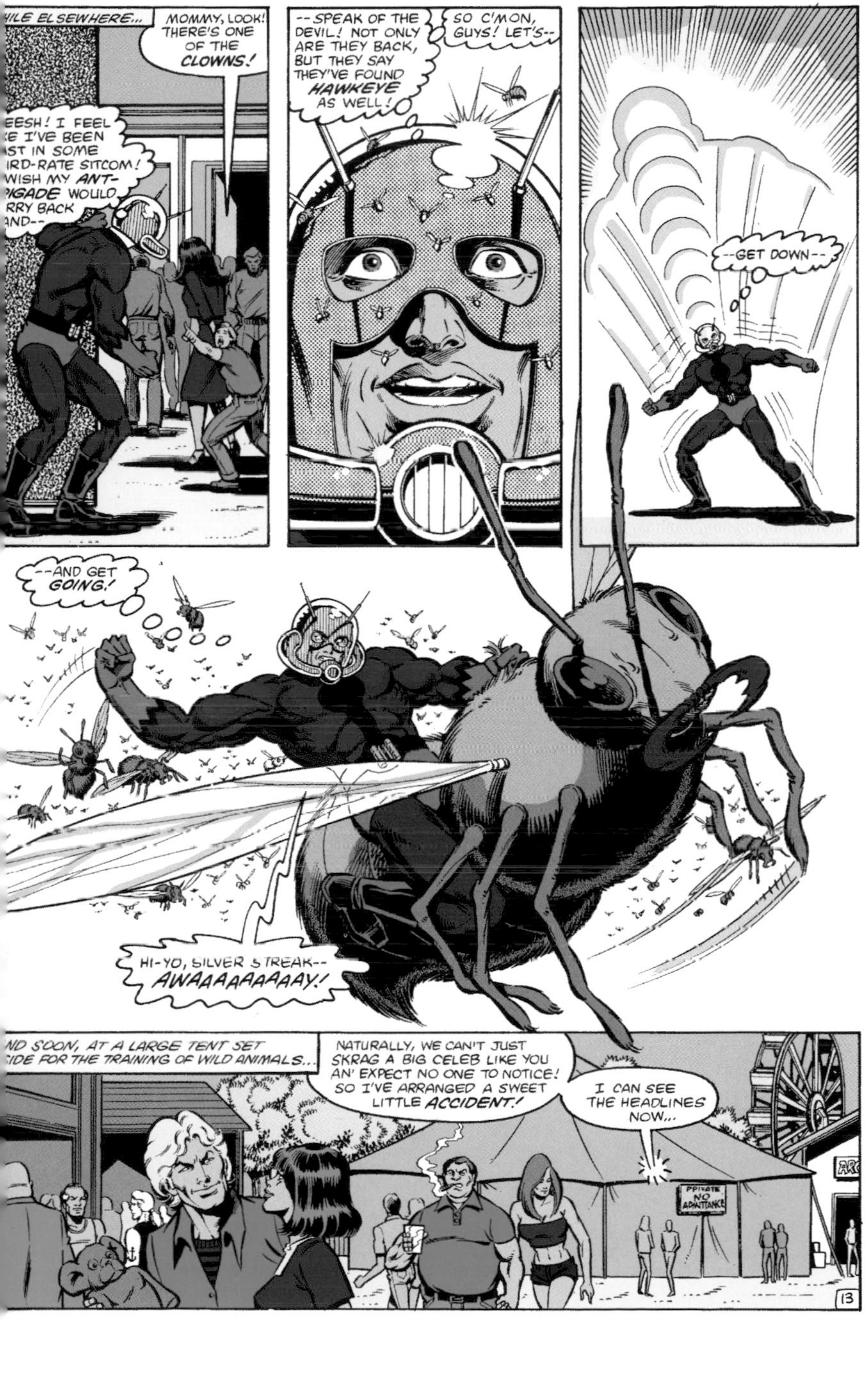

HILE ELSEWHERE...
MOMMY, LOOK! THERE'S ONE OF THE CLOWNS!
EESH! I FEEL E I'VE BEEN ST IN SOME IRD-RATE SITCOM! WISH MY ANT-PIGADE WOULD RRY BACK AND--
--SPEAK OF THE DEVIL! NOT ONLY ARE THEY BACK, BUT THEY SAY THEY'VE FOUND HAWKEYE AS WELL!
SO C'MON, GUYS! LET'S--
--GET DOWN--
--AND GET GOING!
HI-YO, SILVER STREAK-- AWAAAAAAAAAY!
ND SOON, AT A LARGE TENT SET IDE FOR THE TRAINING OF WILD ANIMALS...
NATURALLY, WE CAN'T JUST SKRAG A BIG CELEB LIKE YOU AN' EXPECT NO ONE TO NOTICE! SO I'VE ARRANGED A SWEET LITTLE ACCIDENT!
I CAN SEE THE HEADLINES NOW...
PRIVATE NO ADMITTANCE
13

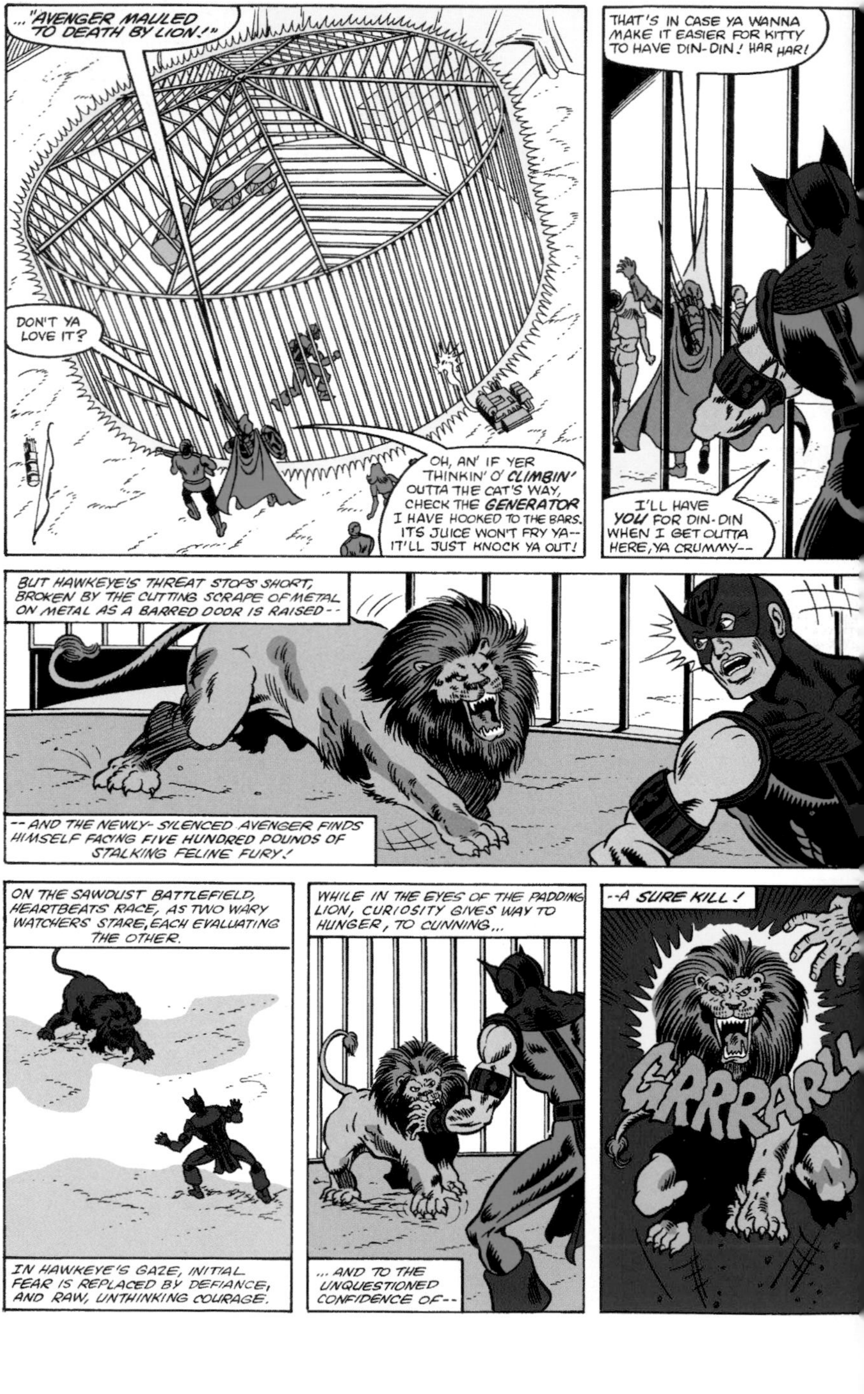
..."AVENGER MAULED TO DEATH BY LION!"
DON'T YA LOVE IT?
OH, AN' IF YER THINKIN' O' CLIMBIN' OUTTA THE CAT'S WAY, CHECK THE GENERATOR I HAVE HOOKED TO THE BARS. ITS JUICE WON'T FRY YA-- IT'LL JUST KNOCK YA OUT!
THAT'S IN CASE YA WANNA MAKE IT EASIER FOR KITTY TO HAVE DIN-DIN! HAR HAR!
I'LL HAVE YOU FOR DIN-DIN WHEN I GET OUTTA HERE, YA CRUMMY--
BUT HAWKEYE'S THREAT STOPS SHORT, BROKEN BY THE CUTTING SCRAPE OF METAL ON METAL AS A BARRED DOOR IS RAISED--
--AND THE NEWLY-SILENCED AVENGER FINDS HIMSELF FACING FIVE HUNDRED POUNDS OF STALKING FELINE FURY!
ON THE SAWDUST BATTLEFIELD, HEARTBEATS RACE, AS TWO WARY WATCHERS STARE, EACH EVALUATING THE OTHER.
IN HAWKEYE'S GAZE, INITIAL FEAR IS REPLACED BY DEFIANCE, AND RAW, UNTHINKING COURAGE.
WHILE IN THE EYES OF THE PADDING LION, CURIOSITY GIVES WAY TO HUNGER, TO CUNNING...
...AND TO THE UNQUESTIONED CONFIDENCE OF--
--A SURE KILL!
GRRRARL

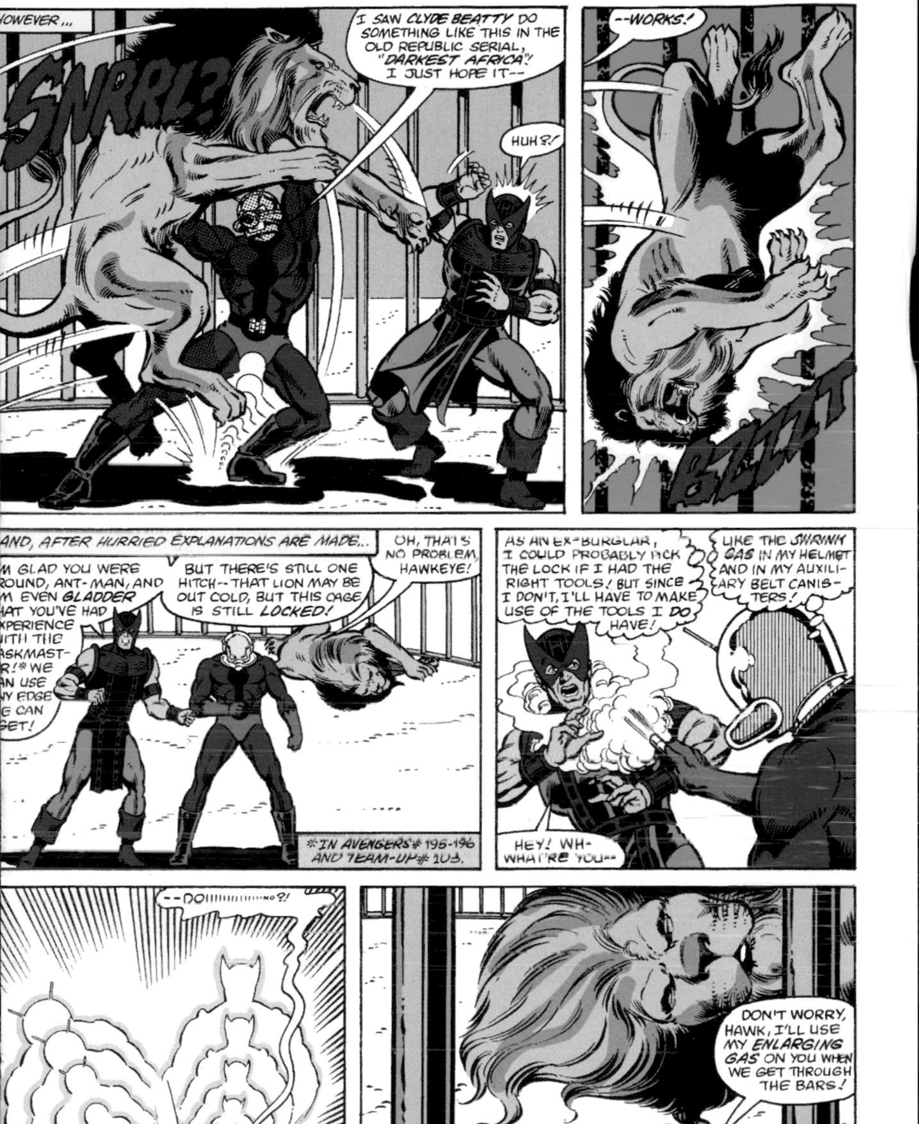
HOWEVER...
SNRRL?
I SAW CLYDE BEATTY DO SOMETHING LIKE THIS IN THE OLD REPUBLIC SERIAL, "DARKEST AFRICA"! I JUST HOPE IT--
HUH?!
--WORKS!
BZZZT
AND, AFTER HURRIED EXPLANATIONS ARE MADE...
M GLAD YOU WERE ROUND, ANT-MAN, AND M EVEN GLADDER HAT YOU'VE HAD XPERIENCE WITH THE ASKMASTER!* WE AN USE NY EDGE E CAN GET!
BUT THERE'S STILL ONE HITCH--THAT LION MAY BE OUT COLD, BUT THIS CAGE IS STILL LOCKED!
OH, THAT'S NO PROBLEM, HAWKEYE!
*IN AVENGERS# 195-196 AND TEAM-UP# 103.
AS AN EX-BURGLAR, I COULD PROBABLY PICK THE LOCK IF I HAD THE RIGHT TOOLS! BUT SINCE I DON'T, I'LL HAVE TO MAKE USE OF THE TOOLS I DO HAVE!
LIKE THE SHRINK GAS IN MY HELMET AND IN MY AUXILIARY BELT CANISTERS!
HEY! WH-WHAT'RE YOU--
--DOIIIIIIIIIIIINO?!
DON'T WORRY, HAWK, I'LL USE MY ENLARGING GAS ON YOU WHEN WE GET THROUGH THE BARS!
GEEZ! E-EVERYTHING IS SO... HUGE! NO OFFENSE, GUY, B-BUT I DON'T THINK I WANNA DO THIS TOO OFTEN! =GULP!=
15

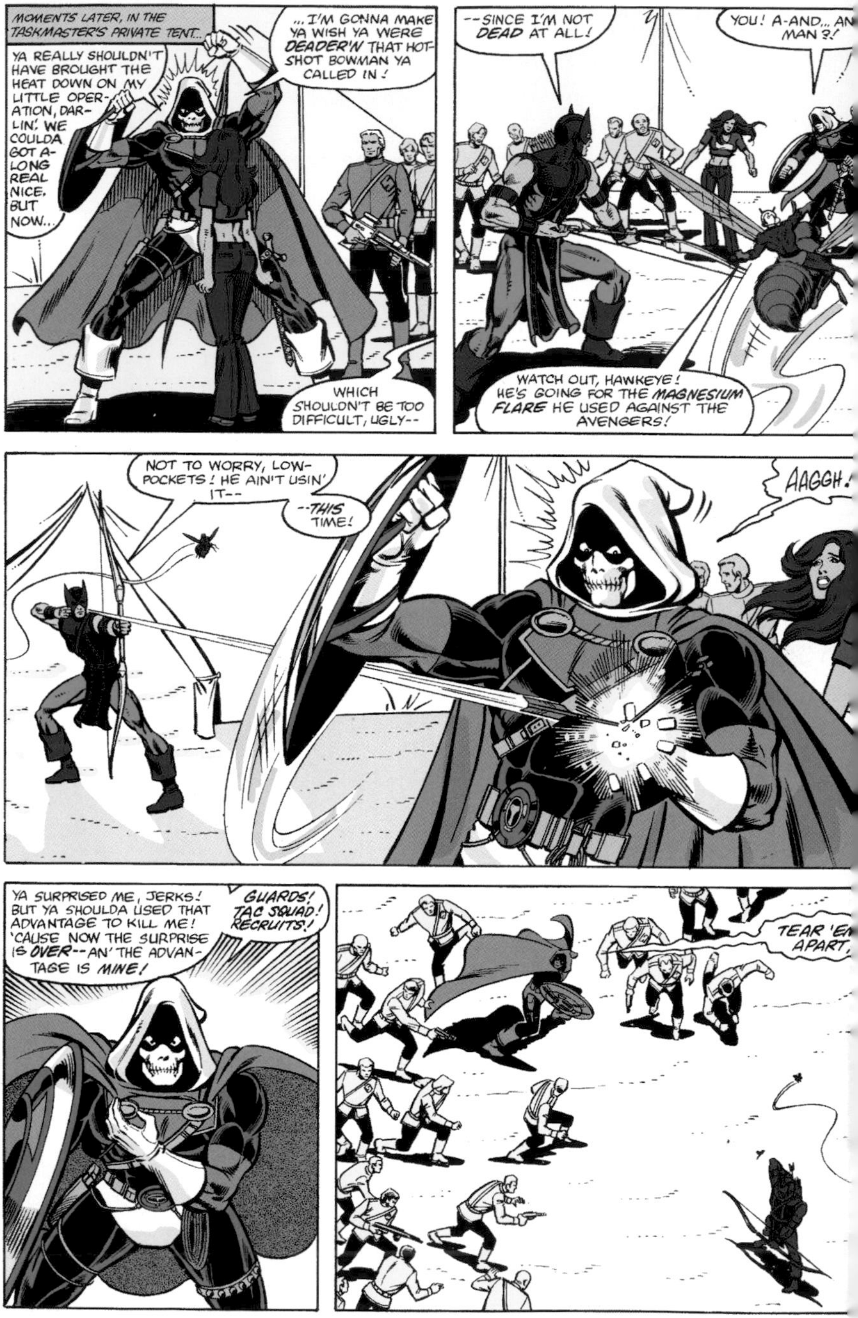
MOMENTS LATER, IN THE TASKMASTER'S PRIVATE TENT...
YA REALLY SHOULDN'T HAVE BROUGHT THE HEAT DOWN ON MY LITTLE OPERATION, DARLIN'. WE COULDA GOT ALONG REAL NICE. BUT NOW...
...I'M GONNA MAKE YA WISH YA WERE DEADER'N THAT HOT-SHOT BOWMAN YA CALLED IN!
WHICH SHOULDN'T BE TOO DIFFICULT, UGLY--
--SINCE I'M NOT DEAD AT ALL!
YOU! A-AND... AN MAN ?!
WATCH OUT, HAWKEYE! HE'S GOING FOR THE MAGNESIUM FLARE HE USED AGAINST THE AVENGERS!
NOT TO WORRY, LOW-POCKETS! HE AIN'T USIN' IT--
--THIS TIME!
AAGGH!
YA SURPRISED ME, JERKS! BUT YA SHOULDA USED THAT ADVANTAGE TO KILL ME! 'CAUSE NOW THE SURPRISE IS OVER--AN' THE ADVANTAGE IS MINE!
GUARDS! TAC SQUAD! RECRUITS!
TEAR 'EM APART,

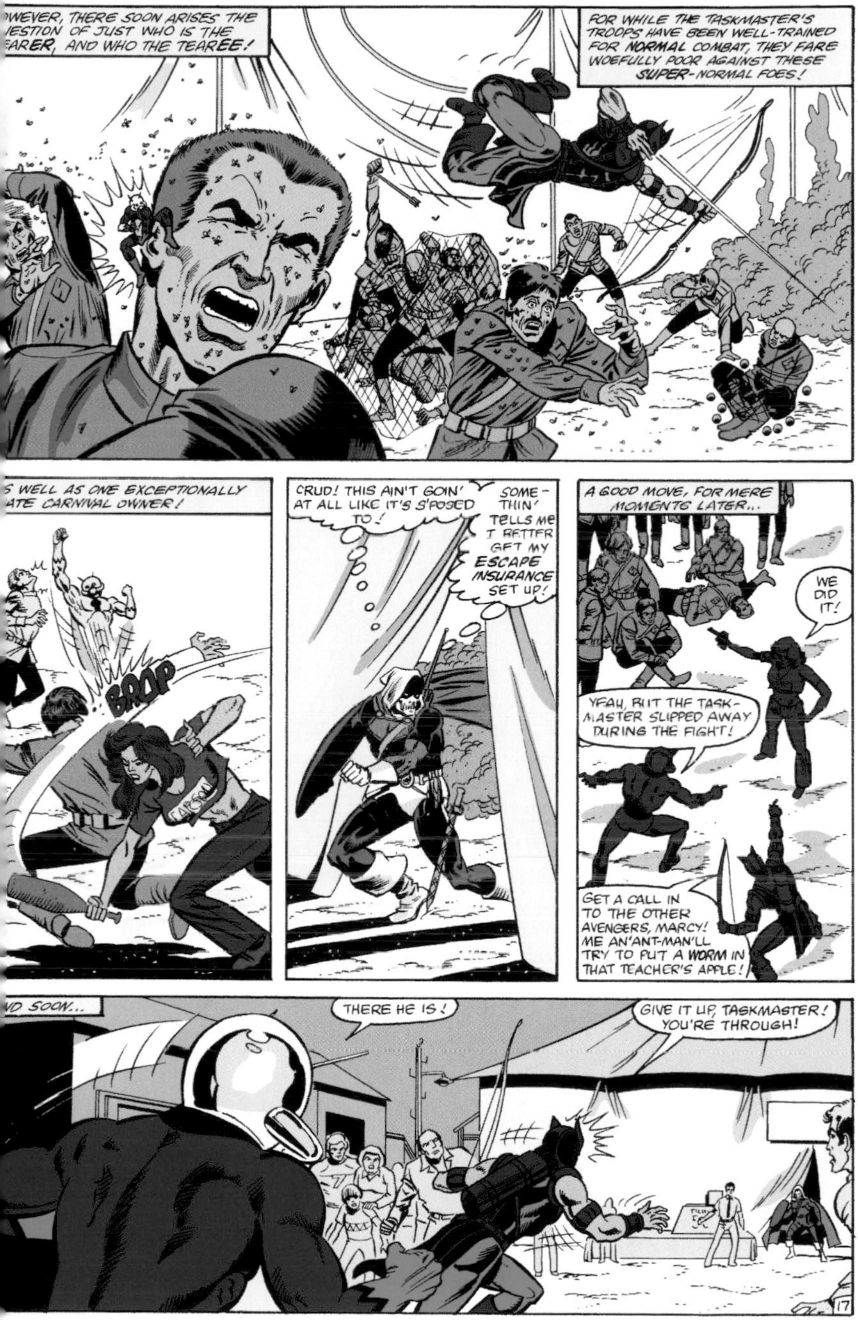

OWEVER, THERE SOON ARISES THE
UESTION OF JUST WHO IS THE
EARER, AND WHO THE TEAREE!
FOR WHILE THE TASKMASTER'S TROOPS HAVE BEEN WELL-TRAINED FOR NORMAL COMBAT, THEY FARE WOEFULLY POOR AGAINST THESE SUPER-NORMAL FOES!
S WELL AS ONE EXCEPTIONALLY
ATE CARNIVAL OWNER!
BRAP
CRUD! THIS AIN'T GOIN' AT ALL LIKE IT'S S'POSED TO!
SOME-THIN' TELLS ME I BETTER GET MY ESCAPE INSURANCE SET UP!
A GOOD MOVE, FOR MERE MOMENTS LATER...
WE DID IT!
YEAH, BUT THE TASK-MASTER SLIPPED AWAY DURING THE FIGHT!
GET A CALL IN TO THE OTHER AVENGERS, MARCY! ME AN' ANT-MAN'LL TRY TO PUT A WORM IN THAT TEACHER'S APPLE!
ND SOON...
THERE HE IS!
GIVE IT UP, TASKMASTER! YOU'RE THROUGH!
17

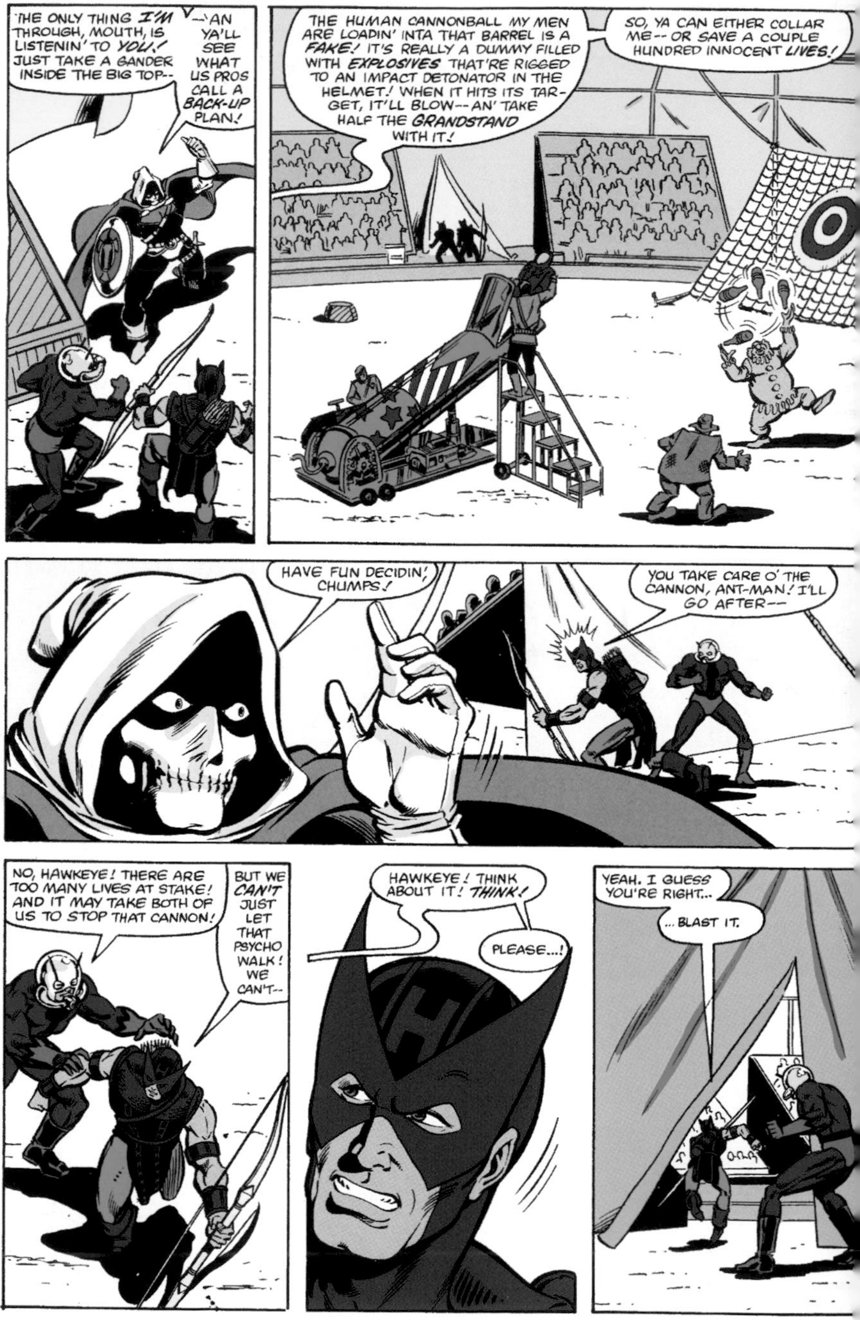
THE ONLY THING I'M THROUGH, MOUTH, IS LISTENIN' TO YOU! JUST TAKE A GANDER INSIDE THE BIG TOP--
--AN YA'LL SEE WHAT US PROS CALL A BACK-UP PLAN!
THE HUMAN CANNONBALL MY MEN ARE LOADIN' INTA THAT BARREL IS A FAKE! IT'S REALLY A DUMMY FILLED WITH EXPLOSIVES THAT'RE RIGGED TO AN IMPACT DETONATOR IN THE HELMET! WHEN IT HITS ITS TARGET, IT'LL BLOW--AN' TAKE HALF THE GRANDSTAND WITH IT!
SO, YA CAN EITHER COLLAR ME--OR SAVE A COUPLE HUNDRED INNOCENT LIVES!
HAVE FUN DECIDIN', CHUMPS!
YOU TAKE CARE O' THE CANNON, ANT-MAN! I'LL GO AFTER--
NO, HAWKEYE! THERE ARE TOO MANY LIVES AT STAKE! AND IT MAY TAKE BOTH OF US TO STOP THAT CANNON!
BUT WE CAN'T JUST LET THAT PSYCHO WALK! WE CAN'T--
HAWKEYE! THINK ABOUT IT! THINK!
PLEASE...!
YEAH. I GUESS YOU'RE RIGHT...
...BLAST IT.

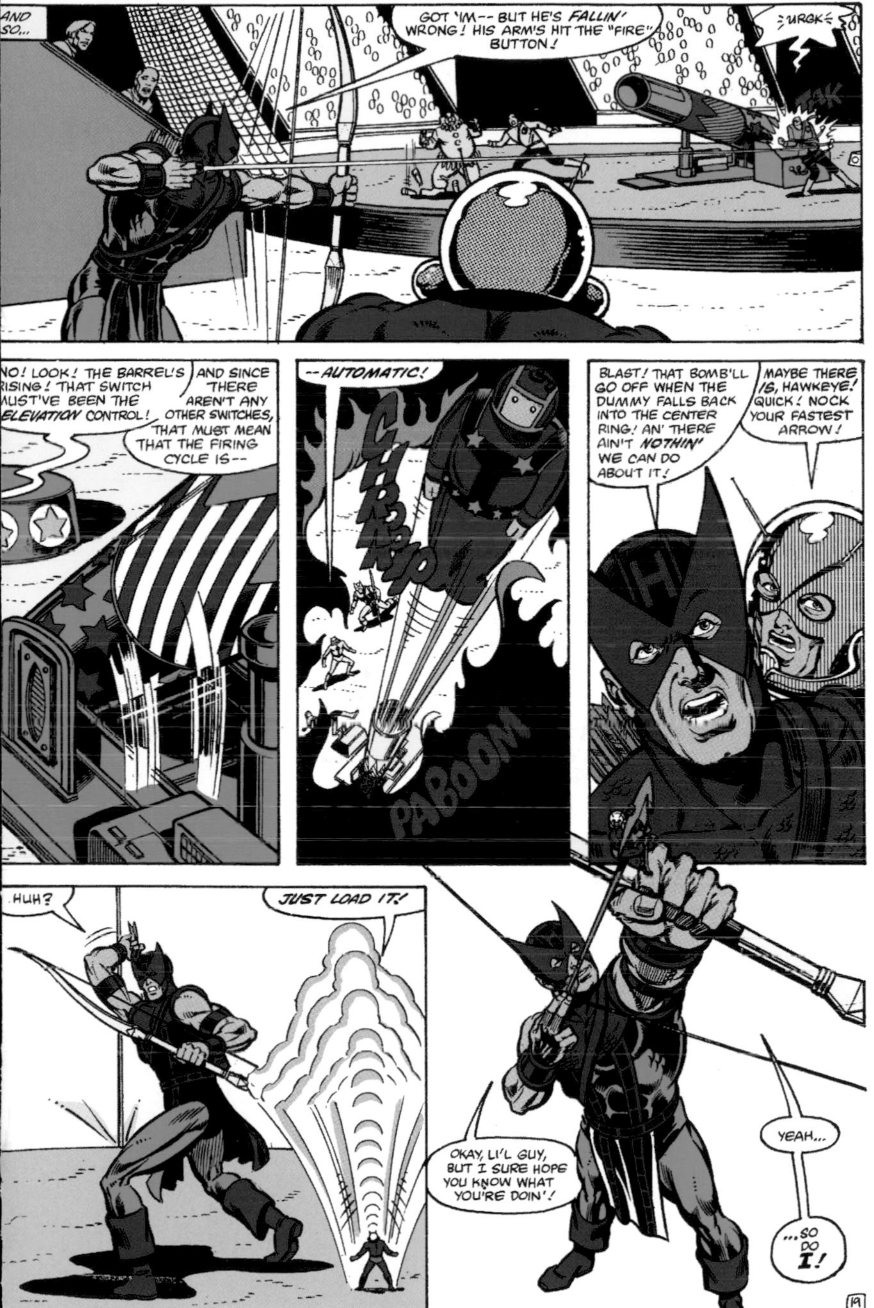
AND SO...
GOT 'IM-- BUT HE'S FALLIN' WRONG! HIS ARM'S HIT THE "FIRE" BUTTON!
URGK
NO! LOOK! THE BARREL'S RISING! THAT SWITCH MUST'VE BEEN THE ELEVATION CONTROL!
AND SINCE THERE AREN'T ANY OTHER SWITCHES, THAT MUST MEAN THAT THE FIRING CYCLE IS--
--AUTOMATIC!
PABOOM
BLAST! THAT BOMB'LL GO OFF WHEN THE DUMMY FALLS BACK INTO THE CENTER RING! AN' THERE AIN'T NOTHIN' WE CAN DO ABOUT IT!
MAYBE THERE IS, HAWKEYE! QUICK! NOCK YOUR FASTEST ARROW!
HUH?
JUST LOAD IT!
OKAY, LI'L GUY, BUT I SURE HOPE YOU KNOW WHAT YOU'RE DOIN'!
YEAH...
...SO DO I!
19

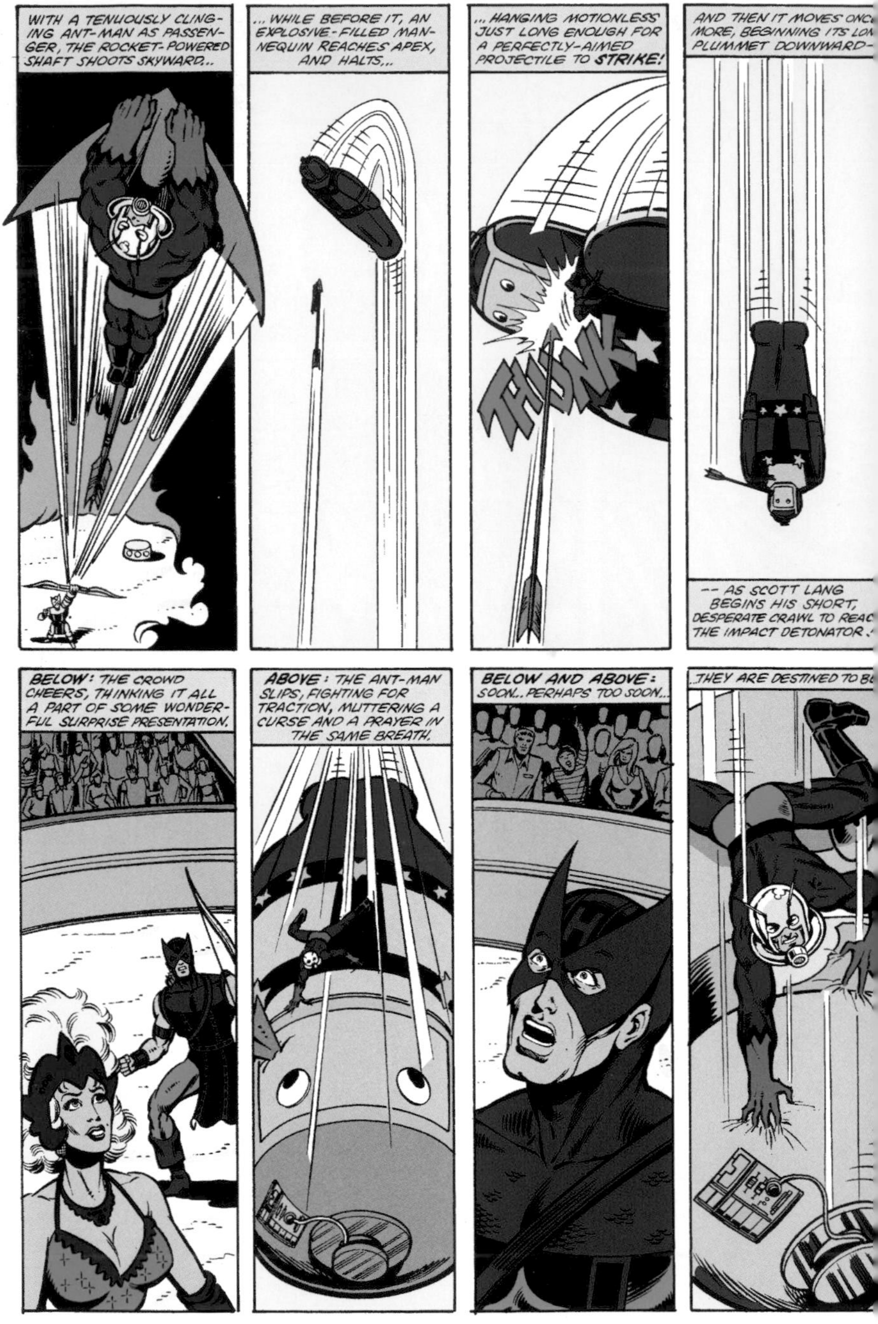
WITH A TENUOUSLY CLINGING ANT-MAN AS PASSENGER, THE ROCKET-POWERED SHAFT SHOOTS SKYWARD...
...WHILE BEFORE IT, AN EXPLOSIVE-FILLED MANNEQUIN REACHES APEX, AND HALTS,...
...HANGING MOTIONLESS JUST LONG ENOUGH FOR A PERFECTLY-AIMED PROJECTILE TO STRIKE!
THUNK
AND THEN IT MOVES ONCE MORE, BEGINNING ITS LON PLUMMET DOWNWARD--
-- AS SCOTT LANG BEGINS HIS SHORT, DESPERATE CRAWL TO REAC THE IMPACT DETONATOR.
BELOW: THE CROWD CHEERS, THINKING IT ALL A PART OF SOME WONDERFUL SURPRISE PRESENTATION.
ABOVE: THE ANT-MAN SLIPS, FIGHTING FOR TRACTION, MUTTERING A CURSE AND A PRAYER IN THE SAME BREATH.
BELOW AND ABOVE: SOON... PERHAPS TOO SOON...
...THEY ARE DESTINED TO BE

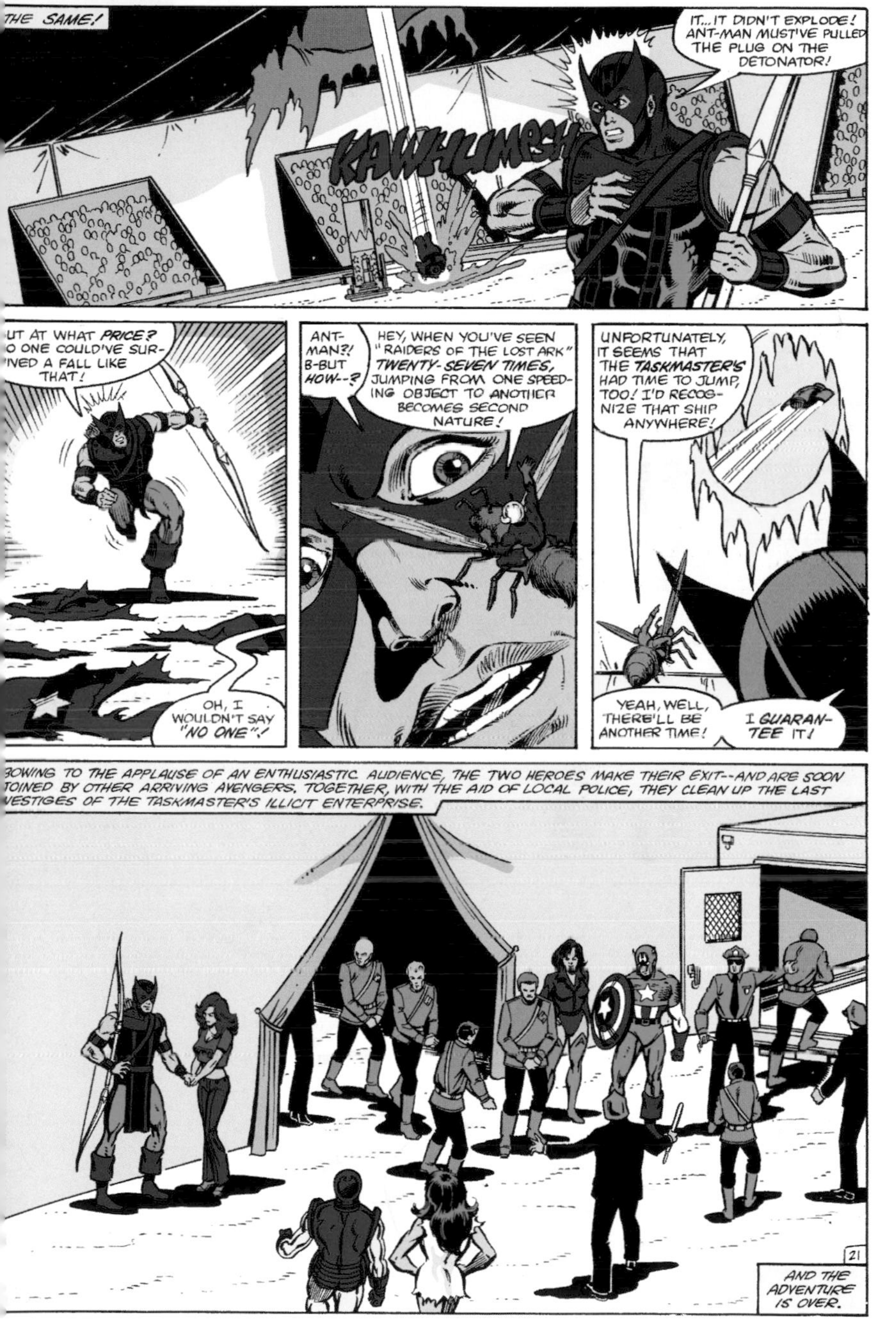
THE SAME!
IT... IT DIDN'T EXPLODE! ANT-MAN MUST'VE PULLED THE PLUG ON THE DETONATOR!
KAWHUMPSH
UT AT WHAT PRICE? O ONE COULD'VE SURVIVED A FALL LIKE THAT!
OH, I WOULDN'T SAY "NO ONE"!
ANT-MAN?! B-BUT HOW--?
HEY, WHEN YOU'VE SEEN "RAIDERS OF THE LOST ARK" TWENTY-SEVEN TIMES, JUMPING FROM ONE SPEEDING OBJECT TO ANOTHER BECOMES SECOND NATURE!
UNFORTUNATELY, IT SEEMS THAT THE TASKMASTER'S HAD TIME TO JUMP, TOO! I'D RECOGNIZE THAT SHIP ANYWHERE!
YEAH, WELL, THERE'LL BE ANOTHER TIME!
I GUARANTEE IT!
BOWING TO THE APPLAUSE OF AN ENTHUSIASTIC AUDIENCE, THE TWO HEROES MAKE THEIR EXIT--AND ARE SOON JOINED BY OTHER ARRIVING AVENGERS. TOGETHER, WITH THE AID OF LOCAL POLICE, THEY CLEAN UP THE LAST VESTIGES OF THE TASKMASTER'S ILLICIT ENTERPRISE.
21
AND THE ADVENTURE IS OVER.

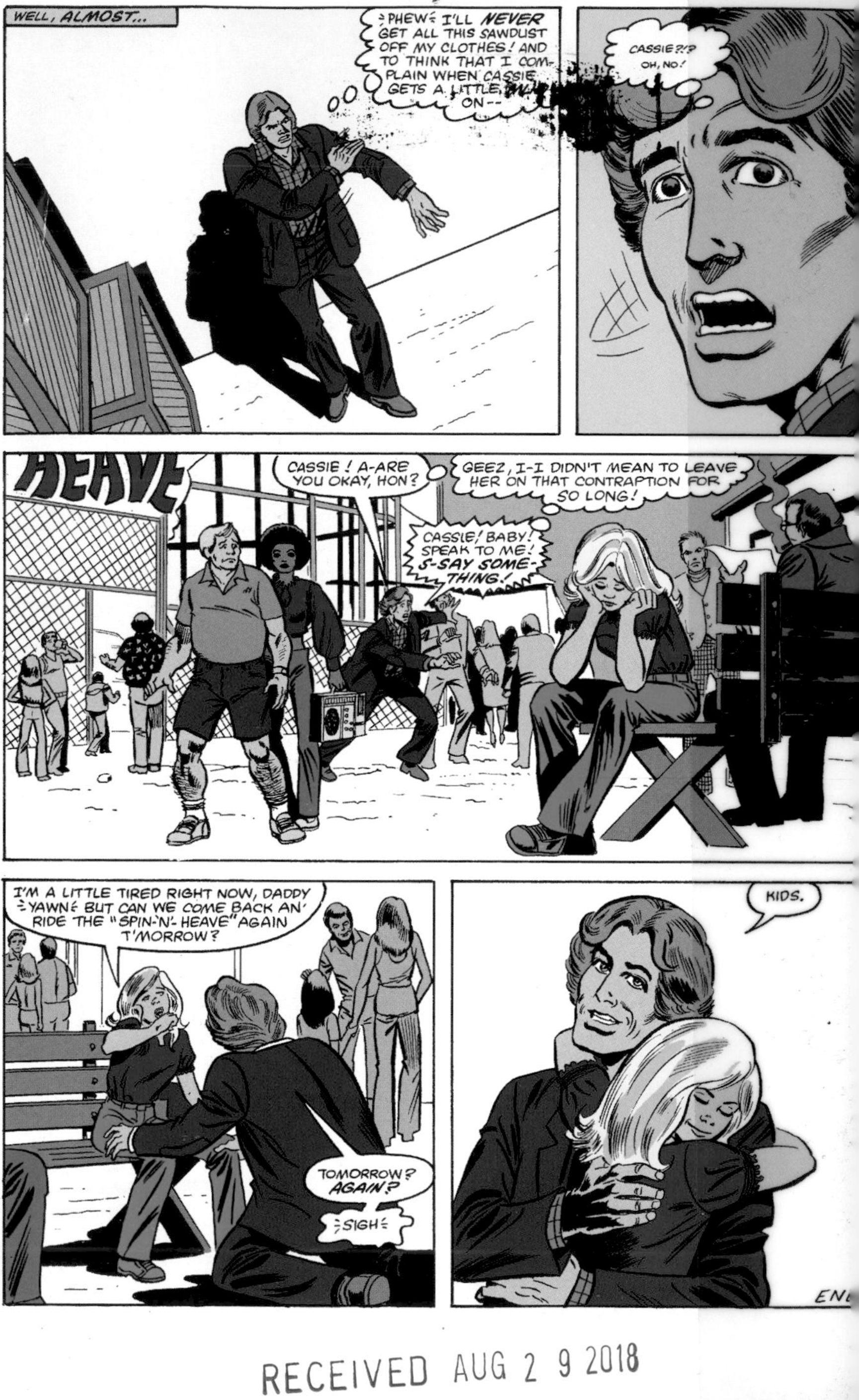
WELL, ALMOST...
PHEW I'LL NEVER GET ALL THIS SAWDUST OFF MY CLOTHES! AND TO THINK THAT I COMPLAIN WHEN CASSIE GETS A LITTLE
ON--
CASSIE?!? OH, NO!
HEAVE
CASSIE! A-ARE YOU OKAY, HON?
GEEZ, I-I DIDN'T MEAN TO LEAVE HER ON THAT CONTRAPTION FOR SO LONG!
CASSIE! BABY! SPEAK TO ME! S-SAY SOMETHING!
I'M A LITTLE TIRED RIGHT NOW, DADDY YAWN BUT CAN WE COME BACK AN' RIDE THE "SPIN-'N'-HEAVE" AGAIN T'MORROW?
TOMORROW? AGAIN?
SIGH
KIDS.